# THE GREAT PHILANTHROPISTS
*And the Problem of "Donor Intent"*

## Martin Morse Wooster

THIRD EDITION REVISED AND ENLARGED

**Capital Research Center**

Copyright 2007 by Capital Research Center
ALL RIGHTS RESERVED


Library of Congress Cataloging-in-Publication Data
Wooster, Martin Morse, 1957-
The great philanthropists and the problem of "donor intent" /
  Martin Morse Wooster.
      p. cm.
Includes bibliographical references and index.
ISBN 1-892934-12-4 (pbk.)
1. Philanthropists–United States.
2. Charities–United States.
3. Family foundations–United States.
4. Charitable uses, trusts, and foundations–United States.  I. Title.

HV91.W6265 2007
361.7'40973--dc22
                                   2007003884


Typesetting and layout by G.P. Begelman, Inc.

# About the Author

Martin Morse Wooster, a Senior Fellow at Capital Research Center, received his undergraduate degree in history and philosophy from Beloit College. He is a contributing editor of *Philanthropy* and a columnist for the *Washington Times*. He has been an associate editor of *The American Enterprise,* Washington editor of *Reason,* an associate editor of *The Wilson Quarterly,* and Washington editor of *Harper's Magazine.* His articles have appeared in the *Wall Street Journal, Washington Post, Reader's Digest, The Weekly Standard, The American Spectator, Policy Review, Elle, Spin, and Air and Space.* His other books are *Angry Classrooms, Vacant Minds* (Pacific Research Institute, 1994) and *Great Philanthropic Mistakes* (Hudson Institute, 2006). His monographs include the sequel to this book, *Should Foundations Live Forever?* (Capital Research Center, 1998), *Return to Charity?* (Capital Research Center, 2000), *The Foundation Builders* (Philanthropy Roundtable, 2000), and *By Their Bootstraps* (Manhattan Institute, 2002). He has also contributed articles on the history of philanthropy to *The Encyclopedia of Civil Rights, The Encyclopedia of Philanthropy, The Encyclopedia of the Victorian Era,* and *Notable American Philanthropists.*

# Dedicated to the Memory of

ANDREW CARNEGIE

HENRY FORD

HENRY FORD II

JOHN D. MCARTHUR

J. HOWARD PEW

JOSEPH N. PEW

JOHN D. ROCKEFELLER, SR.

# Acknowledgements to the First Edition (1994)

This book owes its inspiration to Tim Ferguson and Willa Johnson. In the fall of 1989 Tim Ferguson, then the editorial features editor at the *Wall Street Journal,* read an issue of *Alternatives in Philanthropy* I had written about the Ford Foundation. He suggested that I write an op-ed on what happened to the fortunes of Andrew Carnegie and John D. MacArthur. Like all good editors, he identified a subject that a writer would find interesting, and if it were not for him, I would not have begun my exploration of the problems of donor intent.

In January 1993, I had a meeting with Willa Johnson where I first proposed doing an article on donor intent. She suggested a book instead, and by the end of the meeting we had a contract and I have become a CRC visiting fellow. Thank you, Willa, for your suggestions, your inspiration, and your patience.

Research for this book was done at the Library of Congress, the McKeldin Library at the University of Maryland, and the library in the Foundation's Center's Washington, D.C. office. Special thanks to the Foundation Center's series *The Literature of the Nonprofit Sector,* an invaluable research tool that provided a great many citations for articles and books I might otherwise have missed.

At the Capital Research Center, Daniel T. Oliver did a fine job of editing this book. My research on the Buck Trust was aided by earlier research done by Philip Marcus and Robert Davis.

Several staff members at foundations and corporations provided useful information, particularly Elizabeth Locke at the Duke Endowment, Patrick Modugno at the Conrad N. Hilton Foundation, and Claire Sheehan at TIAA-CREF. Kim Dennis of the Philanthropy Roundtable made several helpful suggestions. Other suggestions, articles, or advice were provided by James Bowman, Charles Hamilton, Sean Haugh, and Rodger Morrow.

# Acknowledgements to the Second Edition (1998)

This new edition shows what happened from 1994-1999 to the foundations I originally wrote about in 1993. It includes new information about almost every foundation I analyzed, as well as substantial new primary material on the Pews and the MacArthurs. In addition, it incorporates much from "Undermining Donor Intenet: Four Case Studies," *Alternatives in Philanthropy,* November 1995, and two paragraphs from "The MacArthur Fellowships: The Oscars of the Multicultural Elite," *Philanthropy, Culture & Society,* January 1996. Other new material about the great philanthropists was uncovered through a search of scholarly material published in the past four years. This second edition has about 12,000 words of new material.

As with the first edition, the book was edited by Daniel T. Oliver and supervised by Robert Huberty. Research for the book was performed at the Library of Congress, the McKeldin Library at the University of Maryland, the library at the Foundation Center's Washington, D.C. office, and the Rockville, Maryland public library.

# Acknowledgements to the Third Edition

This third edition shows what happened to the foundations I write about between 1998–2006. It includes a new section on the Robertson Foundation case (which was not a problem in 1998), and a substantially expanded section on the Barnes Foundation. In addition, a great many more electronic databases (including searchable files of the *New York Times* and the *Washington Post,* as well as America: History and Life, which indexes historical journals) allowed me to deepen my knowledge of foundation history. As a result, this third edition includes about 20,000 words of new material.

This book was edited by Robert Huberty. Research for the book was done at the Library of Congress and the McKeldin Library at the University of Maryland.

Herb Berkowitz and Jennifer Berkowitz, public relations specialists for the Robertson family, went beyond the call of duty in providing documents showing the intentions of Charles Robertson. Thanks to Gay Clyburn and Ann Whitfield of the Carnegie Foundation for the Advancement of Teaching, Michael Hartmann of the Bradley Foundation, and Patrick Modugno of the Conrad N. Hilton Foundation for their help in making sure I was accurate. F.H. Buckley assisted me with the legal research.

# Table of Contents

PREFACE .......................................................xi

INTRODUCTION
**American Philanthropy and
the Problems of Donor Intent** ........................1

CHAPTER I
**The Rockefeller Legacy** ...............................9

CHAPTER II
**Undermining Donor Intent** ..........................25
   The Ford Foundation .................................26
   The Carnegie Corporation of New York ..............46
   The John D. and Catherine T. MacArthur Foundation ........57
   The Pew Charitable Trusts ..........................64
   The Barnes Foundation ..............................78
   The Buck Trust and Marin Community Foundation .........109
   The Robertson Foundation ..........................122

CHAPTER III
**Preserving Donor Intent:** ..........................143
   The JM Foundation .................................143
   The Lynde and Harry Bradley Foundation .............149
   The Duke Endowment ...............................159
   The Conrad N. Hilton Foundation ...................189

CHAPTER IV
**A Legal History of Donor Intent** ...................201

CONCLUSION
**What Donors Can Do** ................................226

NOTES .......................................................232

INDEX .......................................................264

# Preface

By the time the third generation becomes involved with running a foundation, the memory of the founder has often become dimmed. His or her aspirations, motivations, and vision are often no longer compelling. Donor intent may have been appropriate for grandpa, but it doesn't apply to his grandchildren.

Unfortunately, this scenario has been repeated too many times in the history of American philanthropy.

Philanthropic institutions will experience a major inflow of new funds during the next two decades. Those who made their money after World War II will reach maturity, and their estates will be passed to their heirs and to foundations. How will those funds be spent? Is it important to donors who created new wealth that their gifts be used in accordance with their political and philosophical beliefs?

Donors should be aware that clear violations of donor intent—even when that intent is explicitly stated in binding documents—have occurred. The Pew Charitable Trusts, the Buck Trust, the Barnes Foundation, and the DeRancé Foundation have all explicitly violated detailed donor intent statements. The Ford Foundation, the John D. and Catherine T. MacArthur Foundation, the Rockefeller Foundation, the Carnegie Corporation of New York and others do not follow the spirit of their donors' intent. But in these cases the donors did not leave clear mandates of their wishes.

Some foundations regain a lost respect for their donors, but there are not many. The most notable ones are the William H. Donner Foundation and the Buck Trust. Except for the Barnes and the DeRancé foundations and possibly the Donner Foundation, all these abrogations are characterized by a shift away from traditional forms of charity to left-wing advocacy and from a respect for free markets to redistributive political action.

So donor beware. How can someone who wants to create a foundation ensure that his or her wishes will be followed decades from now? What's to prevent trustees, relatives, and lawyers from disregarding, changing, or reinterpreting a donor's intentions to fit their own plans for the money?

Martin Morse Wooster answers these questions in the course of his fascinating survey of the founding fathers of American philanthropy and the great institutions of wealth and generosity they created. He shows how our system of free enterprise and limited government released the entrepreneurial energies of these people, giving them incentives to use their wealth for the benefit of others. He describes the plans and actions of famous entrepreneurs—the Rockefellers, Carnegies, Fords and others less well known—who created vast new wealth and then pondered what would become of it after they died.

But this is also an instructive and cautionary tale for our time. It is a story about how those who were brilliant in the marketplace often failed to understand the very different outlooks of the trustees and foundation executives they entrusted to handle their fortunes.

There is a world of difference between those who can earn great wealth and those who are bequeathed great wealth—and then find themselves responsible for spending someone else's money. Martin Wooster's recommendations should be carefully considered by those who wish to avoid the pitfalls of modern philanthropy.

W. J. Hume<br>
Jaquelin Hume Foundation<br>
San Francisco, California

# INTRODUCTION

## American Philanthropy and the Problems of Donor Intent

*Mr. Rockefeller's method of giving away money impersonally on the basis of investigation by others is careful and conscientious; but it must have cut him off almost completely from the real happiness which good deeds ought to bring the doer, the happiness of giving personally not only one's money, but one's sympathy and labor. He has already done an enormous amount of good, and is going to do much more for many years to come. We all wish that he had got more joy out of it.*

—Charles W. Eliot, Harvard University president and Rockefeller Foundation trustee.[1]

*When you die and come to approach the judgment of almighty God, when you stand before St. Peter in supplication at the gates of heaven, what do you think he will demand of you? Do you for an instant presume that he will inquire into your petty failures and your trivial virtues?...No! No indeed! He will brush all these matters to one side and he will ask but one question: "How did you do as a trustee of the Rockefeller Foundation?!"*

—Frederick T. Gates, philanthropic adviser to John D. Rockefeller.[2]

In 1900, most forms of philanthropy in the United States were locally based. Most of the major national charities either did not exist or were very small. When Clara Barton was ousted as president of the American Red Cross in 1904, the organization's annual budget was only $2,730.

By 1925, the philanthropic world had greatly changed. Large organizations had been created by Andrew Carnegie and John D. Rockefeller. Major national charities, including the American Cancer Society, National Urban League, and National Association for the Advancement of Colored People had also been established. The American Red Cross had grown from a small decentralized charity to a giant nonprofit that collected and spent $400 million during World War I. Increasingly, the typical philanthropy was a large organization with general—and often vague—goals, rather than a small charity with narrow aims.

Most historians treat the creation of large philanthropies as an important advance. Historians Barry D. Karl and Stanley N. Katz argue that large foundations were able to "play a major role in preparing the

1

way for the modern state. For by supporting research and thereby influencing the choice of social policies, the philanthropists were [able to shape] governmental action in what was increasingly identified as the private sector.[3]

But with the growth of large foundations, the problem of donor intent increased. As historian Kathleen D. McCarthy notes,

> neither the donor's motives nor the donor's decisions were beyond question after the turn of the century. Instead, growing ranks of professionals worked to systematize the benevolent impulse and channel it towards responsible ends. Science, rather than simple good will, infused the philanthropic ethos of the Jazz Age. In the process, donors were increasingly asked to pay for projects they often could neither touch nor comprehend, deferring to the wisdom of reformers and managers of every stripe and hue.[4]

This chapter examines several social trends in the late 19th and early 20th centuries that helped to inspire the increasingly widespread ideal of the "disinterested donor"—the belief that donors should calmly leave their fortunes to trained "professionals" to be distributed in ways favored by those professionals. These include the rise of social engineering ideas, the advent of modern fundraising, the creation of community foundations and the massive increase in requests for charity.

**The Rise of Social Engineering**

As Marvin Olasky shows in his historical overview of American philanthropy, *The Tragedy of American Compassion,* until about 1900, most charity in the United States was provided by local organizations that dealt directly with the poor. As the 19th century progressed, however, some charity leaders came to believe that national organizations could better deal with the administration of charities. By 1900, Olasky writes, some poverty-fighters "were beginning to suggest that a central organization, based on the most scientific methods of poverty-fighting, might need to have the power to dominate charity distributions and push others to comply with them."[5]

At the same time, anti-poverty crusaders began to emphasize fighting the alleged causes of poverty rather than merely alleviating symptoms. Instead of working with the poor on an individual basis, ensuring that they reentered the work force, charity workers increasingly focused on such issues as the presumed causes of homelessness and hunger.

A 1906 report by the Charity Organization Society (COS) of New York reviewed 25 years of poverty-relief efforts, concluding that past methods were no longer feasible. "The result to the community in eliminating and diminishing some of the more important causes of pauperism is of infinitely greater value than could have been brought about by the same amount of effort and the same amount of money expended for the relief of individual suffering." The COS therefore "deliberately determined, without neglecting in any way its duty in the relief of individual cases of poverty, to lay emphasis on the field of removing or minimizing the causes of poverty, and to firmly establish and extend these forms of work by organizing them into a department for the permanent improvement of social conditions."[6]

**The Russell Sage Foundation**

In the philanthropic world, the trend toward fighting the presume causes of poverty is best exemplified by the Russell Sage Foundation, created in 1907. Russell Sage was a prominent investment banker of the 1890s. As historian Joseph J. Thorndike Jr. notes, Sage apparently had no charitable impulses, preferring to hoard his wealth rather than spend it. Though he was a millionaire, he routinely walked in order to save streetcar fare. When he died in 1906, he unconditionally left his fortune of $65 million to his widow, Margaret Olivia Sage. The result, says Thorndike, is that he "would certainly have been horrified at what happened..."[7]

At first Mrs. Sage tried to help those in need. But after receiving 20,000 requests for help in six months, she decided to create an endowment as a memorial to her husband. She asked the advice of Robert W. deForest, a long-time president of the Charity Organization Society of New York. DeForest, after consulting with like-minded friends, presented a set of ten options to Mrs. Sage, including building houses for the poor, offering the poor insurance, and subsidizing stores that sold goods at a small profit. But the best way to honor Russell Sage, deForest suggested, was to create a "Sage Foundation for Social Betterment."

Mrs. Sage, however, worried that a foundation might run out of things to do. What if the problems of the poor were solved? DeForest replied that "with the constant change and shift of social conditions,...the future may develop other and greater needs for philanthropic action than any which are now apparent." He even addressed the problem of donor intent by saying that Mrs. Sage's intentions "should be sufficiently elastic in form and method to work in different ways at different times."[8]

This belief was generally applauded by the press. *Charities and the Commons,* the leading journal of the charity movement, saluted the new foundation in a 1907 editorial, saying it had "a field of activity that the most enthusiastic would not call cramped or small...Centuries hence, if the Sage Foundation is still in existence, its managers will not be tied down to any outgrown subject of inquiry or relief."[9]

But the Russell Sage Foundation dispensed with "outgrown subjects" early. Within a month of its incorporation, the board of directors declared that it would "not attempt to relieve individual or family need." Helping individuals would mean that "there would be no money left" for the "peculiar function of eradicating causes of poverty."[10] Instead, the foundation would give money to study poverty, and also help create a nonprofit movement by funding *Charities and the Common* (later *The Survey*), roughly equivalent to the Council on Foundations' *Foundation News & Commentary.*

**The Advent of Modern Fundraising**

The Sage Foundation's grants and its emphasis on centralized philanthropy helped ensure that by 1915 charities in the United States were largely national organizations that addressed general concerns. Nonprofits created between 1900 and 1916 included the Boys Clubs (1906), Federal (later National) Council of Churches (1908), National Association for the Advancement of Colored People (1909), Boy Scouts of America (1910), Camp Fire Girls (1912), American Cancer Society (1913), Girl Scouts (1915), and National Parent-Teacher Association (1915). By 1922, these groups were joined by the National Association of Travelers' Aid Societies, Girls Clubs, Jewish Welfare Board, Child Welfare League of America, American Federation of the Blind, Big Brothers and Big Sisters, and National Alliance of Legal Aid Societies.[11]

Such large charities were also strengthened by the perfection of fundraising techniques between 1900 and 1910. Historian Scott Cutlip credits three men with systematizing and perfecting fundraising: YMCA leaders Charles Sumner Ward and Lyman Pierce, and Harvard fundraiser Abbott Lawrence.

Ward and Pierce created the "campaign clock," in which large sums of money were raised in short periods of time. Their first campaign in 1905, was a 26-day effort to raise $80,000 for the Washington, D.C. YMCA. They were the first fundraisers to hire publicists and convince a prominent business (the Woodward and Lothrop department store) to buy advertisements urging support of charities. They also invented the fundraising dinner in which prominent individuals paid large sums to support a charitable cause.[12] Abbott Lawrence's contribution was to create the long-term campaign, first used in 1904 to raise funds for Harvard University. His techniques generated $2.5 million for Harvard, and by 1915, they had been copied by dozens of institutions nationwide.

Fundraising transformed the nonprofit sector so drastically that by 1917 Ward had successfully launched his first national campaign, raising over $114 million for the American Red Cross between June 18 and June 25, 1917. Americans were bombarded by editorials, lantern slides, streetcar signs, banners and continued exhortations to give. President Woodrow Wilson proclaimed the event National Red Cross Week and semi-nationalized the organization, declaring it the nation's official relief agency. Americans for the first time "saw what large sums could be attained through the intensive fundraising campaign hitherto used only at the community level for charity or a civic or church building."[13]

While such techniques increased the pressure on average Americans to give, the appeals to wealthy donors were even greater.[14] One study commissioned by Mary Harriman, widow of the railroad magnate and mother of diplomat Averell Harriman, found that she received 6,000 requests in 1910 and 1911 for aid totaling $267 million. This was at a time when national giving was $270 million.[15] Given the mountains of mail many rich donors received, it was reasonable for them to create foundations to insulate themselves from grantees.

But the temperament of the times went further than this. William H. Allen, the director of the New York Bureau of Municipal Research (which conducted the study of Harriman's giving), believed that misinformed donors could cause great damage. He denounced "the dead hand," or the legacy that outlived its times. Far worse, however, was "the sympathetic live hand which from misinformation and lack of efficiency standards invites insincerity, evasion, waste, incompetence and incompleteness in the use of its gifts. Energy can be deadened by riches and freedom, as well as by restrictions."[16]

Allen opposed unrestricted gifts, saying that "history proves that they frequently encourage sloth, extravagance, indolence, disregard for social needs...[I]n institution after institution in this city [New York] unrestricted legacies go regularly to make up deficits in current accounts instead of perpetuating the giver's interest.[17] But he also opposed restricted gifts (i.e. donor intent), saying that these "frequently outlive their usefulness; cannot change with changes in social conditions; handicap societies in time of need; frequently result in carrying coals to Newcastle and putting bounty on wolf scalps when all wolves are exterminated except those specially reared for the bounty."[18]

Allen believed that if trustees of a foundation could show that the intentions of the donor "no longer exist or are otherwise met by funds of this or other agencies," they should be free to use funds for any purpose whatsoever 20 years after the donor's death.[19] "Every city needs experts on will making, not only to draft unbreakable wills but to submit unquestionable needs," he added. "There is room for a new profession of consulting experts on will making and large giving."[20] He also called for a national clearinghouse to review all requests for aid, separate "worthy" from "unworthy" requests, and forward the worthy one to suitable donors.

## The Creation of Community Foundations

The ideas of Allen and like-minded individuals were instrumental in creating community foundations. These were intended to eliminate the "dead hand" problem by giving unbiased experts authority to "scientifically" decide how small fortunes, pooled into a large fund, should be used. When the Cleveland Foundation,[21] the first community foundation, was created in 1914, one of the city's newspapers noted that most fortunes went to "weak children—the weaker for having had too much money when young...[I]t is almost as unwise for the man of wealth to endow a charity. He doesn't know how soon the charity may become obsolete and his money serves only to pension useless hangers-on." But a community foundation, the paper opined, was more admirable, as it had "representatives of the public having a continuously freshened say as to how it is to be used. Obviously that is better than having it spoil heirs or galvanize dead or dying charities or pile up power in the hands of entrenched trustees suffering from fatty degradations of the soul."[22]

Allen's views, and the creation of community foundations, indicate the climate of opinion that led to a widespread repudiation of donor intent early in this century. But Allen and his compatriots failed to answer one question. If "experts" would separate worthy from unworthy requests, and if strong donor intent would lead to the use of legacies for unnecessary purposes, why should donors create foundations in the first place? If donors believed their wishes would likely be repudiated or ignored after their deaths, why should they create foundations? This is the subject of Chapter One: "The Rockefeller Legacy."

# CHAPTER I

# The Rockefeller Legacy

*"The immense fortune which is to be left to the [Rockefeller] foundation is to be left without any restriction, except that it is to be devoted to the well-being of the human race. And not Rockefeller himself, but the unborn generations of the future, will determine how the money is to be expended... In the Rockefeller Foundation there is not a sentence, nor a word, which will tie down the people of the twenty-first century."*
—Herbert N. Casson (1910)[1]

The philanthropic careers of John D. Rockefeller (1839-1937) and John D. Rockefeller, Jr. (1874-1960) offer an illuminating example of how the problems of donor intent have become solidified.

John D. Rockefeller was a devout Close Communion Baptist. He believed that helping the less fortunate was a necessary part of life. As biographers John Ensor Harr and Peter J. Johnson note, "there was no question that Rockefeller's exclusive motivation for giving was his religious conviction and the old-fashioned concept of stewardship, not the expiation of guilt or the buying of public favor."[2]

Early in his philanthropic career, Rockefeller gave small gifts of between $50 and $500. But as his wealth exceeded the $5 million mark in the 1880s, he was increasingly burdened by requests. In 1891, he hired Frederick T. Gates, a fellow Baptist, to assist in his philanthropic and business concerns. Gates' first task was to shield Rockefeller from those who wanted part of his fortune. "Neither in the privacy of his home nor at his table, nor anywhere else, was Mr. Rockefeller secure from insistent appeal," Gates wrote in his memoirs. "Nor if asked to write were solicitors willing to do so. If in New York, they demanded personal interviews. Mr. Rockefeller was constantly hunted, stalked, and hounded almost like a wild animal."[3]

Gates swiftly put an end to this. He also found that many Baptist groups Rockefeller funded were deemed unworthy of support by Baptist headquarters. He consequently convinced Rockefeller to practice "wholesale" rather than "retail" philanthropy: instead of giving to individual churches, Rockefeller supported Baptist headquarters or mission boards.

# CHAPTER I

"Wholesale" philanthropy did not mean that Rockefeller was unconcerned with how his money was spent. While he did not try to control the activities of his benefactors, he did seek to ensure that they were financially sound. One early recipient was the University of Chicago.[4] When its president William Harper refused to cut expenses to balance the school's budget, Rockefeller summoned him to his office, where John D. Rockefeller, Jr. told him that the school would receive no more money until it balanced its books. Only when Harper left the school and his successor pursued more frugal policies did grants to the university resume.[5]

In addition, Rockefeller was adamant that his charity not be used to promote dependency. "The most perplexing issue for Rockefeller was how to square philanthropy with self-reliance," notes his latest biographer, Ron Chernow. "His constant nightmare was that he would promote dependence, sapping the Protestant work ethic... He dreaded the thought of armies of beggars addicted to his handouts."[6] As early as the 1880s, Chernow observes, Rockefeller discussed with his brother, Frank, whether or not to contribute to a veterans organization in Cleveland. Rockefeller wondered whether such a contribution would be useful, since he did "not want to encourage a horde of irresponsible, adventuresome fellows to call on me at sight for money every time fancy seizes them."[7]

**The "Tainted Money" Controversy**

After 1900, Rockefeller expanded his philanthropic concerns to other Protestant churches. In early 1905, he gave $100,000 to the American Board of Commissioners for Foreign Missions to promote Congregationalism overseas. Though not himself a Congregationalist, his lawyer, sister-in-law, and Frederick Gates (who had switched churches) were members, so Rockefeller felt no hesitancy in contributing.

But the Congregational Church's moderator, Rev. Washington Gladden vigorously protested. Rockefeller's gift was "tainted money," acquired "by methods as heartless, as cynically iniquitous as any that were employed by the Roman plunderers or robber barons of the Dark Ages. In the cool brutality with which properties are wrecked, securities destroyed, and people by the hundreds robbed of their little, all to build up the fortunes of the multi-millionaires, we have an appalling revelation of the kind of monster that a human being may become." Gladden added, "Is this clean money? Can any man, can any institution, knowing its origins, touch it without being defiled?"[8]

For a few months in 1905, "tainted money" was the issue of the day. The *Chicago Tribune* ran a cartoon featuring a prim pastor pointing to a portly man about to contribute to a collection plate. A sign hanging on the plate said, "ONLY HONESTLY ACQUIRED MONEY ACCEPTED." The caption read, "Wait a Minute! How Did You Get That Dollar?" The phrase was even used in vaudeville routines: "Sure it's tainted," the joke went. "Tain't yours and tain't mine."[9]

But the Rockefeller gift had not come to the Congregationalists by whim or chance. The Foreign Missions Board, it soon became known, had been corresponding with the Rockefellers since 1902, and both John D. Rockefeller, Jr. and Frederick Gates had talked with representatives before the grant was made. In fact, the Foreign Missions Board had asked for $163,000 to fund ten proposals, four of which the Rockefellers had rejected. "I never had any question whatever regarding the propriety and even duty of soliciting help for the needy institutions and work of the Board from Mr. Rockefeller, as from other people of means who are members in good and regular standing of Christian churches," wrote James D. Barton, the Foreign Missions Board's secretary.[10]

**The Rockefeller Legacy**

The tainted money episode, however, greatly damaged Rockefeller's reputation. Senator Robert LaFollette (R-WI) charged that Rockefeller was "the greatest criminal of the age," while President Theodore Roosevelt called him one of the "malefactors of great wealth" who had to be tamed. The Memphis, Tennessee *Appeal* compared Rockefeller to Captain Kidd, the pirate. Rockefeller was particularly vulnerable to such assaults because he would not cooperate with writers who wanted to say good things about him. He believed that posterity would show his business dealings to be ethical and just, and that he therefore needed no favorable press. Further, he was a very private man. Unlike Andrew Carnegie who wrote several books and took part in the issues of the day, Rockefeller wrote very little and usually responded to public criticism with silence.[11]

Continued attacks gave Gates an opening. He had for some time been needling Rockefeller to dispose of his fortune. As early as 1896, he warned, "Your fortune is rolling up, rolling up like an avalanche! You must distribute it faster than it grows! If you do not it will crush you and your children and your children's children!"[12] Because of the tainted

# CHAPTER I

money episode, most denominations, at least for a time, refused to accept Rockefeller money. This meant that much of Rockefeller's charity had to be redirected.

**Rationale for the Rockefeller Foundation**

On June 3, 1905, Gates wrote Rockefeller a letter that would change the history of nonprofits. "I have lived with this great fortune of yours for nearly fifteen years. To it, and especially its uses, I have given every thought. It has been impossible for me to ignore the great question of what is to be the end and use of all this wealth. You have not made me the confidant of your thoughts in this, which neither surprises nor grieves me..."

"Two courses seem to me open," Gates continued.

> One is that you and your children, while living, should make final disposition of this great fortune in the form of permanent corporate philanthropies for the good of mankind. It seems to me that either you and those who live now must determine what shall be the ultimate uses of this vast fortune, or at the close of a few lives now in being it must simply pass into the unknown, like some other great fortunes, with unmeasured and perhaps sinister possibilities.

"To me, of course, beyond decent provision against want for the unborn who may come after, this great fortune should be dedicated to and legally secured for the service of mankind by those who live," Gates added.

> It seems to me that any other course than this is morally indefensible... If you and Mr. John [D. Rockefeller] Junior are, therefore, to discharge this trust while you live, there is only one thing possible to be done, and that is to provide legally incorporated endowment funds under competent management, with proper provision for succession, which shall be specifically devoted to the promotion of human well-being."[13]

After listing ideas for several such funds, including one for higher education, one for medical research, and one for "the promotion of fine arts and refinement of taste," Gates concluded that "these funds should be so large that to become a trustee of one of them would make a man at once a public character. They should be so large that their administration would be a matter of public concern, public inquiry, and public criticism. They should be so large as to attract the attention and the intelligence of the world, and the administration of each would command the highest expert talent."[14]

Gates' letter was followed on June 21, 1905 by a letter from John D. Rockefeller, Jr., who told his father that "Mr. Gates' letter to you seems to me a powerful and unanswerable argument... and I endorse it most heartily."[15] In 1906, he made another suggestion to his father that he create "a large trust fund to which you would turn over considerable sums of money to be devoted to philanthropy, education, science, and religion."[16]

But not until 1909 did John D. Rockefeller give $50 million in Standard Oil Company stock to an organization to be known as the Rockefeller Foundation. As part of the deed of trust, Rockefeller said that "I direct said trustees as soon as can advisedly be done, to apply to the Congress of the United States, or to the legislature of such state as they deem advisable, for a suitable corporate charter."[17]

**The Ill-Fated Congressional Charter**

In his memoirs, Frederick Gates explains that one of the reasons for a government charter was to restrict John D. Rockefeller's ability to use his fortune.

> As a private American citizen he could use his means in any amount anywhere in the world for any lawful purpose. Indeed, the charter, in so far as he used it, would restrict his liberty rather than enlarge it, for it would take away from him altogether and place in the hands of an independent and self-perpetuating board the distribution of the funds contributed to it. But on the other hand, Mr. Rockefeller personally was mortal, the charter would be immortal, and confer on his philanthropies the priceless boon of perpetuity, besides securing for them through competent Trustees a higher and broader efficiency than any single intelligence, however able, could compass."[18]

# CHAPTER I

This, however, does not explain why Rockefeller sought a con-gressional charter rather than a more easily obtainable state charter. There were two reasons for this. First, as historian Raymond B. Fosdick notes, most nonprofits at the time sought national recognition, including most of the organizations created by Andrew Carnegie, the Russell Sage Foundation, and such scholarly enterprises as the American Academy in Rome and the American Historical Association. "To Mr. Rockefeller's advisers, therefore it seemed appropriate to follow the same course."[19]

Second, however, these advisers had devious motives. A con-gressional charter would provide an impetus for placing the Rockefeller Foundation under "nonpartisan" control, ensuring not only that Rockefeller's wishes need not be followed but also that they would be irrelevant. Rockefeller's lawyer, Starr Murphy, told a Senate committee that

> it is eminently desirable... that the dead hand should be removed from charitable bequests and that the power to determine to what specific objects that should be applied should be left in the hands of living men who can judge *of* the necessities and the needs in the light of the knowledge which they have as contemporaries, and not that they shall find their hands tied by the will of the man who *is* long years dead. The wisdom of living men will always exceed the wisdom of any man, however wise, who has been long since dead.[20]

Rockefeller believed the passage of a congressional charter would be simple; after all, the General Education Board, a Rockefeller charity that helped Southern black students, had easily obtained one in 1903. Moreover, the chief sponsor of the effort, Senator Nelson Aldrich of Rhode Island. was John D. Rockefeller, Jr.'s father-in-law. But neither Rockefeller nor his advisers foresaw intense opposition from those who distrusted anything Rockefeller might do. A federal lawsuit that would ultimately force the Standard Oil Company to divide into five parts was wending its way through the courts, and there was great suspicion that Rockefeller's efforts to acquire a charter were part of a nefarious scheme.

When Aldrich introduced the charter bill in 1910, opposition swiftly formed. Attorney General George Wickersham wrote to President William Howard Taft, saying a charter would give the trustees of the Rockefeller Foundation absolute control of the income of $100,000,000 or more, to be expended for the general indefinite objects described in the bill, [which] might be in the highest degree corrupt in [their] influence. The medieval statutes against mortmain were enacted to prevent just such perpetuation of wealth in a few hands under the cloak of such a charitable purpose as this... It was not without much reason that the English common law and English statutes required bequests for charitable purposes to be definite and specific in their terms. Such legislation was the result of experience with the indefinite charities which the monastic and other medieval institutions erected, and which were the occasion of so much scandal and corruption...

Moreover, Wickersham noted, the Rockefeller Foundation's statement of purpose, including "the acquisition and dissemination of knowledge" and the "promotion of any and all of the elements of human progress," was so vague that one could not "imagine anything that might not be made to fall within one of these purposes." President Taft's reply was succinct, expressing firm opposition to the charter. "I agree with your characterization of the proposed act to incorporate John D. Rockefeller.[21]

Aldrich's bill passed the Senate Judiciary Committee in 1910 but went no further. Aldrich then allowed amendments that would have limited the foundation's endowment to $100 million; required that the foundation spend interest from its endowment rather than reinvest it; prohibited the foundation from investing more than 10 percent of its endowment in stocks; and barred a new trustee from joining the foundation if a majority of the following persons disapproved: the President of the Senate, the Speaker of the House of Representatives, and the presidents of Harvard, Yale, Columbia, Johns Hopkins, and the University of Chicago. Had Congress authorized a charter with these amendments, the Rockefeller Foundation could well have become a quasi-governmental organization along the lines of the Smithsonian Institution.

Rockefeller also tried to advance the charter through covert diplomacy. On April 25, 1911, Sen. Aldrich, John D. Rockefeller, Jr., and the younger Rockefeller's wife, Abby Aldrich Rockefeller, lunched at the White House with President Taft. To ensure that the lunch was secret, Rockefeller, Jr., and his wife went though a side entrance, and their presence was not recorded in official White House guest books. Writing to his mother, Laura, the younger Rockefeller said that President Taft was "most agreeable and kindly" and that the president opined that the charter would not pass until the Standard Oil antitrust case was settled (which happened a few months afterwards).[22] But the private presidential luncheon did little good. The charter bill was introduced again in 1911, 1912, and 1913. It passed the Senate Judiciary Committee again in 1913, but was never reported out of committee in the House. After Congress adjourned in 1913, Rockefeller went to the New York state legislature, which quickly passed a bill giving the Rockefeller Foundation a state charter.

**The Rockefeller Foundation's Early Years**

Shortly before the creation of the Rockefeller Foundation, Jerome W. Greene, the foundation's first secretary, circulated a memorandum that asked, "How shall the Trustees of the Rockefeller Foundation keep responsive to the will and intelligence of the people through future generations?" Greene wished to create a "Public Council" comprised of one person from each state who would be nominated either by the state university or a leading private institution. Although his idea was never tried, these advisors would have represented "better than anyone else, the wisdom and good will of the community in matters affecting the general well-being."[23]

Pressure to dilute the Rockefeller Foundation board by adding new "independent" members continued. "It is very important to add to the number of Trustees of the Rockefeller Foundation persons of independent position, and known to the country, or at least to the State of New York, as publicists, philanthropists, and educators," Harvard University president Charles W. Eliot wrote to Jerome Greene in 1915. "The fundamental criticisms of the Socialists and Labor-leaders can be met in no other way."[24]

According to historian Robert E. Kohler, Rockefeller Foundation trustees split into two factions. The liberals, including Jerome Greene, Starr Murphy, medical researcher Abraham Flexner and former commissioner of police Arthur Woods, wanted the foundation to address "criminology, alcoholism, drug addiction, feeblemindedness, venereal disease, family structure, incomes policy, and delinquency." They were opposed by Frederick Gates and others, who believed the foundation should deal with less partisan scientific and medical issues. Gates called

Greene's proposal "scatteration," as it would give many small grants rather than a few large ones.[25]

Kohler also notes that Gates and Greene disagreed on who would control the foundation. Gates foresaw Rockefeller's descendants as wielding control while Greene believed professional middle managers would predominate. Significantly, neither side seemed to believe that John D. Rockefeller's ideas or principles would matter. By 1914, many foundation trustees and employees were looking for ways to exclude Rockefeller from the foundation's affairs. One incident in particular helped contribute to that effort.

**The Ludlow Massacre**

In October 1913, the United Mine Workers of America launched a strike against Colorado Fuel and Iron, a company controlled by the Rockefellers since 1912. On April 20, 1914, after a seven-month standoff, private guards and members of the Colorado National Guard surrounded the strikers' camp and began firing. At one point, a tent was set ablaze, and the smoke caused two women and 11 children trapped in a cellar below to die of suffocation. The remaining strikers began to attack Colorado Fuel and Iron property. Ten days later, President Woodrow Wilson ordered other National Guard units into the area to suppress the uprising.

The "Ludlow Massacre" quickly became a *cause celebre* for the left. Novelist Upton Sinclair picketed John D. Rockefeller's home, and in New York City, four members of the Industrial Workers of the World, a radical union, died when a bomb exploded prematurely in their apartment. As historian Priscilla Long notes, "it was generally believed that the bomb had been intended for the Rockefeller townhouse."[26]

The Rockefellers reacted swiftly. John D. Rockefeller, Jr. (a member of the Colorado Fuel and Iron board of directors) went to Colorado, where he met with prominent union organizers, including Mary Harris "Mother" Jones.[27] The Rockefellers also hired Ivy Lee, one of America's first public-relations specialists, to help deal with the aftermath. However, they made a fatal mistake of involving the Rockefeller Foundation in the Ludlow affair.

John D. Rockefeller, Jr. had long been interested in public policy, believing the foundation should be involved in nonpartisan research on public issues. He decided that a study of the Ludlow incident might lead to better relations between labor and management. On the advice of

# CHAPTER I

Jerome Greene and Harvard University president Charles Eliot, he decided to interview W.L. Mackenzie King, a Canadian politician and industrial relations specialist.

Mackenzie King was at first hesitant, fearing that working for the Rockefellers might jeopardize his career in Canada's Liberal Party. But in December 1914, he accepted a five-year grant with a salary of $12,000 a year, which could be cancelled at any time if the Liberals, then out of power, made a comeback.[28] At the time, Mackenzie King was not just a liberal but a radical. Historian H.M. Gitleman notes that on April 6, 1917, he toasted America's entry into World War I with Raymond Fosdick, who later became president of the Rockefeller Foundation, the foundation's historian, and John D. Rockefeller, Jr.'s biographer. After denouncing John D. Rockefeller, Jr.'s opposition to a Wilson Administration proposal to boost income-tax rates on wealthy Americans, Mackenzie King and Fosdick "agreed that in the not too distant future the state would act to level out all of the great fortunes. Before the evening was out, they concluded that socialism was inevitable and desirable,' that workers would one day own the factories in which they toiled, and that society would take proper title to all natural resources."[29]

The mere fact that the Rockefeller Foundation had appointed someone to study Rockefeller businesses was ammunition for Rockefeller's foes. No enemy was more vigorous than Frank Walsh, chairman of the U.S. Commission on Industrial Relations, a federally funded agency that investigated labor-management relations. On January 27, 1915, John D. Rockefeller, Jr. testified before the commission. The hearing included an audience that, according to historian Graham Adams, Jr., consisted "chiefly of Single-Taxers, Socialists, anarchists, AFL members," and members of the Industrial Workers of the World.[30]

John D. Rockefeller, Jr., charmed them all. Commission member Mary Harriman decided that John D. Rockefeller, Jr. was not "a psalm-singing, cold-blooded capitalist," but an "intensely human" person. Even *The Masses*, the leading leftist journal of the day, said the younger Rockefeller was "apparently frank," "gentle," and "Christianish."[31]

But Frank Walsh was not through with the Rockefellers. He believed the commission should go beyond "challeng[ing] the wisdom of giving public sanction and approval to the spending of a huge fortune through such philanthropies as that of the Rockefeller Foundation," and that "the huge philanthropic trusts, known as foundations, appear to be a menace to the welfare of society" since they enabled the wealthy "to become molders of public thought" and to influence public policy.[32] At the hearings, Walsh grilled both Ivy Lee and Mackenzie King about their involvement with the Rockefellers. When the U.S. Commission on Industrial Relations terminated, Walsh formed a nonprofit to criticize the Rockefellers.

Eventually, the Ludlow affair subsided. Colorado Fuel and Iron formed a union to give workers more benefits. Mackenzie King completed his report and returned to Canada, where he eventually became Prime Minister in the 1930s and 1940s. He and John D. Rockefeller, Jr. remained close friends for the rest of Mackenzie King's life. However, the Rockefellers' image had been further scarred.

**The Rockefellers Relinquish Control**

In 1916, John D. Rockefeller transferred his fortune to his children. John D. Rockefeller, Jr. was given most of the estate that did not go to the Rockefeller Foundation or other Rockefeller charities. Nearly all the younger Rockefeller's advisers were liberals or leftists, and they continually urged him to abandon the stalwart confidence in free markets that his father had.

After John D. Rockefeller, Jr. testified before the U.S. Commission on Industrial Relations, Mackenzie King wrote that

> when it is remembered that Mr. Rockefeller, Jr. is at present only administering his father's affairs and is not free to act of his own responsibility in complete measure, when further, it is remembered that it has been his father's friends... who have been his immediate advisers, the progress which has been made by him toward a modern, progressive outlook is remarkable indeed. What is particularly satisfying about it is the circumstance that every bit of it is based on conviction. He has said absolutely nothing that he does not with his whole heart and mind believe."[33]

Raymond Fosdick also helped persuade the younger Rockefeller to abandon the principles of his father. As historian Robert Kohler notes, Fosdick "worked hard to wean Rockefeller, Jr. away from the family's hidebound conservatism."[34] By 1921, Fosdick's brother, noted left-wing

# CHAPTER I

theologian Harry Emerson Fosdick, wrote to Fosdick praising him for helping the younger Rockefeller replace "old Tory" board associates of the elder Rockefeller with more liberal ones.[35] Indeed, John D. Rockefeller, Jr. became his own man after the Ludlow Massacre, and he was heartily approved by liberals. His first significant act after taking control of the Rockefeller fortune was to serve as head of a committee that temporarily combined seven major nonprofits—including the YMCA, Young Women's Christian Association (YWCA), Jewish Welfare Board, Salvation Army, and National Catholic War Council—in a huge charity devoted to the war effort. He was also active in a failed effort to amalgamate existing Protestant denominations into an interdenominational "Church of the Living God."[36]

As biographers John Ensor Harr and Peter J. Johnson note, the main lesson John D. Rockefeller, Jr. learned from the Ludlow episode was to erect a firm wall between the Rockefeller Foundation and the Rockefellers' personal affairs.[37] Though he continued to be a Rockefeller Foundation trustee, he personally repudiated the family's interest in the foundation. Likewise, the Ludlow Massacre severed the elder Rockefeller's associations with the foundation. Though he was a trustee until 1922, he never attended a board meeting, having delegated this task to his son.

When John D. Rockefeller gave the initial grant of $100 million to the Rockefeller Foundation, it was given with a stipulation he called "founder's designations." "It is a condition of this gift that from the income of the Foundation the sum of Two Million Dollars ($2,000,000) annually, or so much thereof as I shall designate, shall be applied during my lifetime to such specific objects within the corporate purposes of the Foundation as I may from time to time direct."[38] But under pressure from his son, Rockefeller rescinded this clause on July 29, 1917, saying that "in view of the increasing demand upon the funds of the Foundation, especially those arising in connection with the great war for human freedom in which our country is now engaged, which have led the Foundation to appropriate a part of its principal, as well as all of its income, I hereby release the conditions."[39]

Rockefeller did, however, make one last effort to assert his will. In 1919, he wrote to his lawyer, Starr Murphy.

> I could wish that the education which some professors furnish was more conducive to the most sane and practical and possible

views of life rather than drifting, as it does, in cases, toward socialism and some forms of Bolshevism. It seems to me that some influences ought to be brought to bear upon the universities and colleges with reference to the textbooks which, from my standpoint at least, are calculated to lead astray and do harm rather than good.

Murphy was aghast. Having helped create the Rockefeller Foundation to block Rockefeller's wishes, he was determined to stop Rockefeller's plan. "The placing of limitations upon... academic freedom must be left to the trustees and faculties of the institutions," Murphy wrote. "[As] it would be extremely unwise for any donor to attempt to place limitations on the character of the teaching which shall be given in an institution to which he contributes, it is hardly less objectionable for him to make the determination as to whether or not he will give to any particular institution dependent upon that matter... I have sufficient faith in the truth," Murphy added, "to believe that in an atmosphere of freedom it will ultimately vindicate itself."[40]

Though Rockefeller lived 18 years after this exchange, he is not known to have asserted his wishes again. He spent the rest of his life in quiet retirement, allowing Ivy Lee and other public-relations people to remold his image. The Rockefellers eagerly took the advice of Lee and his associates. If the John D. Rockefeller of 1915 was a ruthless capitalist who held the world in octopus-like tentacles, the Rockefeller the press portrayed in 1925 was a kindly eccentric who delighted in giving dimes to children. The favorable publicity, however, was won only by severing John D. Rockefeller from the philanthropies he created.

John D. Rockefeller, Jr. took one more step to distance the family from the Rockefeller philanthropies. In the early 1920s, he greatly expanded the trustees of Rockefeller Foundation board. While trustees of the foundation in 1920 were mostly Rockefeller friends, business associates, and family members, by 1925 many had retired. (Frederick Gates retired from the board in 1923.) Their successors were leading businessmen and scholars. From the early 1920s onwards, note Harr and Johnson, the board "could be compared favorably at any time with the Cabinet of the U.S. president-and indeed many trustees later served as Cabinet members."[41]

But there was a crucial difference between the Rockefeller Foundation board and the President's cabinet. While the President can

# CHAPTER I

dismiss cabinet members, John D. Rockefeller, Jr. abdicated his role as leader of the foundation. The board was free to act without regard for the sources of wealth that made the foundation possible. Indeed, a main reason John D. Rockefeller, Jr.'s sons John D. Rockefeller 3rd, Nelson, Laurence, Winthrop, and David created the Rockefeller Brothers Fund in 1941 was to reassert ties between the Rockefeller family and the charities John D. Rockefeller, Jr. had created.

## The Problem of Donor Intent Is Solidified

By 1925, the wealthy donor had two main types of foundations from which to choose: those created by Andrew Carnegie and those created by John D. Rockefeller. In both cases, donor intent was ignored, either because, in the Carnegie Corporation's case, the donor had run out of ideas for disposing of his wealth (see Chapter Two), or in the Rockefeller Foundation's case, the donor had chosen not to assert his will. Not surprisingly, most foundations after 1925 distanced themselves from the sources of their wealth.

However, two major donors of the 1920s did assert their wishes and manage to ensure that these were preserved. Tobacco magnate James Buchanan Duke structured the indenture of the Duke Endowment so it could only be broken by a massive legal effort. Further, he was a regional donor who limited his charity to North and South Carolina. (See Chapter Three for a discussion of the Duke Endowment.) Likewise, Julius Rosenwald, a long-time Sears, Roebuck executive and a prominent liberal philanthropist of the 1920s and 1930s, also asserted his wishes, though by different means. A long-time critic of foundations that outlived their donors, Rosenwald in 1928 gave the Julius Rosenwald Fund $20 million worth of Sears, Roebuck stock on condition that the fund cease to exist within 25 years of his death:

> I am not in sympathy with this policy of perpetuating endowments and believe more good can be accomplished by expending funds as Trustees find opportunities for constructive work than by storing up large sums of money for long periods of time. By adopting a policy of using the Fund within this generation, we may avoid those tendencies toward bureaucracy and a formal or perfunctory attitude toward the work which almost inevitably develop in organizations which prolong their existence indefinitely. Coming generations can be relied upon to provide for their own needs as they arise... [In] accepting the

shares of stock now offered, I ask that the Trustees do so with the understanding that the entire fund in the hands of the Board, both income and principal, be expended within twenty-five years of the time of my death."[42]

In two articles in *The Atlantic Monthly*, Rosenwald explained his reasons for imposing "term limits" on foundations. Narrowly imposing one's wishes on the future meant the creation of philanthropies that out-lived their usefulness, such as an endowment given to Bryn Mawr College that protected students against hunger by giving them baked potatoes. But it was also true, Rosenwald argued, that organizations with vague charters could quickly succumb to institutional hardening of the arteries, becoming preoccupied with self-preservation rather than the purpose for which they were created. "I think it is almost inevitable that as trustees and officers of perpetuities grow old they become more concerned to conserve the funds in their care than to wring from those funds the greatest possible usefulness," Rosenwald wrote. "That tendency is evident already in some of the foundations, and as time goes on it will not lessen but increase. The cure for this disease is a radical operation. If the funds must exhaust themselves within a generation, no bureaucracy is likely to develop around them."[43]

Rosenwald also argued for what today might be called a marketplace of ideas in philanthropy. A donor with a worthy notion, he said, would have that notion funded by others. Yale University was begun with an initial endowment of 600 pounds and a few hundred books. John Harvard created Harvard University in 1638 with a legacy of 300 books and 750 pounds. But these institutions thrived, Rosenwald said, because "they were recognized to be meeting a human need, and this recognition has been expressed in financial support generation after generation... Real endowments are not money, but ideas... Desirable and feasible ideas are of much more value than money, and when their usefulness has once been established they may be expected to receive ready support as long as they justify themselves."[44]

The employees of the Julius Rosenwald Fund accepted Rosenwald's conditions. In fact, they spent the money faster than Rosenwald asked. The Rosenwald Fund terminated in 1948, only 15 years after Rosenwald's death. While a few philanthropists followed Rosenwald's example, most did not. Not until John M. Olin created the Olin Foundation in 1953 was a major foundation organized with a

# CHAPTER I

term limit. Rosenwald himself said the main reason his example would probably not be followed was that trustees of perpetual foundations with vague charters could easily ignore the wishes of their founders."[45]

So by 1925 the problems of donor intent were firmly established. As detailed in the following chapters, the conflicts between donors and philanthropies would harden, not weaken, over time.

# CHAPTER II

# Undermining Donor Intent

How firm a Foundation, we saints of the Lord.
We've built on the faith of our excellent Ford.
We've laundered and lightened the Trustees' Report.
And left for California,
And left for California,
And left for California,
The place to resort.

How firm the Foundation has been for E.C.A.
And for Hutchins, for Davis, what those boys get ain't hay.
What more can we do than for them we have done?
Way out in Pasadena,
Way out in Pasadena,
Way out in Pasadena,
We bask in the sun.

How firm a Foundation, we've Funds by the score.
Have you an idea? We'll establish one more.
We smile through the smog; (some say that we smirk);
Out here in Pasadena,
Out here in Pasadena,
Out here in Pasadena,
The funds do the work.

How fine a Foundation; we are for peace;
We live peaceful lives, and we hope wars will cease.
We've heard mankind cry, and we've answered the call;
We're out in Pasadena,
We're out in Pasadena,
We're out in Pasadena,
Away from it all.

How firm a Foundation; we've three times the dough,
And ten times the brains that any other can show.

# CHAPTER II

> The hell with Rockefeller, and Carnegie, too.
> We've left for California,
> We've left for California,
> We've left for California,
> The hell with you.
>
> – Robert Maynard Hutchins, associate director,
>   Ford Foundation (1952)[1]

The extremities to which the millionaire is reduced by this closing up of old channels of bequest are such that he sometimes leaves huge sums to bodies of trustees "to do good with," a plan as mischievous as it is resourceless; for what can the trustees do but timidly dribble the fund away on charities of one kind or another?
— George Bernard Shaw, "Socialism for Millionaires" (1896)

## The Ford Foundation

In judging whether the Ford Foundation violates donor intent, one must assess the intentions of two men: Henry Ford (1863-1947) and his grandson, Henry Ford II (1917-1987). (Edsel Ford, son of the first Henry Ford and father of the second, died before he could wield control of the Ford fortune. In this family, power passed from grandfather to grandson.) The two men were quite different. Henry Ford was a man who never outgrew his agrarian background, while Henry Ford II was a pillar of the Establishment who attended Hotchkiss and Yale (though he never was graduated from college.)

The evidence suggests that the Ford Foundation routinely violates every charitable principle of Henry Ford, and in a lesser way, those of Henry Ford II. In his last years, even Henry Ford II, who was certainly not conservative, railed against "the liberals" who had seized control of the foundation.

The conventional history of the Ford Foundation is that Henry Ford left no instructions on how his money should be used, thus leaving the trustees free to do whatever they pleased with his fortune. According to foundation historian Waldemar Nielsen, who worked for the Ford Foundation for many years, when Henry Ford died in 1947, four lawyers, supervised by Maurice N. "Tex" Moore (brother-in-law of

Henry Luce), combed Ford's personal and corporate papers and "were unable to find a single sentence or a single note from old Henry expressing any interest in, or ideas about, his philanthropy."[2]

It is true that Ford left no explicit instructions on how his money should be spent. But his philosophy of charity was very clear, and was consistently expressed throughout his life. His views were simply ignored by those who staffed and led the Ford Foundation.

### George Bernard Shaw's "Socialism for Millionaires"

According to William Greenleaf, author of the most extensive study of Henry Ford's charity, Ford gave $37,641,627 during his lifetime. This was not as much as Andrew Carnegie, who gave $325 million, John D. Rockefeller, who gave $600 million, or John D. Rockefeller, Jr., who gave $400 million. But Ford nonetheless donated one-third of his income to charity, and was far more generous than most Americans of his generation.

Greenleaf notes that between 1922 and 1936, millionaires in America on average gave less than five percent of their incomes to charity; Ford's annual donations, however, were in excess of 15 percent of income. Nearly two-thirds of this was not only not tax-deductible, but subject to a surtax. "As gauged by outlay in ration to taxable income," Greenleaf wrote, "the record speaks well for Ford's intentions and performance as a donor."[3]

According to Greenleaf, Ford derived his philosophy of charity from "Socialism for Millionaires," an 1896 essay by George Bernard Shaw. Shaw warned that the millionaire should not try to help the poor directly. Giving money to "the utterly worthless, the hopelessly, incorrigibly lazy, idle, easy going good-for-nothing," Shaw believed, "would soon exhaust the resources of even a billionaire. It would convince the most sentimental of almsgivers that it is economically impossible to be kind to beggars."[4]

Shaw illustrated this point by describing how he once offered to pay someone two pounds to copy a book in the British Museum's reading room. He first offered the job to a former teacher "whose qualifications were out of date, and who, through no particular fault of his own, had drifted into the reading-room as less literate men drift into Salvation Army shelters." The teacher, more interested in leisurely reading than work, subcontracted the job to someone else, who hired someone else, who then hired "the least competent and least sober female copyist in

## CHAPTER II

the room, who actually did the job for five shillings, and then turned it into a handsome investment by making it an excuse for borrowing endless sixpences from me from that time to the day of her death."[5]

Instead of direct aid, Shaw advised the rich to support large projects that government was unwilling to assume.

> I confess I despise a millionaire who dribbles his money away in fifties and hundreds, thereby reducing himself to the level of a mere crowd of ordinary men, instead of planking down sums that only a millionaire can. The millionaire should ask himself what is his favorite subject? Has it a school, with scholarships for the endowment of research and the attraction of rising talent at the universities? Has it a library, or a museum? If not, then he has an opening at once for his ten thousand or his hundred thousand.[6]

### Henry Ford's Philosophy of Giving

These ideas guided Henry Ford throughout his life. He created philanthropies that outlived him and still honor his wishes. Ford N. Bryan, the most authoritative historian of the Ford family, says that Henry Ford began contributing small amounts to charity as early as 1908. By 1910, Ford was a steady contributor to causes such as the Anti-Cigarette League of the United States and Canada. He also served on the board of Detroit's Protestant Orphan Asylum.[7]

But his major works were the Henry Ford Hospital in Detroit and two related efforts in Dearborn, Michigan-Greenfield Village and the Edison Institute (now the Henry Ford Museum). The Henry Ford Hospital is still one of Detroit's leading hospitals, and millions of visitors flock to Greenfield Village each year to see the historic houses that Ford collected and reassembled.

Throughout his life, Ford was besieged by requests for aid. As early as 1914, after introducing one of the nation's first profit-sharing plans, swarms of people lined up outside his house. By 1915, he received 200 letters a day for aid; by 1924, the number had climbed to 10,000 a week, and a team of private secretaries sent out over fifty form letters in response.[8]

Ford often gave money spontaneously to poor people he met during his travels. But he always refused to give to organizations he could not directly control. He would not give to community chests, the predecessors of the United Way, and he consistently opposed any form of charity that might reward idleness.

In *Today and Tomorrow* (1930; co-written with Samuel Crowther), Ford explained at length his views on charity.

> We hold that it is part of our industrial duty-that is, part of our service that supports the wage motive-to help people to help themselves. We believe that what is called being charitable is a particularly mean *form of* self-glorification-mean because, while it pretends to aid, it really hurts. The giver to charity gets a certain cheap satisfaction out of being regarded as a kind and generous man. That would be harmless enough in itself were it not that the recipients *of* charity are usually destroyed-for once you give a man something for nothing, you set him trying to get someone else to give him something for nothing.

"Charity creates non-producers, and there is no difference at all between a rich drone and a poor drone," Ford added. "Both are burdens on production. It will easily take a generation to wipe out the effects of the dole upon the peoples of Europe."[9] In a 1924 interview, he said,

> I believe in living wages-I do not believe in charity. I believe we should all be producers. Organized charity and schools of philanthropy and the whole idea of 'giving' to the poor are on the wrong track. They don't produce anything. If a railroad had a bad piece of track that wrecked cars every day and piled them in the ditch it would cure nothing to merely build a fine repair shop. The track itself should be fixed. Charity and philanthropy are the repair shops and the efficiency, however high, does not remove the cause of the human wrecks.[10]

For those who had experienced misfortune and were willing to work, Ford had plenty of jobs at good wages at his plants. He prided himself on taking people that others might have considered hopeless and turning them into productive workers. He routinely hired the disabled. In 1919, nearly 20 percent of his workers had some sort of disability, including one employee who had lost both hands, four whose legs or feet were gone, four who were totally blind, 123 who only had one hand or arm, and 1,560 with hernias.[11]

CHAPTER II

Former criminals—even violent ones—were routinely hired at Ford plants, and many performed well. Between 1914 and 1920, Ford hired between 400 and 600 convicted criminals, including one convicted of forging the name "Henry F. Ford Jr." on a $15 check.[12] Ford's policy was not to ask for references or a work history, but to judge employees by how well they did on the job. "We do not care anything about references, and a man is kept or discharged solely on his record with us," Ford wrote in *Moving Forward* (1930; also co-written with Samuel Crowther). "The man stands on his own feet and nearly always he becomes a valuable employee once he has gained his self-respect and the knowledge that he is not going to be hounded for anything that he has done in the past."[13]

**The Revitalization of Inkster**

Ford's belief in self-help also extended to blacks. In 1931, Ford heard of the plight of the largely black city of Inkster, a distant suburb of Detroit. Wracked by the Great Depression, most residents were out of work and heavily in debt. The city was bankrupt and had laid off its police and garbage collectors, and could not even afford to turn on the street lights.

Ford decided to help, not by offering charity, but jobs. He hired dozens of residents to work in his factories at six dollars a day, while others were paid a dollar a day to pick up trash, clean the streets, and grow crops. He loaned trucks to pick up garbage and tractors to plow fields. Ford factories crushed slabs of concrete from demolished buildings for use in paving streets and roads.

As biographer Keith Sward notes, "Inkster, in no time at all, became a shining little oasis, immune from the worst ravages of depression." By 1936, Ford had recovered most of his investment. But as William Greenleaf says, his "final achievement was the recovery of usefulness and self-respect by the Inkster residents through their own efforts. This is as Ford would have wanted it."[14]

In May 1932, in the frostiest period of the Depression, Ford ran an advertisement saying that the Inkster experiment was a better way to fight poverty than government welfare. "I do not believe in routine charity," Ford wrote. "I think it a shameful thing that any man should have to take it, or give it. I do not include human helpfulness in the name of charity. My quarrel with charity is that it is neither helpful [nor] human. The charity of our cities is the most barbarous thing in our system, with the possible exception of our prisons." Ford wrote that the residents of Inkster would not have become productive workers "by paying out welfare funds [in] the orthodox manner. The only true charity for these people was somehow to get under their burdens with them and lend them the value of our experience to show them what can be done by people in their circumstances."[15]

**"A Chance and Not Charity"**
Given his belief in self-reliance, Ford always told reporters that he planned to use his wealth to create jobs and cars, not a foundation. "Mr. Ford," William L. Stidger asked in 1923, "the people want to know what you are going to do with your huge fortune when you die?"

"Why do they want to know?" Ford replied.

"I presume because it is getting to be a habit with wealthy men to do some useful and social thing with the vast sums of money that they accumulate. Take Mr. Rockefeller, he has established the Rockefeller Foundation," Stidger said.

"So they want to know what I'm going to do with my money. Well, you can tell them there is no "going to do" about it. I am doing it now! I am investing my money in men; every cent of it, and will continue to do so. When people ask me what I am going to do with my money they usually mean what bunch of secretaries or societies I am going to select to dole out my 'charity.' My money is going to keep on going where it is going now–into men," Ford said.

"Then the business itself is to be the Ford Foundation?" Stidger asked.

"That's right. The organization is to be the Ford Foundation. I want that Foundation to be the life-saving opportunity of millions of men and women to be self-supporting and self-sustaining. My old motto, 'A chance and not charity,' will be the spirit of the Ford Foundation. I do not believe in giving folks things. I do believe in giving them a chance to make things for themselves!"[16]

**Enemy of the New Deal**
Henry Ford's belief in self-reliance and community self-help was coupled with an intense dislike of government. As early as 1925, he told journalist Judson C. Welliver that he worried how inheritance taxes would affect his estate and the Ford Motor Company. "Mr. Ford has never taken much out of his business," Welliver wrote. "He questions

## CHAPTER II

whether the Government ought to be more severe with it than he has been... But some day he will have to relinquish control. When that time comes, the Government will demand the extreme limit of inheritance taxes. To pay them will require liquidating a considerable portion of the estate. The problem will be to take care of the business and at the same time liquidate a sufficient part of it to pay the taxes."[17]

If Ford worried about inheritance taxes in the comparably benign administration of Calvin Coolidge, he had much more to fear under Franklin Roosevelt. An ardent critic of the New Deal, Ford was the only major industrialist who refused to take part in the National Recovery Act, a system of government-organized cartels that was later declared unconstitutional by the Supreme Court. "Through all of his career the conservative grimoires of the American free enterprise system regarded him with alarm," wrote biographer Garet Garrett. "He was a dangerous maverick, almost a revolutionary, at the least a menace, an anticapitalist capitalist-certainly the last man you could trust to defend the premises with his life. And yet, when the New Deal came, he was the one who had the will and the courage to stand against it, *and he stood alone.*"[18]

In 1935, partly inspired by Senator Huey Long's calls to "share the wealth" and "soak the rich," Congress passed the Revenue Act, which Roosevelt declared would change the tax code to fight "unjust concentration of wealth and power."[19] Under the act, taxes on estates rose to 50 percent of assets over $4 million and 70 percent of assets over $50 million.

The Ford Motor Company had always been a closely held, family-run business. Between them, Henry and Edsel Ford held 96.9 percent of the company's stock. If either died, the estate could pay taxes on that man's share of the Ford Motor Company. But if both died, the tax burden might well mean the end of the family enterprise.

Some politicians sided with Ford in his efforts to stop the Revenue Act. In August 1935, Senator Arthur Vandenberg (R-MI) argued that the bill was specifically designed to dismember the Ford Motor Company. "The Ford example seems to have been chosen, even by the authors of the plan themselves, as the most important and challenging clinical test," said Vandenberg. "There need be no speculation as to what will happen to the great Ford industrial enterprise under this proposed tax confiscation. It will be driven into diversified ownership which can come only through enormous ultimate stock sales to the public."[20]

## Creation of the Ford Foundation

On January 15, 1936, Henry Ford took the only option he could to preserve family control of the Ford Motor Company. He created the Ford Foundation. The existing Ford Motor Company stock was converted into two types: non-voting Class A common stock, which comprised 95 percent of the total stock, and voting Class B common stock. Ford drafted a will leaving the Class A shares to the Ford Foundation and the Class B shares to his son and grandchildren. Edsel Ford drafted a similar will. The Ford estate was thus divided into two parts, leaving the wealth Ford created to philanthropy and the Ford Motor Company to the family.

Ford did not create the Ford Foundation out of altruism or to restore his reputation. Unlike the great fortunes created before the Income Tax Act of 1913, no one called Ford a "robber baron" or wicked capitalist. Nor was he seen as a paragon of conspicuous consumption. He lived simply and reinvested most of the profits he made back into his business. "Much of the public was extremely hostile to the fortunes of Carnegie, Rockefeller, and Mellon, which were largely diverted into endowments and foundations," write Ford biographers Allan Nevins and Frank Ernest Hill. "Comparatively few were hostile to Ford's, which people felt was usefully employed for social purposes just where it stood."[21]

Further, the Ford Foundation was created in great secrecy. Ford never announced its creation. The press found out only when the head of Michigan's corporation and securities division told reporters that Ford's lawyers had filed the necessary papers. These lawyers refused to talk to the press, and only Edsel Ford had anything to say: "The foundation will take care of the various charitable, educational, and research activities that I don't care to do personally. It will be on a small scale and I have no intention of making it larger."[22]

For the first few years of its existence, the Ford Foundation was, in fact, small and inconspicuous. During World War II, the Ford Motor Company reached its lowest ebb. After Edsel Ford's death in 1943, Henry Ford resumed control of the company. But he was in his eighties and ailing. He delegated control to Harry Bennett, a hard-headed union buster whose extraordinary incompetence as Ford CEO caused the value of the company to plummet.[23]

## CHAPTER II

### Henry Ford II Rescinds Control of the Foundation

In a power struggle in 1945, Henry Ford II triumphed over Harry Bennett and began a 34-year tenure as chairman of the board of the Ford Motor Company. Two years later, the elder Henry Ford died. Given that both Henry and Edsel Ford were dead, the provisions of their wills took effect, and the Ford Foundation became the wealthiest foundation in America.

From its beginnings, the Ford Foundation was eager to spend money. According to historian Francis X. Sutton, the foundation went $31 million into debt before a single share of Ford Motor stock was acquired by borrowing against the value of the shares it was to receive. In 1948, as the wills of Edsel and Henry Ford were being probated, Henry Ford II signed a statement that he would later regret. He declared that the Ford family would make no effort to use the inheritance of his father and grandfather to control the Ford Foundation. Henry Ford II would be chairman of the board of the foundation and his brother Benson would be a trustee, but their influence would be no greater than any other Ford Foundation employee.

The best explanation of why Henry Ford II signed this document comes from testimony he gave before a House committee (known as the "Cox Committee") in 1952.

> We thought that the amount of funds that would be available in this public instrument was of such magnitude that it would hardly be right for one family to have the decision as to the distribution, in how they should be spent for educational, charitable, and scientific purposes. Further than that, I think it was said, and probably justifiably so, that people who have left their moneys [sic] to charitable organizations so that this trust was so large that the family should not have control of it.
>
> Naturally we want to—we feel that we have an obligation as a family to—carry out to the best of our ability the desires of our forebears, and we intend to do so. I am speaking of my brothers and myself. We intend to do our part as a trustee of the foundation. However, we felt that for the benefit of the whole thing it would be better to have the members and the trustees the same, and also have a majority who were not connected with the Ford Motor Co. or members of our family, so that, if a

matter came to the vote within the foundation, we would not have the control.[24]

By signing this document, Henry Ford II ensured that the intentions of his family would be steadily undermined.

**The Foundation's Early Years**

If Henry Ford was such a firm advocate of free markets and voluntarism, how did the Ford Foundation become such a bastion of the welfare state? Part of the answer lies in the different political views of Henry Ford and Henry Ford II. Some of Henry Ford's views, such as his support of prohibition, were peculiar. Others, such as his support of traditional dancing, were eccentric.[25] Finally, some of Henry Ford's views, particularly his anti-Semitism, were reprehensible. Nonetheless, he championed free enterprise and fought government intervention.

Though not a leftist, Henry Ford II was moderately liberal. He was what pundits of the 1950s called a "modern Republican," a pillar of the establishment who preferred Dwight Eisenhower to Robert A. Taft, and whose relations with Lyndon Johnson were so friendly that, in 1968, he was appointed to head the liberal National Alliance of Businessmen.

Historian Thomas C. Reeves describes Henry Ford II's political views. He was the sort of man

> who had no basic quarrels with the New and Fair deals, who respected academic credentials, who liked Ike (and Adlai), who contributed to *Harper's*, subscribed to *Foreign Affairs*, and read *Time* and *Newsweek*, who professed belief in racial equality, who supported foreign aid and the United Nations, who played prominent (the Far Right frequently used 'conspiratorial') roles in national political conventions, and who was often appointed to positions of authority by both parties.[26]

Henry Ford II supported most of what the Ford Foundation did in its early years. He was, however, bored by some of its activities. In 1951, Paul Hoffman, the Ford Foundation's first president, was leading a discussion about proposed grants to Indonesia when Henry Ford II asked, "My God, where is this place Indonesia that you're talking about? And why in God's name should we be interested in it anyway?" According to Francis Sutton, Hoffman "just shriveled," and was overheard later to say that "he was not going to devote his life to educating this young ignoramus."²⁷

In 1952, the feud between Hoffman and Henry Ford II escalated when Hoffman took an extended leave of absence to work on the Eisenhower presidential campaign. During this time, Henry Ford II acted as president of the Ford Foundation, although he wished to leave the post as quickly as possible. "I want to make cars," he told top Ford Foundation executive W.H. "Ping" Ferry.²⁸ Hoffman, on his return, was forced to resign, and was replaced by Rowan Gaither. The Ford Foundation moved its offices from Pasadena to New York City.

**The Legacy of Robert Maynard Hutchins**
Hoffman's lasting achievement was the appointment in 1950 of Robert Maynard Hutchins as an associate director. Hutchins was a long-time chancellor at the University of Chicago and a leading authority on education. In 1950, he had Senator William Benton (D-CT) visit Henry Ford II. "I spent an hour and a half at breakfast with Henry Ford II this morning," Benton wrote to Hutchins on February 9.

> He is expecting you to call him and have lunch with him the next time you are in Detroit. You are recommended to join Paul Hoffman *in* heading up the Ford Foundation but it was felt that you would bring enemies along with you! I assured Henry Ford that no one would have enemies when he had his hands on half a billion dollars. He doesn't seem to realize the enormous impact himself. My own suggestion *is* that you don't wait too long on a Detroit visit.²⁹

From the start, Hutchins and Henry Ford II disliked each other. The aversion appears to have been personal rather than ideological. Hutchins was an originator of the "Great Books" program of liberal education, while Henry Ford II was a Yale dropout. The feud between them was the proximate cause of Henry Ford II's later resignation as chairman of the board of the Ford Foundation.

**The Fund for the Republic**
Robert Maynard Hutchins chafed while in Pasadena. He wrote satirical poetry about the Ford Foundation, calling it "Itching Palms." But in 1952 the foundation reorganized. Among the changes was the

creation of several specialized funds. To study civil liberties, the foundation created the Fund for the Republic with $15 million. Hutchins became its first and only president.

Hutchins was eager to head the organization. "I've got a new job," he wrote to his friend Thornton Wilder. "It's spending $15 million stolen from the Ford Foundation on civil liberties & racial & religious discrimination, if you know what I mean. It's not bad. It's better than the Ford Foundation."[30] As early as August 1951, Hutchins wrote a memo saying he would deal in "unpalatable causes," and offered ways for the Ford Foundation to distance itself from possible controversy.

In an unsolicited memo to the Ford Foundation board, W.H. "Ping" Ferry explained that the Fund for the Republic was

> not in conflict with the real interest of the Ford Motor Company, although it may sometimes prove irritating to some of its officials, and may embarrass, temporarily, members of the Ford family. In the long run it will bring more credit to the Ford name than the easy and innocuous course of making impressive contributions to established activities or undertaking programs that cannot arouse criticism or opposition. Here it should be remembered that the reputation of the Ford Motor Company largely centers around Henry Ford's lifelong preoccupation with experimentation and pioneering ventures.[31]

Ferry's predictions were to prove radically wrong. In its early years, the Fund for the Republic, which Hutchins called a "wholly disowned" subsidiary of the Ford Foundation, saw itself as a bold, path-breaking venture. As Hutchins declared,

> The Fund should feel free to attack the problem of the freedom of the press; of migrant workers; of the immigration laws and the McCarran Act; of loyalty investigations; [of] the House Unamerican Activities Committee; of conscientious objectors; of academic freedom and teachers' oaths; of racial and religious discrimination in all its manifestations, from lynching to inequality of educational opportunity; of disfranchisement; of dishonesty in government; of the liberties guaranteed by the First and Fourteenth amendments; of the administration of justice, etc.[32]

# CHAPTER II

Hutchins condensed this into a decoration in his office, which consisted of a sampler embroidered with the words, "FEEL FREE." During its short life, the Fund for the Republic acted like a bullfighter waving a red cape at conservatives and daring them to attack. Among its activities were spending hundreds of thousands of dollars for a report on Hollywood black-listing, having *Washington Post* cartoonist Herbert Block prepare a television documentary on civil liberties, and hiring political scientist Clinton Rossiter to write a report on American communism. (Rossiter in turn hired Earl Browder, former head of the Communist Party U.S.A., as a consultant. Browder was at the time under indictment for perjury.)

Some conservatives were troubled by the Ford Foundation even before the Fund for the Republic was created. Columnist George Sokolsky charged that Henry Ford "made nearly all the money in this country, but Paul Hoffman, who is spending that money, seems to be placing [it] in remote bottomless pits and [expending] it for meaningless purposes such as an investigation as to why the world is full of refugees when, in fact, it always has been."[33] The most ardent critic was probably Fulton Lewis, Jr., a newspaper columnist and radio commentator. Every night, millions of radio listeners heard Lewis comment on the issues of the day. For three months in 1955, Lewis's nightly topic was the Fund for the Republic.

A typical example of Lewis' critique was a broadcast of August 25, 1955. After describing efforts to distribute liberal publications, including a book by Harvard University's Erwin Griswold, a television interview on book censorship, and 25,000 copies of the *Bulletin of the Atomic Scientists,* Lewis said that

> in all I have read to you, from these projects of the Fund for the Republic, there *is* not one penny for anything to benefit the farmers of the nation, the man and his wife who run the corner grocery store and provide jobs for a couple of other neighbors... nothing about bringing up healthier kids, or better education, or *better* salaries for school teachers and policemen and postmen... just the same old lines of agitation from the policy book of the CIO Political Action Committee and the Americans for Democratic Action.[34]

Henry Ford II was caught between the Fund for the Republic and American conservatives. According to foundation observer Waldemar Nielsen, the foundation's trustees had "gone for the storm cellar" when the conservative critique began, while Henry Ford II stood steadfast.[35] But the foundation's critics were not just complaining—they were launching boycotts of Ford Motor products. These were actions that Henry Ford II could not ignore. According to Thomas C. Reeves, Henry Ford II received at least 1,200 letters complaining about the Ford Foundation or the Fund for the Republic. Historians Leonard Silk and Mark Silk say that one Ford Foundation officer kept a box with "choice samples of the intimidating missives," and that after reading some of them at the Links Club, Henry Ford II was so irritated by them that he emptied the box into a fire, leaving the foundation officer frantically grabbing ashes for scarred scraps of evidence.[36]

Many of these letters were from Southerners bothered by the Fund's attitude towards race relations. Its "activities have seriously frightened Ford dealers in this region," Charleston (S.C.) *News and Courier* editor Thomas R. Waring wrote to Ford Foundation executive Walter Millis, on July 20, 1956. "[This] may be unfair but nevertheless is a demonstrable fact."[37] In fact, so many Southern Ford dealers complained that Henry Ford II had a form letter printed that said, "it is not Ford Motor Company policy to attempt, directly or indirectly, to influence the personal beliefs of Southerners."[38]

## Resolution of the Controversy

By 1956 the problem of the Fund for the Republic had been settled. On November 29, 1955, *National Review* editor William F. Buckley, Jr., wrote to Henry Ford II about the Fund for the Republic. "What is your own judgment on those activities of the Fund for the Republic that are at public issue?" Buckley asked. "Do you believe that the present management of the Fund is faithfully and effectively carrying out the intentions of the Foundation in establishing the Fund?"[39]

A week later Henry Ford II answered Buckley's charges by replying to a letter sent by John K. Dunfey, chairman of the Anti-Subversive Committee of the American Legion's Post 41 in Syracuse, New York. "Despite the fact that I have no legal right to intervene in the affairs of the Fund for the Republic," Henry Ford II wrote, "I have exercised my right as a private citizen to question the manner in which the Fund has attempted to achieve its stated objectives. Some of its actions, I feel, have been dubious in character and inevitably have led to charges of poor judgment. I am satisfied, however, that no public trust can expect to fulfill its responsibilities if it does not respond to intelligent and constructive public criticism."[40]

Henry Ford II's letter was the apogee of the Fund for the Republic controversy. Some of the Fund's more controversial programs, such as the Herblock television project, were canceled, and Robert Maynard Hutchins conducted himself in a less fiery manner. Eventually, the Fund for the Republic became the Center for the Study of Democratic Institutions, an organization that, while still liberal, did little that was controversial, or even interesting. "When the center set up in Santa Barbara in September 1959 it was intended as a near-total change of life," W.H. "Ping" Ferry noted in a 1988 memoir. "We were to become reflective, not active; quiet, not noisy."[41] In fact, the Center's hottest controversy during its 28 years of existence was a 1975 dispute over whether or not Alex Comfort wrote *The Joy of Sex* and *More Joy* while working as a Center fellow, and whether the Center was entitled to royalties.

But the Fund for the Republic controversy illuminated the problematic relationship between the Ford Foundation and the Ford Motor Company. Since the Ford Foundation's endowment consisted mostly of Ford Motor stock, and since the foundation had no influence in Ford Motor affairs, it was unable to determine the size of its endowment. Conversely, the Ford Motor Company was often blamed for the activities of a large philanthropic enterprise over which it had no control.

The Ford Motor Company and the Ford Foundation were also often confused in the public's mind. According to a 1957 article in *Holiday*, a California trucking magnate celebrated his daughter's receipt of a Ford Foundation fellowship by buying dozens of Ford trucks; another man in Florida insisted on buying Lincolns in the hope that the foundation would take note and give grants to schools and hospitals in the area. An Indian government official had trouble understanding why he did not have to buy Ford cars and trucks after receiving a Ford Foundation grant.[42]

Other conflicts revolved around the Ford Foundation's television programs. According to *Holiday*'s Joe McCarthy, Henry Ford II was "a little put out, to say the least" when he learned that the foundation-subsidized television show *Omnibus* had sold commercials to Willys, one of Ford Motor's competitors. Henry Ford II was enough of a Republican partisan to be incensed when the foundation gave money to a children's television show called *Excursion*, which asked former president Harry S. Truman to be a guest.[43]

## The Foundation in the 1960s

By 1957, all Henry Ford II could do about the Ford Foundation was complain. In 1956, the nightmare the elder Henry Ford had sought to avoid came true. The Ford Foundation, in the largest stock offering of its time, began selling its Ford Motor shares. Because of New York Stock Exchange prohibitions against selling non-voting corporate stock, the shares were converted into voting-class stock. Although the Ford family was able to retain control of 40 percent of the voting shares, the Ford Motor Company was now a public enterprise.

Leonard Silk and Mark Silk say that Rowan Gaither agonized about what to do with the Ford Foundation's newfound wealth, spending many late-night walks brooding about what to do with the money and then not doing anything. At one point, say the Silks, Ford Foundation trustee Donald David proposed that the foundation give all the money to hospitals and spend itself out.[44]

The board's response was to force Gaither out, replacing him with Henry Heald. They then announced that their 1956 grantmaking would include $550 million from the stock sale, including $198 million to private hospitals, $90 million to private medical schools. and $260 million to private liberal arts colleges to be used to raise faculty salaries.

"The purpose of the huge giveaway was unabashedly political," the Silks write. "The hospital grants were deliberately arranged so that there would be some Ford money flowing into every congressional district." But the Silks charge that two of the $250,000 hospital grants had to be recalled after the "hospitals" turned out to be "coyly named whorehouses."[45]

At the same time, Henry Ford II resigned as chairman of the Ford Foundation board of trustees, preferring to concentrate on Ford Motor affairs. With every share of Ford Motor stock sold, his influence on the foundation declined. As president of the Ford Motor Company, he

# CHAPTER II

commanded one of the world's largest companies. But as a Ford Foundation trustee, he cast only one of 16 votes.

During the 1960s, the Ford Foundation continued to grow. In a 1969 report, *The Law and the Lore of Endowment Funds*, the foundation addressed the issue of how colleges and universities could ensure that their endowments would grow relatively free of restrictions, thus touching on the problems of donor intent. "The courts in all jurisdictions pay at least lip service to the necessity of observing the donor's intent," authors William L. Cary and Craig B. Bright wrote. "In practice the attempt to ascertain that intent is often an exercise in futility, which ultimately ends with the predilections of the court masquerading as the wishes of a deceased donor who is no longer able to speak for himself."[46] Technically, Cary and Bright's views were not those of the Ford Foundation, but their advice was nonetheless a fair example of what the foundation was receiving.

In the late 1960s, the divorce between the Ford family and the Ford Foundation was completed. In 1967, Detroit suffered a severe riot, and Henry Ford II resolved to rebuild the city. He led an effort to construct the Renaissance Center, a major office building, and hired thousands of unemployed blacks to work in Ford Motor plants. According to Peter Collier and David Horowitz, Cristina Ford (Henry Ford II's wife) urged him to help the Henry Ford Hospital, which was still serving Detroit as it had since the elder Henry Ford created it. However, it was now in a bad neighborhood and needed funds. Henry Ford II's brother, Benson, asked the Ford Foundation three times for money for the hospital, and was rejected each time. Henry Ford II also asked Ford Foundation president McGeorge Bundy for a grant, but was told, "giving to hospitals is not part of our program."

Cristina Ford, Collier and Horowitz say, was outraged. "How can you do this?" she told Bundy. "Do you forget that the old man left three billion dollars to the foundation? He gave it to you instead of to his own children!" Bundy was not persuaded, so Cristina Ford went to Ford Foundation trustee Robert McNamara and told him how bothered she was that the foundation would spend $45 million on a new headquarters building but nothing on one of Henry Ford's favorite charities. McNamara said he would do what he could. Henry Ford II also conducted an intensive lobbying effort. In 1973, the Ford Foundation gave $100 million to the Henry Ford Hospital, but McGeorge Bundy announced that this was a "terminal grant."[47]

## Henry Ford II's Resignation

The Henry Ford Hospital affair further estranged Henry Ford II from the foundation. In October 1976, Henry Ford II's mother died. Three months later, he went to the Ford Foundation trustees meeting and resigned. He had several reasons for doing so, including concern over at least three grants the foundation had made:

• A 1967 grant to the Congress for Racial Equality for a voter-registration drive in Cleveland. Newly enfranchised voters voted en masse for Democrat Carl Stokes, ensuring a narrow victory;

• A 1969 grant to several members of assassinated Senator Robert Kennedy's staff to "ensure their transition into private life." However, several of these people, such as Peter Edelman and Frank Mankiewicz, were resuming law practices and earning up to $500,000 a year;[48]

• A 1974 grant to S. David Freeman, who became chairman of the board of the Tennessee Valley Authority during the Carter Administration, to study problems relating to energy. Freeman's report called for massive controls on oil companies and energy production. "I felt that Freeman was not the fellow to do the study, but they picked him," Henry Ford II told *New York Times Magazine* writer Lally Weymouth.[49]

Henry Ford II was also disturbed by the management practices of McGeorge Bundy. According to Collier and Horowitz, he believed Bundy was an executive very much like Lee Iacocca, who served under Henry Ford II before beginning his checkered career with Chrysler Corporation. Henry Ford II, say Collier and Horowitz, thought Bundy was "a philanthropic analogue of Iacocca-someone devoted to self-aggrandizement and empire-building at the expense of the institution itself."[50] During Bundy's tenure, the Ford Foundation lost a billion dollars of its endowment—a third of its assets—due to a combination of bad investments and massive grant programs.[51] As Waldemar Nielsen notes, the effects of inflation made the loss even greater: "by dint of had financial and investment management [the foundation] has dissipated almost three fourths of the real value of its assets [since 1970], a loss of something in the order of $6 billion of philanthropic resources measured in current dollars. No disaster of comparable magnitude has ever been recorded."[52]

By late 1976, Henry Ford II had lost patience with the Ford Foundation. "I don't think I can stand this much longer," he told long-time associate Walter Hayes. "This place is a madhouse."[53] Unable to stop the abuses he saw, he could only call attention to them by resigning. In a letter to the trustees, he said, "after 33 years I have come to the point where I have pretty much done all there is to do as a trustee and have said all there is to say." He urged the trustees to have more respect for the free-enterprise system that had created the fortune they were spending. "In effect, the foundation is a creature of capitalism," he wrote, "a statement that, I'm sure, would be shocking to many professional staff people in the field of philanthropy. It is hard to discern recognition of this fact in anything the foundation does. It is even more difficult to find an understanding of this in many of the institutions, particularly the universities, that are the beneficiaries of the foundation's grant programs." He added, "I'm not playing the role of the hard-headed tycoon who thinks all philanthropoids are Socialists and all university professors are Communists. I'm just suggesting to the trustees and the staff that the system that makes the foundation possible very probably is worth preserving."[54]

Accompanying his letter was a cartoon from a 1964 issue of the *New Yorker*, which showed a prim man in a tight suit confronting a subordinate who was throwing currency out an open window. "Just a minute, young man," read the caption. "That's not the way we do things at the Ford Foundation." Henry Ford II personally inscribed the cartoon in a firm, unwavering hand. "To my fellow trustees with warm and high regard. Maybe this fellow has a better idea."[55] For a while, the cartoon hung in the Ford Foundation's lobby. In 1987, a *USA Today* reporter searched the foundation offices for some trace of the Ford family. He found one grainy portrait of Henry Ford in a development officer's suite—the only evidence that the Ford Foundation respected the memory of Henry Ford, Edsel Ford, and Henry Ford II.

After his resignation, Henry Ford II regretted his 1948 decision to abandon control of the Ford Foundation. In a late 1977 interview, he said that if he could live again, he would have divided his grandfather's estate into three parts-one-third for Greenfield Village and the Henry Ford Museum, one-third for the Henry Ford Hospital, and one-third for the Ford Foundation. The foundation would have been only "one-third as big, and therefore it wouldn't have gotten into so many different kinds of things, but nevertheless might have been able to do a substantial job in the meantime."[56]

Additional evidence of Henry Ford II's intentions comes from a series of oral histories that he taped for the Henry Ford Museum in the early 1980s. These tapes were sealed until five years after Henry Ford II's death, and were unearthed by *Detroit News* reporter Jon Pepper, who used them for a multi-part series in 1994. The tapes refer at least twice to the Ford Foundation. "I made a big mistake on the Ford Foundation," Henry Ford II said. "I had the Ford Foundation in my hand at one time. Then I lost it, and lost it on my own volition. I gave it away on my own. I was young, inexperienced, and stupid. I just muffed it. It got out of control, and it stayed out of control. And now it's gone, of course."

In a second passage, Henry Ford II referred to how easy it would have been for the Ford family to ensure that the Ford Foundation did what the family wanted. "It could have been done so easily. It could have been done with a pen-in four seconds. We had three trustees. We could have done anything we wanted. We could have taken the [Ford Motor] stock and given it to any nonprofit company, nonprofit Edison Institute [now the Henry Ford Museum], nonprofit Henry Ford Hospital, nonprofit Fair Lane, [Henry Ford's house, now a conference center], nonprofit whatever you want. And done a much better job for the whole family than I did. I did it all on my own and made a horrible mistake. I'll never live it down, and I regret it sincerely. But what the hell can I do about it? I can't do anything about it. Just have to lie and die with it."[57]

In a 1990 biography of Henry Ford II, Walter Hayes, a long-time friend and former Ford Motor vice-president, recalled a 1979 conversation with Henry Ford II. Ford said that if he had not abandoned family control of the Ford Foundation, it would have remained in Detroit with a primary purpose of serving the local area. There would have been national programs, Hayes recalled, but the main goal would have been to aid the needy in Detroit.

Could Detroit's institutions have absorbed all the Ford Foundation's wealth? Would a Detroit-based foundation have done as much good as a global philanthropy? "They couldn't have done a worse job than the one that has been done," Henry Ford II replied, "no matter what they did."[58]

The controversy over Henry Ford and Henry Ford II's intentions was revived in 2006, when Michigan Attorney General Mike Cox announced a probe of the Ford Foundation to see if the foundation was spending enough of its money in Michigan. Because of the foundation's incorporation in Michigan, General Cox claimed that the investigation fell within his oversight.

## CHAPTER II

Patricia E. Moordian, president of the organization that managed the Henry Ford Museum, told the *Chronicle of Philanthropy* that the last grant by the Ford Foundation to the museum was in 1973. She said that the museum "is definitely supportive of the A.G.'s efforts. The need is very, very big in southeast Michigan."[59]

In June 2006, state representatives Andy Dillon and Bill Huizenga introduced a bill in the Michigan state legislature that would require foundations incorporated in Michigan to spend half their grants in the state. The bill would affect not just the Ford Foundation, but also other large foundations as the Charles Stewart Mott, Kresge, and Kellogg foundations, none of whom spent half their grants in Michigan.

Attorney General Cox said he supported the legislation. He told the *Detroit News* that the bill "applies to all foundations so it'll make them all nervous—which is fine with me."[60]

As of this writing, no action had been taken on the bill, and Attorney General Cox's investigation had come to no conclusions. Critics of the efforts said that the actions were a wrong way to enforce donor intent, given the Ford Foundation's vague charter and Henry Ford II's 1948 renunciation. "The Ford experience is an argument for donors to be more careful about setting up their philanthropic organizations, not for government to take control whenever there is a dispute," said *Detroit News* columnist Thomas Bray.[61]

"Whatever its flaws," adds *National Review* reporter John J. Miller, the Ford Foundation "is a private institution in a free society. It should not have to endure political shakedowns, even when they come from well-meaning conservatives."[62]

## The Carnegie Corporation of New York

The philanthropic enterprises of Andrew Carnegie (1835-1919) are both good and bad examples of donor intent. The organizations Carnegie endowed before 1911—the Carnegie Foundation for the Advancement of Teaching, the Carnegie Institute of Pittsburgh (now Carnegie-Mellon University), the Carnegie Institution of Washington, and the Carnegie Endowment for International Peace—still reflect Carnegie's wishes. But his last creation, the Carnegie Corporation of New York, evolved in a way that undermined the positions and causes Carnegie supported.

Unlike most entrepreneurs of his day, Carnegie was a prolific writer, producing four books and scores of magazine articles. His views remained remarkably constant throughout his life. A student of Herbert Spencer and William Graham Sumner, he championed free enterprise (with the exception of protectionism, which he favored for the United States) and opposed expanding government.

Carnegie's major work, *Triumphant Democracy* (1886; revised 1893), is a 500-page salute to American inventiveness and ingenuity. Carnegie delighted in attacking socialism ("a domain of foreign cranks") and the income tax, which he correctly predicted could only be administered by "a thorough system of espionage and minute examination... not in harmony with the spirit of free institutions."[1] He was particularly harsh on efforts to establish government welfare. These, he warned, would "foster the idle and improvident at the expense of the industrious and prudent... Whenever paupers regard charity as a right, they are apt to demand it in cases where they would hesitate to ask for favors."[2]

### "The Gospel of Wealth"

Documents unearthed by David Nasaw, who is writing a biography of Carnegie, showed that he spent years thinking about what to do with his fortune. In an 1885 letter to British Prime Minister William Ewart Gladstone, Carnegie said that he would give away his fortune during his lifetime. And in an 1887 pre-nuptial agreement with Louise Whitfield Carnegie, Carnegie stated that "Andrew Carnegie desires and intends to devote the bulk" of his fortune to charity "and said Louise Whitfield sympathizes and agrees with him in said desire."[3]

Carnegie explained his philosophy of philanthropy in "The Gospel of Wealth," the famous 1889 essay that also continued his critique of socialism.

> The Socialist or Anarchist who seeks to overturn present conditions is to be regarded as attacking the foundation upon which civilization itself rests, for civilization took its start from the day when the capable, industrious workman said to his lazy and incompetent fellow, "If thou dost not sow, thou shalt not reap," and thus ended primitive Communism by separating the drones from the bees.[4]

# CHAPTER II

"The Gospel of Wealth" was the first essay to recognize the problems of donor intent. Carnegie noted that there were three ways a wealthy person could dispose of his fortune: leave it to his children, leave it to charities, or give it away during his lifetime. Carnegie believed that while giving *some* money to one's children was desirable, giving heirs great wealth would make them soft and indolent. "Wise men will soon conclude that, for the best interests of the members of their families, and of the State, such bequests are an improper use of their means."[5]

Carnegie was also critical of creating charities that outlived a donor's death. "Knowledge of the results of legacies bequeathed is not calculated to inspire the brightest hopes of much posthumous good being accomplished by them," he wrote. "The cases are not few in which the real object sought by the testator is not attained, nor are they few in which his real wishes are thwarted. In many cases the bequests are so used as to become only monuments of his folly."[6]

Carnegie argued that philanthropists should, after deducting expenses for a modest life, give money during their lifetimes. But they should not, he believed, randomly give to people they did not know. The "main consideration" of the philanthropist "should be to help those who cannot help themselves, to provide part of the means by which those who desire to improve may do so; to give those who desire to rise the aids by which they may rise; to assist, but rarely or never to do all."[7] For him, libraries, hospitals, colleges, astronomical observatories, parks, concert halls, and the like would enrich the lives of many, and were thus worthy objects of philanthropy.

Carnegie expanded these views in an 1895 address dedicating Pittsburgh's Carnegie Library. He reiterated his belief that donors should give during their lifetimes, saying that "the aim of millionaires should be to deserve such eulogy as that upon the monument of Pitt: 'He lived without ostentation, and he died poor'."[8] But the goal of giving, he insisted, was not to redistribute income. If a rich man divided his fortune equally among the poor, the result would be to increase, not decrease, poverty, since lower-income workers would stop working in order to receive aid. Rather than trying to help the poorest, he argued, it was more important to aid "the vastly more precious class" of "the swimming tenth—the industrious workers who keep their heads above water and help themselves, though sometimes requiring our assistance, which should never be withheld in times of accident, illness, or other exceptional cause, and always deserving our sympathy, attention, and recognition, and the outstretched hand of brotherhood."[9]

## Carnegie's Early Philanthropy

Until 1905, Carnegie followed the principles set forth in "The Gospel of Wealth." He either gave communities things they needed, such as libraries and church organs, or created institutions with narrow, specific aims. Frederick Lynch, a New York pastor who worked with Carnegie on peace issues, recalled in a 1920 memoir that even Carnegie's "most intimate friends could seldom persuade him to give large sums to anything in which he was not personally interested or of which he had not made a special duty."[10] On one occasion, a group of friends urged Carnegie to give money to medical research. He responded, "it's a great thing; but that's Rockefeller's sphere. Get him to do it."[11]

In at least one case, Carnegie's aims were impossible to achieve and were altered. In 1906, he became worried about college professors who lacked funds for retirement, and created the Carnegie Foundation for the Advancement of Teaching. This provided free pensions for professors with at least 15 years of service, as well as for widows married to eligible participants for at least 10 years and also for "librarians, registrars, recorders, and administrative officers of long tenure."[12] By 1909, 96 institutions were informed of their eligibility. Because the pensions were free, historian William C. Greenough notes, everyone wanted one. Even Woodrow Wilson, after resigning from the presidency of Princeton University in 1910 to run for governor of New Jersey, demanded one.

Carnegie began the program with a grant of $10 million. Over the years, the Carnegie Corporation of New York gave the Carnegie Foundation for the Advancement of Teaching another $12 million, and loaned another $15 million. This, however, was insufficient, and in 1918, with Carnegie's approval, the pension program was transferred to the Teachers Insurance Annuity Association of America (TIAA), a newly created for-profit enterprise. Later named TIAA-CREF, this giant insurance company still sells pensions to most of America's college and university professors. But eligible academics and their widows (widowers were apparently not eligible) still receive Carnegie pensions, even though the list of potential recipients was sealed in January 1931. As of July 2006, the Carnegie Foundation for the Advancement of Teaching was paying pensions to one eligible widow. Since 1918, it has paid $87.4 million-substantially more than the $10 million to $15 million Carnegie thought the program would require.[13]

# CHAPTER II

## The Carnegie Corporation of New York

The nature of Carnegie's philanthropy began to change between 1905 and 1910, when he created the Carnegie Endowment for International Peace. After nearly two decades as America's leading philanthropist, Carnegie was growing weary of the part. Biographer Joseph Frazier Wall notes that by 1906, "Carnegie was tired of the game," and by 1910, "he was desperately sick of it." As Carnegie wrote to a friend, "The final dispensation of one's wealth preparing for the final exit is... a heavy task—all sad... You have no idea the strain I have been under."[14]

That strain grew as Carnegie aged. In 1908, Carnegie asked several of his friends, including Harvard president Charles W. Eliot and Columbia University president Nicholas Murray Butler, for suggestions on what sort of organization would be worth an additional $5 or $10 million. Butler's biographer, Michael Rosenthal, noted that while Eliot did not ask for money for Harvard, Butler was blunter. "I know of no other way in which more useful work could be done for the civilization of the United States and of the world than by making it possible for the one great metropolitan University to do the work of leadership and enlightenment which lies ready at hand." In fact, Butler argued, to make Columbia the equal of universities in London, Berlin, and Rome as "a real lighthouse of humanity," Columbia would need, not just $10 million, but "up to twenty millions" of Carnegie money.[15]

Carnegie had no interest in giving to university endowments, except for universities that he created. But Butler's proposal contained one clause that $10 million of Carnegie funds could be used to create an institute that could produce "a great body of international opinion which would not tolerate the brutalities and immoralities of war, with all that war meant and involves."[16]

This idea intrigued Carnegie. He was long interested in international peace, and had been a steady contributor to peace societies. Carnegie spent the next two years mulling about Butler's idea. His decision was accelerated in 1909, when textbook magnate Edwin Ginn announced that he would create a peace organization (which eventually became the World Peace Foundation) and endow it with $1 million upon his death.[17]

Ginn's announcement acted as a catalyst for Carnegie to create his own peace organization. Another spur to Carnegie took place in 1910, when he became convinced that President Taft would sign treaties with

Great Britain and France ensuring that all disputes between them and the United States would be submitted to binding arbitration. The move by President Taft, observes Michael Rosenthal, "ignited Carnegie as all the complicated persuasion by Butler and his colleagues had not... Carnegie's belief that a genuine system of international arbitration could be the key to perpetual peace now seemed not a dream, but an actual political possibility."[18]

As historian Larry L. Fabian notes, Carnegie rewrote the deed of trust for the Carnegie Endowment for International Peace several times, and only agreed to transfer $10 million in United States Steel bonds to the organization when Taft seemed ready to support the arbitration treaties.[19] But the endless negotiations and lobbying that created the endowment wore Carnegie out. He was 73, and still in possession of vast wealth. What was he to do?

On the advice of Theodore Roosevelt's Secretary of State, Elihu Root, Carnegie used $125 million in 1911 to create the Carnegie Corporation of New York. Root's biographer, Philip Jessup, observes that Carnegie went to Root with a plan to create a large foundation that would come into existence after Carnegie's death. Root advised Carnegie to create an organization during his lifetime, because the courts could easily declare a posthumous trust invalid, as had happened with the will of presidential candidate Samuel Tilden.[20]

Carnegie gave the Carnegie Corporation only one instruction: to provide pensions for former presidents of the United States and their widows. Otherwise, "I give my Trustees full authority to change policy or causes hitherto aided, from time to time, when this, in their opinion, has become necessary or desirable. They shall best conform to my wishes by using their own judgment."[21]

As Joseph Frazier Wall notes, when Carnegie created the Carnegie Corporation of New York, he "had been forced to abandon almost all of the basic tenets of philanthropy he had expressed in the "Gospel of Wealth."[22] Moreover, he quickly found that his deed was irreversible. Biographer Burton J. Hendrick tells how a few years after the Carnegie Corporation was created, Carnegie wanted to create a similar organization in Great Britain. He tried to transfer $10 million of the Carnegie Corporation's endowment to a new institution. "Carnegie was astonished when the question was raised as to the legality of this step," Hendrick writes. He went to Elihu Root, "who served as a kind of supreme court when points like this were at stake," and was told that his deed could not be altered and that his wishes no longer mattered. (Carnegie, however, used money he had saved for his retirement to create the British organization.)[23]

Fortunately, during Carnegie's remaining years the Carnegie Corporation of New York did not become a bureaucratic hierarchy. According to historian Robert E. Kohler, it "was more like an old-fashioned family charity than a modern foundation,"[24] with Carnegie personally involved in most gifts and with much of the money given to other Carnegie philanthropies. However, some of Carnegie's instructions were contradicted. In 1918, a year before Carnegie's death, the trustees voted to end pensions for former presidents. (Only William Howard Taft received one.)

But while Carnegie was still alive, the trustees of the Carnegie Corporation violated his wishes a second time, by slowing down and nearly eliminating the library program. As historian Theodore Jones notes, by 1914 it was clear that many communities were misusing Carnegie's funds for libraries. The town of Clarksville, Texas, for example, received a $10,000 grant in 1902 for a library. But by 1905, the librarian was tired of working without pay and left. The town mayor asked Carnegie if he could turn the library into offices, and was refused. Eventually, according to Jones, "tramps moved in and warmed themselves by burning books and bookshelves." In 1910, a local barber tried to buy the long-vacant building for $1,000 but was refused on the grounds that he would have to pay the money directly to Andrew Carnegie."[25]

The Carnegie Corporation decided to investigate, and hired Cornell University economist Alvin Johnson to travel across America to see how the library funds were used. Johnson found that many libraries were soundly run, but still others were badly managed. In some cities, he found that library board members "thought reading a futile and usually an injurious activity."[26] "I found relatively few towns in which the library had been located where it would be most accessible," Johnson recalled in his memoirs, "and some towns where the library had been located on a practically inaccessible site, to oblige some powerful real-estate owner."[27]

Johnson recalled that he was summoned to a meeting of the Carnegie Corporation board in November 1916 to discuss his report. He proposed that the corporation eliminate most of the money spent on libraries, divert the funds to training librarians, and tighten procedures by which communities could obtain Carnegie libraries. After Elihu Root read the report, Andrew Carnegie's private secretary, James Bertram, confronted Johnson. "Your proposals, Doctor Johnson, fly straight in the face of Mr. Carnegie's intentions," Bertram said. "He wanted to give libraries to communities and leave the communities absolutely free to manage them any way they might see fit. He abominated centralized, bureaucratic control. That is exactly what you want to introduce. Mr. Carnegie never wanted an unnecessary cent to be spent in the administration of his charities. I have administered the whole huge enterprise of establishing libraries with just one secretary, with a desk in my room. To do what you propose would require twelve secretaries and at least six rooms—a big unnecessary expense."

"Not so huge an expense," Johnson replied, "for keeping track of an investment of fifty millions." "A big expense, and unnecessary," Bertram repeated. "And as for library training, Mr. Carnegie never believed in it. He believed in having books where anybody could get hold of them. What made him, he used to say, was a private library a philanthropic gentleman opened to him. A librarian's business is to hand out the books. That doesn't require a long, expensive training."[28]

After the board meeting, Elihu Root invited Johnson to his office and explained that the board, with the exception of Bertram, supported Johnson's findings. "Bertram was in Carnegie's service for years," Root said. "He loved Carnegie, and Carnegie was devoted to him. And we can't do anything to hurt the old fellow, who retires before the year is out. However, as you will see, your recommendations will presently be in force." (At the time of this conversation, Bertram was 44. He remained with the Carnegie Corporation until his death in 1934.)[29]

One year later, the Carnegie Corporation board voted to terminate library construction grants except for those already in the pipeline. Of the 1,419 libraries built with Carnegie's money, only six new grants were made after 1917, with the last, to American Fork, Utah, made in 1919. Historian Theodore Jones notes that there is no evidence as to what Carnegie's reaction was to the corporation's decision to terminate the library program.[30]

**The Erosion of Carnegie's Views**

After Carnegie's death in 1919, the erosion of donor intent at the Carnegie Corporation was slow. The foundation's president, James R. Angell, tried to end all grants to Carnegie philanthropies and, for that matter, to anything except graduate schools. This was too radical, and Henry S. Pritchett, also president of the Carnegie Foundation for the Advancement of Teaching and the TIAA insurance company, succeeded Angell. Pritchett, says Kohler, decisively "turned back to tradition"[31] and supported other Carnegie charities, including the bailout of the ill-fated pension program. However, his successor, Frederick Keppel, gradually cut funding to Carnegie charities. Grants to maintain public libraries ended in 1925; to medical programs in 1929; and to scientific research in 1931. In fact, Keppel spent most of his tenure ending old programs without creating new ones. He read all proposals, and "what did not appeal to him went off the desk into the waste basket, what did appeal to him was approved."[32] Consequently, the Carnegie Corporation remained small.

Not until after World War II did the Carnegie Corporation become a large foundation comparable to those created by the Rockefeller family. As the organization grew, it moved steadily away from the beliefs that Carnegie had espoused. As Ellen Condliffe Lagemann shows in *The Politics of Knowledge* (1989), a history of the Carnegie Corporation, the foundation was responsible for many of the ideas of the Great Society. Under the presidency of John Gardner (1955-1965), it specialized in education, and many of the ideas it championed (such as increased educational aid to the poor) were implemented when Gardner left to become Secretary of Health, Education, and Welfare in the Johnson Administration.[33] When Alan Pifer was president (1965-1982), the foundation became, in the words of foundation observer Waldemar Nielsen, "the quintessential liberal, activist, entrepreneurial foundation: more of a combat force than a traditional charity."[34] Under Pifer, it spent millions on grants to the Children's Television Workshop for production of "Sesame Street."[35] It was also a major supporter of the Children's Defense Fund in its early years, and continues to support the organization.

The Carnegie Corporation quietly forgot Carnegie's belief in free enterprise, limited government, and self-help. In 1977, the foundation issued *All Our Children,* a report that included the following propositions:

• "The society we want... would be a society where a parent would be seen as an honorable calling, a form of work as worthy of public support as the defense of the nation or the construction of superhighways...."

- "It would be a society where present excessive inequalities of income, power, and dignity were much reduced."
- "It would be a society where the rights of parents and children were more adequately represented in the courts and throughout the land."
- "It would be, in short, a society that took seriously and had translated into its basic outlooks and policies today's rhetoric that claims children to be our 'most precious natural resource' and calls families 'the building blocks of our society.'"[36]

In 1985, 300 representatives of the many Carnegie philanthropies met in Dumfermline, Scotland (Carnegie's European home) to celebrate the Carnegie sesquicentennial. Though the leaders of the organizations talked about Carnegie projects (a telescope in Chile, a genetics program in Washington, D.C.) and were entertained by a Scottish actor impersonating Carnegie, no one, according to a report in the *Chronicle of Higher Education,* discussed Carnegie's support of capitalism, limited government, and voluntarism. Carnegie Corporation president David Hamburg told the *Chronicle* that Carnegie's failure to leave instructions on how the foundation's money should be spent showed "a tone of receptivity to new information and ideas and a sensitivity to changing circumstances. He would have liked that we took the time to fundamentally reconsider what we do, and he would have seen in our new programs a continuing commitment to three major themes that shaped his philanthropy: peace, education, and social justice."[37] Hamburg did not explain how Carnegie supported "social justice"—often a euphemism for government wealth redistribution.

The Carnegie Corporation continues to be a champion of expanded government. Recent grant recipients include the Children's Defense Fund, National Council of La Raza, National Urban League, and the Council on Economic Priorities. When the Clinton Administration took office in 1993, three members of the Cabinet-Secretary of State Warren Christopher, Secretary of Health and Human Services Donna Shalala, and National Economic Council chairman (and future Treasury Secretary) Robert Rubin had served as Carnegie Corporation trustees.[38]

In 1996 Vartan Gregorian, a former president of Brown University and the New York Public Library, became Carnegie Corporation president, and Thomas Kean, former governor of New Jersey, was named chairman of the board of trustees. In an interview with the *New York*

# CHAPTER II

*Times Magazine,* Gregorian explained that, in his view, the Carnegie Corporation should support affirmative action, world peace, and education issues. When asked if foundations could replace government social programs, he stated that, in his view, the foundation's role should be to "stimulate, assist, ask questions, and risk being critical. They cannot replace ongoing, sustained national commitments" by government.[39]

The Carnegie Corporation is also engaged in an extensive effort to expand the federal government's role in childcare. In 1991, it established the Carnegie Task Force on Meeting the Needs of Young Children. In 1994, the task force issued a report, claiming that America was "beginning to hear the rumblings of a quiet crisis" about child care, and calling for more state regulation of child care centers, government subsidies to increase the pay of child care workers, and developing networks so that child-care providers could receive more state and private grants. In 1996, the corporation gave $175,000 to the National Governors Association to ensure that the states had policies "that promote young children's healthy development and school readiness."[40]

In 1999, the Carnegie Corporation decided to commemorate the millennium by awarding $15 million in library grants. None of the money (far less, before adjusting for inflation, than the $56 million Carnegie spent on library construction) went to new libraries, but instead went to the budgets of existing libraries. In Houston, the grants went to programs designed to reach Latino patrons. The Cleveland Public Library said it would use the funds for new programs for day care providers and to provide new library cards for the city's children. These grants, said Thomas M. Kean, chairman of the Carnegie board, were designed "to highlight the central role of America's public libraries in preparing young people, adults, and newcomers for a new century."[41]

In 2001, the Carnegie Corporation said it honored its founder's legacy by presenting the first annual Andrew Carnegie Medals of Philanthropy. It was unclear how the winners of this prize—Leonore Annenberg, Brooke Astor, Irene Diamond, William H. Gates Sr, David Rockefeller, George Soros, and Ted Turner—upheld Carnegie's faith in limited government and free enterprise. (Astor and Diamond, however, upheld one principle of Carnegie's by running term-limited foundations that spent themselves out of existence.)

Vartan Gregorian said that he still kept a photograph of Carnegie in his office. "Every day," Gregorian said, "I ask him, 'How'm I doing?'" [42]

# The John D. and Catherine T. MacArthur Foundation

Like Carnegie, John D. MacArthur (1897-1978) was a champion of free enterprise. In 1935, he bought Bankers Life, a bankrupt insurer, for $2,500. It grew by selling policies at lower rates than competitors and by being the first insurance company to hire large numbers of part-time and handicapped workers. MacArthur, the sole owner, reinvested most of the profits in real estate in Florida and New York City. When he died, he was one of only two billionaires in America. His holdings included thousands of acres in Florida and 19 office buildings and 6,000 apartments in New York City. (As late as 1992, the MacArthur Foundation was still one of the largest holders of undeveloped land in Palm Beach County, Florida.)

MacArthur's innovative strategies brought him scores of enemies, particularly in government. He fought the Internal Revenue Service, the Post Office, the Federal Trade Commission, and the insurance commissions of scores of states. At one point in 1951, the Illinois insurance commissioner held what *Fortune* called "a grand inquisition" in which the insurance commissioners of 14 states tried-and failed-to prove that Bankers Life had broken the law.[1] All these investigations left MacArthur with an intense dislike of bureaucracy and regulation. He refused to give money to politicians[2] and denounced environmentalists who sought to block development of his Florida properties as "bearded jerks and little old ladies" who "are obstructionists and just throw rocks in your path."[3] "A staunch conservative with political views to suit his nineteenth-century personality," Lewis Beman noted in *Fortune* in 1976, "he (MacArthur) complains that environmental regulations require heavy investments in sewage treatment, buried utility lines, and other improvements." Planners, MacArthur told Beman, "think alligators are more important than people."[4]

MacArthur also quarreled with his son, J. Roderick "Rod" MacArthur (1920-1984). While the elder MacArthur was fairly conservative, Rod MacArthur was liberal and a self-proclaimed "draft-dodger" who spent the Second World War in the ambulance corps. As Joshua Muravchik notes, in 1972 Rod MacArthur organized the Chicago branch of Republicans for McGovern, "although friends doubt that he really was a Republican."[5] In 1984, he received the Roger Baldwin Lifetime Achievement Award from the American Civil

# CHAPTER II

Liberties Union—an award given only five times in 60 years. "Rod MacArthur was the kind of guy who harangued total strangers in restaurants about PCB levels in white-fish," Kenneth W. Hope, director of the MacArthur Foundation's fellows program, told the *New York Times Magazine*.[6]

Rod MacArthur spent most of his career starting businesses that failed. In the late 1960s, he founded a company to produce lava lamps just as they were becoming unfashionable. In 1973, however, he created the Bradford Exchange, a successful collectible-plate business. John D. MacArthur, who advanced Rod MacArthur $70,000 for the business, promptly sued, claiming that he owned 51 percent of the company. The senior MacArthur even padlocked the doors of the warehouse where the plates were stored, also seizing the firm's customer lists and bank accounts. Rod MacArthur took his revenge by breaking into the padlocked warehouse and taking the plates out.

In 1975, Rod MacArthur bought out his father for $100,000 and became owner of the Bradford Exchange. The firm continued to thrive. Rod MacArthur told the *New York Times* in 1977 that his pre-tax profits were $1.6 million in 1975 and $4 million in 1976.[7] Rod MacArthur used profits from the Bradford Exchange as well as Hammacher Schlemmer, a mail-order firm acquired in 1980, to endow the J. Roderick MacArthur Foundation, which supports left-wing causes. After his death in 1984, these were passed on to his three children, most notably John R. "Rick" MacArthur (born 1956). According to Forbes, Bradford Exchange profits in 1992 were about $20 million, much of which went to the J. Roderick MacArthur Foundation."[8]

**Creation of the Foundation**

From 1970 onwards, John D. MacArthur worried about disposing of his fortune. He spent much of his last decade in the coffee shop at the Colonnades Hotel in Palm Beach, Florida (which he owned).

Writing in the *New York Times* in 1973, Jon Nordheimer found MacArthur to be "quite possibly the nation's most accessible billionaire." "Women in straw hats and bathing suits trot by his table on the way to the beach," Nordheimer wrote, "passing a steady stream of petitioners and hucksters who line up each day to curry favor from Mr. MacArthur, who sits stone-faced and skeptical between a Silex coffee pot and a telephone."

"This is the greatest racket," MacArthur said. "If I took these guys up to my office [in the hotel penthouse], I'd have to be courteous to them. Here I can just get up and walk off into the kitchen and hide."⁹

MacArthur did not wish to leave his fortune to his children and he was also concerned about estate taxes. So he quietly decided to leave his wealth to two foundations: the Retirement Research Foundation, a small think-tank that analyzes pension programs, and the John D. and Catherine T. MacArthur Foundation. Together, these two organizations received 99 percent of MacArthur's fortune.

Like Carnegie, MacArthur willed his fortune without instructions on how his wealth should be used. MacArthur's lawyer, William Kirby, told *Foundation News* in 1982 that MacArthur told him during at the Colonnades Hotel, "Bill, I'm going to do what I know best. I'll make it (money). But you people, after I'm dead, will have to learn how to spend it."

Kirby said that at point he asked MacArthur to "do something big for charities." MacArthur erupted, saying, "Forget it. The hell with it." He then added, "It's not because I'm cheap. Do you have any other client who is going to give as much money as I will? So I'm charitable. If I was going to decide who to give the money to right now, I couldn't sit at this coffee table, because I'd be bothered day and night. They'd all be after me to try and get my money, and I couldn't lead the life I want to lead. So let me alone in peace. Don't worry—you're going to get all the money."¹⁰

Kirby, who stayed with the foundation until his death in 1990, said that he saw "two beautiful ironies" in the MacArthur Foundation. The first was that MacArthur, well known for his thrift,¹¹ would leave his money to philanthropy. Second, that a man "who ran the business, a single owner-some would say a tyrant-turned control over completely to us."¹²

When the MacArthur Foundation was created, it had five board members: William Kirby, two executives from Bankers Life and Casualty, radio commentator Paul Harvey, and Rod MacArthur. Paul Harvey told Joshua Muravchik that in selecting them, MacArthur "knew we mostly feel the same way about things that he did." Said another board member, "We're mostly a bunch of Midwestern businessmen devoted to free enterprise and opposed to more government controls."¹³

# CHAPTER II

## Controversy over the Foundation's Course

Between 1979 and 1981, Rod MacArthur fought for control of the MacArthur Foundation. He threatened lawsuits alleging that the board had conflicts of interest since two members were top executives of Bankers Life. He also charged that the foundation's assets had been mismanaged. "Rod was a forward-thinking guy on the giving side," William Kirby said, "but on this control question we felt that we couldn't give and we wouldn't give."[14]

As a compromise, the board was expanded. The Bankers Life executives appointed two members, former Treasury Secretary William Simon and former University of Illinois president John Corbally. Rod MacArthur nominated two members, scientist Jonas Salk and physicist Murray Gell-Mann. Three other members-former Attorney General Edward Levi, former M.I.T. president Jerome Wiesner, and Gaylord Freeman, former board chairman of the First National Bank of Chicago-were appointed to be neutral members with no ties to Rod MacArthur or Bankers Life. But with these additions, Muravchik notes, "the board was no longer dominated by John MacArthur's associates but by prominent national figures."[15] Moreover, some of the new members, particularly Wiesner and Salk, were as liberal as Rod MacArthur.

For the next two years, the board engaged in lively disputes over what the MacArthur Foundation would become. "Board members, unable to work together, established separate fiefdoms not only for grant-making decisions but for the complex affair of getting Bankers ready for sale," Brenda Shapiro reported in *Chicago* magazine.[16] While many of these disputes were ideological, others were more personal. Rod MacArthur and William Simon "fought openly," particularly over a $100,000 grant to the U.S. Olympic Committee, an organization Simon chaired at the time. In 1981, according to Shapiro, Simon tried to oust Rod MacArthur, but William Kirby blocked the effort. Shortly thereafter, Simon resigned, ensuring that the MacArthur Foundation would become one of America's largest liberal foundations.

Simon's departure, however, did not end Rod MacArthur's quarreling. He continued to fight with the MacArthur Foundation until his death in 1984. According to John Corbally, the MacArthur Foundation's first president, "for a while the board was devoting only about one-quarter of its meeting time to programs and the rest to litigation." "I recall counting more than 30 lawyers at one board meeting—there literally was not a seat available," added MacArthur

Foundation vice-president James M. Furman in a 1987 interview with the *Chronicle of Higher Education.*[17]

**Bastion of Liberalism**

Today, the MacArthur Foundation is best known for its fellowship program of "genius awards," which gave $103,933,322 between 1981 and 1992. These occasionally go to conservatives, most notably philosopher Leszek Kolakowski and the National Center for Neighborhood Enterprise's Robert Woodson. But for every conservative, a hundred liberals receive the honor. This may be because those who nominate candidates are mostly liberals. As Anne Matthews reports in the *New York Times Magazine,* the list of nominators in 1981 included two conservatives—University of Chicago philosopher Allan Bloom and Woodrow Wilson Center director James Billington—but at least 11 liberals: University of Pennsylvania English professor Houston Baker, Jr.; Carnegie Foundation for the Advancement of Teaching president Ernest Boyer; author Ralph Ellison; author Frances Fitzgerald; critic Alfred Kazin; National Public Radio president Frank Mankiewicz; author Toni Morrison; Equal Employment Opportunity Commission chairman Eleanor Holmes Norton; theater director Joseph Papp; cartoonist Garry Trudeau; and Harvard University English professor Helen Vendler. Since 1981, liberals known to have served as nominators include Children's Defense Fund chair Marian Wright Edelman, historian John Hope Franklin, and biologist Jonas Salk.[18]

In at least one case, a MacArthur Fellowship was awarded to a recipient that John D. MacArthur personally disliked. According to author Denise Shekerjian, at an unspecified time (probably in the 1970s) Patrick Noonan," who later became president of the Nature Conservancy and Conservation Fund, went to MacArthur's Palm Beach coffee shop to seek funds. "You know, Mr. MacArthur, sir... saving the parklands... important wetlands... national heritage... ecology..." Noonan was swiftly interrupted. "Young man," MacArthur said, "I've never given anything away in my life, and I'm not about to start now." As Noonan left, MacArthur told him to pay for his coffee.[19] (In 1985, Noonan became a MacArthur Fellow, and in 1989, the land Noonan asked MacArthur to donate became the John D. MacArthur State Park.)

According to the *Chronicle of Higher Education,* in 1988 the MacArthur Foundation considered revising its MacArthur Fellows program to include separate fellowships for scientists and for business

## CHAPTER II

leaders. Kenneth Hope, former director of the program, told the *Chronicle* that the foundation would probably never recognize a successful capitalist, because "we're competing with other programs that reward people, and prominent among them is the marketplace. There's little case for giving it (a grant) to a millionaire."[20]

The evidence suggests that the MacArthur Fellows Program has gone through three stages. First, under the leadership of Kenneth Hope, the foundation funded liberal activists and the occasional non-liberal (such as essayist Stanley Crouch). Catharine Stimpson's brief tenure (1993-96) shifted funding towards the multicultural race-and-gender left. Among the most notorious fellows under her tenure were musicologist Susan McClary, who declared that Beethoven's Ninth Symphony was about "the throbbing music rage of a rapist incapable of obtaining release," and historian Patricia Nelson Limerick, whose work *The Legacy of Conquest,* as *U.S. News and World Report* columnist John Leo wrote, argued "that the settling of the West was essentially one long spasm of greed, racism, sexism, and violence that isn't over yet."

Leo concluded, "The truth is that the MacArthur Awards, launched in 1981 to reward high achievement and high promise, are not what they once were. The science awards still seem to be given out fairly, but other selections pretty clearly have much more to do with politics than with achievement of potential."[21]

Under the leadership of Daniel Socolow, who has overseen the MacArthur Fellows Program since 1997, grants are no longer given to political activists. Instead, the foundation prefers to give money to tenured academics in endowed chairs.

It's far from clear that the fellows program has done much to allow "genius" to thrive. In 2005, *Crain's Chicago Business* investigated the MacArthur Fellowships given for literature and found that 88% of the fellows wrote their most award-winning works before they received the fellowships. Many winners published little or nothing after receiving their prize, most notably Ernest J. Gaines, author of *A Lesson Before Dying,* who published nothing after winning his MacArthur Fellowship in 1993.[22]

"Many of the people" receiving MacArthur Fellowships, observed Stanley Katz, a professor at Princeton's Woodrow Wilson School, "are the usual suspects, who aren't going to produce much more, The program's track record on unknowns isn't that much better than anyone else's."[23]

Though the fellowship program is probably the best-known part of the MacArthur Foundation, it is a relatively small project. The foundation's educational programs, led by Peter Martinez, formerly with the Saul Alinsky Institute, have given millions to education reform proposals, including a ten-year $40-million grant to the Chicago Education Initiative, a major backer of the Chicago school reform program, which seeks to decentralize schools to give parents more say in setting budgets and in hiring and firing teachers. The foundation is also the nation's largest private funder of mental-health research, and has given millions to environmental causes, most notably a $15-million grant in 1982 to create the World Resources Institute, a major command-and-control environmental group.

One of the MacArthur Foundation's more controversial projects is the Peace and International Cooperation Program, which has dispensed $150 million since 1984. As Joshua Muravchik reports, grant recipients include the socialist Institute for Policy Studies and three independent organizations created by IPS: the Center for National Security Studies, Center for International Security Studies, and Policy Alternatives for the Caribbean and Central America. Peace grants have also gone to former IPS employees Eqbal Ahmad (once indicted for conspiring to kidnap Henry Kissinger and blow up government office buildings), Todd Gitlin (a University of California sociologist and New Left veteran), Daniel Ellsberg, David Cortright, William Arkin, Daniel Siegel and Jenny Yancey. At least three former Sandinistas-Alejandro Bendana of the Nicaraguan foreign ministry, foreign trade minister Alejandro Martinez, and ambassador Carlos Tunnerman-have received MacArthur Foundation grants since the defeat of the Sandinista government in the 1990 elections. The foundation also gave $55,000 for research on a biography of radical attorney Leonard Boudin.

Under the leadership of Jonathan Fanton, who has headed the MacArthur Foundation since 1999, the foundation has remained a pillar of political liberalism MacArthur Foundation grantees oppose the death penalty, support increased environmental regulation, support failed public housing programs, and support international bureaucracies, On nearly every issue, MacArthur grantees favor ever-expanding, more intrusive government.[24]

The MacArthur Foundation is an enormously inefficient one. *Chicago Sun-Times* reporter Cheryl L. Reed found in 2004 that "For every dollar it doles out, the MacArthur Foundation spends another 40 cents for expenses, ranking it first out of the nation's top 10 charitable

CHAPTER II

foundations in its ration of expenses to payout." Reed also discovered that the foundation paid its leading officers very well; in 2002, Jonathan Fanton earned $525,181, while chief financial officer Lyn Hutton earned $764,904. Three other MacArthur Foundation officers—vice-president William Lowry, vice-president and secretary Arthur Sussman, and general counsel Joshua Mintz—earned over $350,000.

Paul Harvey, who served on the MacArthur Foundation board from 1978-2002, said that John D. MacArthur if he were alive would have denounced the foundation's extravagance. MacArthur, Harvey said, "would have been exasperated. Embarrassed, frustrated and utterly unsympathetic" to the high salaries paid to MacArthur officials. "He would have loved to bang some heads together."

Rick MacArthur agreed with Paul Harvey, ""If my grandfather were alive today, he would have utter contempt for the MacArthur Foundation. There's no question that my father and grandfather wanted the lowest overhead possible."[25]

## The Pew Charitable Trusts

Oil baron Joseph N. Pew, Jr, was an old-time Republican Party boss who despised government regulation and whose oil refinery in Marcus Hook, Pa., emitted noxious fumes that made the town's air almost uninhabitable. The senior executive of Sun Oil in Philadelphia in the '40s and '50s was called many things in his life: humorless, corrupt, Roosevelt-hater. "Environmentalist" was not one of them. But 35 years after his death, a family charity started by Pew is one of the leading funders of the American environmental movement, pumping an expected $22.5 million this year into causes that Pew himself might well have loathed. In particular, the Pew Charitable Trusts played a key role in convincing President Clinton to adopt tough air pollution regulations that the oil industry strenuously opposed. "The founders of Pew would be rolling in their graves if they knew," said Robert Scheffer, a Boston-based consultant to environmental groups."

— Scott Allen, reporter, *Boston Globe* (1997)[1]

> When I speak of the free enterprise system at its best, I mean when it is entirely free—free from monopoly, private or governmental; free from government control or intimidation; free from trade agreements which result in price or production control after the matter of the cartel systems of Europe.
>
> — J. Howard Pew (1938)[2]

With the possible exception of the Barnes Foundation, the foundation that has committed the gravest violation of donor intent is the Pew Charitable Trusts. The Pews believed in free markets, limited government, and traditional virtues. They practiced their charity quietly, without any desire for publicity or fame. The professional philanthropists who succeeded them believe in self-promotion, big government, and communitarianism.

The Pew family's wealth came from the Sun Oil Company. Sun's founder, Joseph N. Pew Sr. (1848-1912), had participated in the Spindletop oil strike in Texas in 1901, and he was one of the few independent oil refiners who would not be bought out by Standard Oil. By the 1930s, Sun Oil had become a major oil producer and refiner as well as a manufacturer of oil tankers for itself and its competitors. All the Pews were Republicans. But as Sun Oil historian August W. Giebelhaus notes, "some... took more active political roles than others."[3] The two most energetic children of Joseph N. Pew Sr. were Joseph N. Pew, Jr. (1894-1963) and his brother, J. Howard Pew (1882-1971).

**Champions of Free Enterprise and Traditional Charity**

Joseph Pew was a corporate lobbyist who led the successful effort to overturn FDR's National Recovery Act. In the late 1930s, he began to purchase magazines, including the *Farm Journal* and *Pathfinder*, a rural news weekly, which he transformed into market-oriented publications opposed to government growth.

Joseph Pew's political activity was not limited to words. When the New Deal began, according to a 1939 article in *Fortune*, Pew decided to visit the state Republican Party in Philadelphia. "Mr. Pew had visualized the Republican party as occupying sizable, busy offices, something on the order of a large corporation. Instead he found an office deserted except for a handful of underlings... His business friends, even those who were substantial contributors, couldn't tell him where the Republican party was, but assured him that it must be where it had

## CHAPTER II

always been."[4] Pew spent $1 million to revitalize the Pennsylvania Republican Party and $200,000 more to help Arthur James take the governorship in 1938.

He also sought to influence national politics. "The Republican Party stands today where the Continental Army stood at Valley Forge," Pew said in 1940, "and if Haym Salomon and Robert Morris could empty their purses to keep that army alive, so can we."[5] By 1940, after failing to secure the Republican presidential nomination for Robert Taft over Wendell Willkie, Pew had come to regard the New Deal as "a gigantic scheme to raze U.S. businesses to a dead level and debase the citizenry into a mass of ballot-casting serfs."[6] A 1944 article in the *New Republic* called him the leading "Roosevelt-hater" in the United States, a man whose "rabid antipathy to the New Deal" was far more virulent than any member of the Mellon or DuPont families.[7] Pew's fundraising for Republican presidential candidate Thomas Dewey in 1944 was the subject of a speech by Democratic National Committee chairman Robert E. Hannegan, who denounced Pew as "one of the wealthy group of little-known, power-hungry men whose steady stream of money dominates the Republican party."[8]

Joseph's brother, J. Howard Pew, was president of Sun Oil during the Great Depression. He was less active politically, but his many speeches in defense of free enterprise are among the most eloquent ever written by an American corporate executive. "The competitive enterprise system," he said in 1945, "has given us the highest standard of living ever achieved by any country at any time in the world's history."[9] Pew supported many causes but refused to contribute to any organization he believed leftist, including those that favored government welfare. He thought most seminaries were too radical and gave millions to create the Gordon-Conwell Theological Seminary "to turn out the kind of ministers he sought."[10]

By all accounts, J. Howard Pew presented himself in public as a grim and austere man who, in the words of *Institutional Investor* reporter Jack Willoughby, "believed in stiff-backed Christianity, small-town individualism, and local philanthropy." "He was always the chairman of the board, stiff and distant," Pew's grandson, George Black, told Willoughby. "I don't think I ever saw him out of a three-piece suit."[11] One anonymous source told *Fortune* in 1941 that J. Howard Pew was so grim that he looked "like an affidavit all over."[12]

It is important to note the connection of J. Howard Pew's views on economics and theology. The clearest expression of his theological outlook is contained in a 1954 debate among members of the National Council of Churches. At the time, Pew was chairman of the National Lay Committee, which advised the Council on public questions. At one point, Bishop William C. Martin said many Christians disagreed with Pew's support for limits on government. Citing Christ's teaching that "Ye shall know the truth, and the truth shall make you free," Pew answered that "Socialism, Welfare-Stateism, Government intervention, or any other term used to describe Collectivism enforced by the power of Government, appears to be directly antithetical to the above ideals." "Jesus depended on the power of persuasion," Pew continued. "He did not coerce individuals. He saw clearly that attitudes of the heart cannot be changed by coercion, by law and penalty. He depended entirely on the persuasive power of his mission. When Christians lose faith in the message of Jesus and seek to reform society by the power of the state, they are in effect appealing from God to Caesar; they are trying force because they have lost faith in the power of their religion."[13]

Pew continued to continued to critique the Presbyterian Church for the rest of his life. In 1960, for example, he said that delegates to the Presbyterian Church annual convention should not "meddle in secular affairs" by endorsing collective bargaining and birth control and opposing capital punishment. Such positions, Pew said, were contrary to "natural law and the freedom and rights guaranteed by the Constitution" as well as being pronouncements that "frequently coincide with Communist objectives."[14]

Pew was also a generous contributor to conservative and libertarian organizations. "There seems little question that Mr. J. Howard Pew of Philadelphia is one of the biggest contributors to Rightist causes," noted Anti-Defamation League of B'Nai Brith officials Arnold Forster and Benjamin B. Epstein in the 1964 book *Danger on the Right*, "quite apart from the support provided such organizations by him and his family." They noted that the Pew family was the major donors to the Christian Freedom Foundation, a pro-capitalist Christian organization. They also said that Pew contributed to the Foundation for Economic Education, Americans for Constitutional Action, and the John Birch Society, although they provided no evidence of whether or not Pew was active in the Birch organization.[15]

In the 1940s, the Pews began to create several trusts to administer

## CHAPTER II

their estates. There would eventually be seven, and some had typically vague charters. The Pew Memorial Trust, created in 1948, was designed to "help meet human needs through financial support of charitable organizations or institutions in the area of education, social services, religion, health care, and medical research."[16]

The J. Howard Pew Freedom Trust, created in 1957, was different. Pew specifically instructed that it be used to "acquaint the American people" with "the evils of bureaucracy," "the values of a free market," "the paralyzing effects of government controls on the lives and activities of people," and "to inform our people of the struggle, persecution, hardship, sacrifice and death by which freedom of the individual was won." Such "forms of government" as "Socialism, Welfare stateism [and] Fascism... are but devices by which government seizes the ownership or control of the tools of production."[17]

Like Henry Ford, the Pews appear to have created trusts to retain control of the family company while avoiding inheritance taxes. The Pews willed 45 percent of Sun Oil stock to their estates while retaining 55 percent—enough to ensure family control of the enterprise. This tax-avoiding move ensured that the Pew Trusts would become very large. Nearly all of J. Howard Pew's $100-million estate went to the Freedom Trust. Joseph N. Pew left $30 million from his $36-million estate; Mabel Pew Myrin (1889-1972) willed $84 million of her $88-million estate; and Ethel Pew (1884-1979) left $59 million of her $61-million estate to charitable causes.

Moreover, there's some evidence that the Pews worried about the Tax Reform Act of 1969, which altered the rules governing foundations. One provision of the Act required that foundations disburse annually at least six percent of their assets. But soon thereafter, Congress reduced the payout rate to five percent. According to a report in the *New York Times*, Rep. Herman Schneebell (R-PA) on behalf of the Pews and the Kellogg Foundation introduced the bill changing the payout rate. At the time Sun Oil and Kellogg Company dividends were less than six percent, and this meant that the assets of the foundations would be sure to shrink in a bear market."[18]

**Radical Restructuring**

Until the late 1970s, the Pew Trusts were devoted to two causes: charities in the Philadelphia area, which received the largest share, and conservative and libertarian projects. In 1974, for example, the Trusts' largest contributions were to the University of Pennsylvania ($2.8 million), Lankenau Hospital in Philadelphia ($1.1 million), Grove City College ($1.1 million), Children's Hospital in Philadelphia ($1 million), Christianity Today ($500,000), and Presbyterian-University of Pennsylvania Medical Center ($500,000). The Trusts also donated $435,000 to Gordon-Conwell Theological Seminary, $320,000 to the American Enterprise Institute, and $300,000 to the Christian Freedom Foundation.[19]

As the trusts' founders died, however, few members of the family were willing to take part in managing them. This ensured that there would be changes in the recipients of Pew gifts. At the same time, the number of Pews steadily increased, as the great-grandchildren and great-great grandchildren of founder John Pew came into their inheritances.

"With at least 1,000 third, fourth-, and fifth-generation descendants of John Pew," the *New York Times*'s David Diamond noted in 1981, "dispersed throughout the country, the family no longer functions as a cohesive clan."[20]

Some change occurred during the presidency of Robert Smith, a former Sun Oil vice-president who served as administrator of the Pew Charitable Trusts from 1972 to 1977 and president from 1977 to 1986. Smith began giving money to Ivy League schools and "mainstream social agencies."[21] In 1979, the Pew Memorial Trust issued an annual report for the first time, showing its assets (which, of course, didn't include the other six trusts) at $890.2 million, making it the nation's second-largest foundation at the time.[22]

But not until Thomas W. Langfitt became president of the Pew Charitable Trusts in 1986, however, did the foundation undergo radical change. In his first two years as administrator, Langfitt fired 95 percent of the trusts' staff. In 1988, he hired Rebecca Rimel, a self-described "high school cheerleader turned executive feminist," as executive director of the foundation. According to the *Chronicle of Philanthropy*, Rimel's main goal was to increase "access and justice for disadvantaged groups in our society."[23]

Shortly after assuming the Pew presidency in 1986, Langfitt called for placing the Pews' principles "within the context of the world in the late twentieth century." The trusts now would espouse "empowerment of the individual" and "preservation of our American heritage."[24] Langfitt also advocated "more government funds" for welfare, hoping that "public and private agencies [would] join hands [in the 1990s] to provide the human and financial resources needed to empower people."[25]

**Disregarding Donor Intent**

Roger Williams reports in *Foundation News* that the Pew Charitable Trusts have "eliminated almost all of their right-wing grantmaking and embraced a broad range of projects, including some that manifestly oppose the business interests the old Pews held inviolable." He adds that many grants would "send the late J. Howard Pew and Joseph N. Pew, Jr. spinning in the family crypt."[26] In an interview with *Town and Country*, Rimel explained her political beliefs. "If we could reinfuse the idealism of the Sixties into our work, it could get the country out of this morass of feeling that problems are insoluble. We have to assume that if we're committed, innovative and thoughtful, there's nothing we as a country can't solve."[27]

An analysis of Pew grants by the *Philadelphia Inquirer* shows that the amount given to Philadelphia institutions fell from 56 percent of total grantmaking in 1980 to 23 percent in 1991. The trusts have also ended gifts to many of the Pew family's favorite charities. Mabel Pew Myrin willed her home and 350 surrounding acres in Chester County, Pennsylvania to create Camphill Village at Kimberton Hills, a place for retarded people to live and work. When her granddaughter, Karin Myrin sought a grant from the Pew Charitable Trusts, she found that the Pew staff often would not return phone calls. "There's been such a turnover of staff at Pew that a lot of them don't even know my name," she told the *Philadelphia Inquirer*.[28]

In fact, few members of the Pew family are now involved with the Pew Charitable Trusts. According to Lucinda Fleeson, the Pew heir "who was closest philosophically to the trust founders,"[29] John G. "Jack" Pew (a cousin of Joseph and J. Howard Pew) found himself consistently outvoted at Pew board meetings, and was forced to resign. The family member most involved in the trusts is R. Anderson Pew, a great-nephew of Joseph and J. Newton Pew. His notion of the purpose of the Pew Charitable Trusts is expressed in a 1990 interview with the *New York Times*. According to reporter Kathleen Teltsch, he professed to be "mystified" by the idea that the Pews were conservative, because "Our Aunt Harriet Pew in Civil War days ran an underground railroad helping slaves from Parker's Landing in Virginia. You can't get much more liberal than that."³⁰ (Harriet Pew had no involvement in creating the Pew Charitable Trusts.)

Perhaps the Pew Charitable Trusts most directly violate the beliefs of the Pew family by making grants in the area of energy exploration and development. As Dan Rottenberg of *Town and Country* reports, the trusts have supported environmentalists who favor restrictions on oil drilling in the Alaskan wilderness. This strikes directly at the source of wealth that made the Pew Charitable Trusts possible.

Rebecca Rimel summed up her views of the Pew family in an interview with *Foundation News*. She praised the family for having "humility, a quiet style, a conviction that one doesn't dictate through grants." Nonetheless, she said, "the political ghosts" of the Pews "are gone."³¹ In an interview with the *Chronicle of Philanthropy*, she noted that half the members of the Pew board are either Pew family members or people "who knew the donors and are familiar with the donors' wishes."³²

In a letter to the author, Rimel states that the Pew Charitable Trusts board still follows the wishes of their founders. "The Trusts' four founders were, as you describe, conservative in their thinking," Rimel wrote, "but they were also passionate in their commitment to hospitals, churches, schools, universities, and organizations that encouraged civic engagement and democratic principles. The Trusts today have not wandered from these founding precepts. As time has passed, they have necessarily shaped their giving to accommodate evolutionary changes in society. To the extent the Trusts have changed, it is in a way that the founders would likely have saluted."³³

Readers may judge whether Rimel's statements are accurate by the following account of recent Pew Charitable Trusts activities. Politically, both Rimel and her staffers describe themselves as non-ideological. Thomas Langfitt, in a 1997 interview with *National Journal*, describes the Pew board as having "no ideological bias," adding that there was ideological bias on the board in the past, presumably because it was conservative.³⁴ In an interview with the *Washington Post*, Paul C. Light, director of Pew's public-policy program, claimed that he was a moderate who gave money to both the left and the right.³⁵

But an analysis of Pew Charitable Trusts giving done for the Capital Research Center by Dr. Robert Lerner and Dr. Althea Nagai found that the Trusts gradually increased spending on liberal causes and decreased it

CHAPTER II

for conservatives. In 1981, the Trusts gave $2.4 million to conservative organizations; by 1993, they had eliminated all grants to the right, although they did give $150,000 in 1994. By contrast, spending on liberal causes and organizations steadily increased. In 1986, the Trusts gave three times as much money to the left than to the right; by 1994, liberals were getting 40 times as much Pew Charitable Trusts money as conservatives.[36]

These spending patterns have continued. In 1996, for example, the Trusts' public-policy program did give $237,500 to the American Enterprise Institute to support a project by AEI fellow Norman Ornstein on campaign-finance reform. It also gave $300,000 to the Hudson Institute "to strengthen nongovernmental research institutes in the Baltic States." But, in the name of J. Howard Pew, the trusts also gave money to the Brookings Institution ($150,000), the Center for Responsive Politics ($660,000), the League of Women Voters Education Fund "in support of the Money + Politics: People Change the Equation Project" ($450,000), and Rock the Vote Education Fund ($660,000). Despite the severe restrictions in the Pew Freedom Trust indenture, the Pew Trusts also began to give money to radical environmental groups, including the Tides Center ($245,000) and the Environmental Information Center ($770,000).[37]

The Pew Charitable Trusts also continues to be a major funder of environmental programs. Green groups who received 1996 grants include the American Conservation Association ($267,500), the Environmental Information Center ($2.4 million), Green Seal, the National Audubon Society ($300,000), the Natural Resources Defense Council ($375,000), the Pesticide Action Network North America Regional Center ($225,000) the Sierra Club Legal Defense Fund ($200,000), the Tides Center ($1.3 million), the Wilderness Society ($800,000), and the World Wildlife Fund ($100,000). Most gravely, the Pew Charitable Trusts in 1996 gave $550,000 in the name of Joseph N. Pew to the Henry A. Wallace Institute for Alternative Agriculture, even though Wallace, vice-president between 1941 and 1945 (and a communist fellow-traveler) was a man Joseph N. Pew undoubtedly despised.[38]

Among other activities of the Pew Charitable Trusts in recent years:
• It divested its endowment of all Sun Oil stock, reducing its share of Sun Oil common from 24.1 percent in 1993 to nothing as of August 1997.[39]

- It undertook a major effort to re-shape the environmental movement, giving more money to environmentalists than any other single donor. "We're not purists. We believe that people ought to be able to cut down trees," Rebecca Rimel told the *Baltimore Sun* in 1997. "But it ought to be done in a sustainable way. That way, there are jobs, trees, owls—everybody wins."[40]

- Under the leadership of Joshua Reichert, former director of the Veatch Foundation and a former employee of Cesar Chavez, Pew money has created four organizations, most notably the Environmental Information Center.[41] In 1995 and 1996, the Environmental Information Center bought advertisements denouncing "the new Congress" as "bedding down with corporate polluters." (However, the Center claimed that because the advertisements did not specify "The Republican Congress" and because they ceased before the 1996 primaries, they were non-partisan.)[42]

- Pew has given millions in support of the "civic journalism" movement. In 1993, it created the Pew Center for Civic Journalism, headed by Ed Fouhy, a former producer for NBC News. Unlike other foundations, Pew gives money directly to newspapers and other for-profit enterprises. (To ensure that Pew money does not violate federal law that prohibits nonprofits from giving money to for-profit enterprises, Pew supports the Tides Center, which then funds newspapers.) According to Alicia Shepard, Pew money has been used to pay for polls, hold town meetings, and conduct focus groups. Between 1994-1997, Pew gifts paid for 34 projects in 24 cities, involving 22 newspapers, 24 television stations, and 20 radio stations. For example, in Norfolk, Virginia, according to a 1996 *Wall Street Journal* article, Pew civic journalism money allowed the Norfolk *Virginian-Pilot* "to turn a U.S. Senate race into something resembling a job interview," as the newspaper's readers quizzed Republican Senator John Warner and his defeated Democratic rival, Mark Warner, on their views on the issues of the day.[43] Journalists continue to debate the wisdom of allowing recipients of nonprofit grants to work for profit-making enterprises, and they question whether nonprofits can promote "civic-mindedness" or "good government" while remaining objective in writing Pew-funded news articles that do not endorse any particular proposal, idea, or point of view.

- As part of its effort to promote "civic engagement," Pew sponsored the National Commission on Civic Renewal, headed by

## CHAPTER II

former Georgia Democratic Senator Sam Nunn and Heritage Foundation fellow William Bennett. The commission created an "Index of National Civic Health" which determined that Americans were 25 percent less civic in 1996 than in 1972. Among the recommendations of the commission were calls for nonprofits to boycott shows featuring "violence, sexual license, and the pursuit of immediate, intense sensation that a decent civic life seeks to moderate." It also endorsed community development corporations, charter schools, the character education movement, and voluntary national testing.[44]

• Pew also founded Americans Discuss Social Security with a $10 million grant. The organization produced advertisements with different views on Social Security reform and plans to conduct polls and sponsor a book on Social Security by Rudy Abramson, a former *Los Angeles Times* reporter.[45]

Allied with the "civic journalism" movement is a Pew-funded campaign led by former *Washington Post* reporter Paul Taylor to provide free airtime for political candidates. In May 1998, Taylor formed the Alliance for Political Campaigns, which will lobby television stations to "donate" more time for campaign commercials and speeches. Other non-profits receiving money in the $7-million campaign are the Annenberg School of Communications at the University of Pennsylvania and the Campaign Management Institute at American University which plans to work with 200 campaign consultants to "improve" their campaign advertisements. Pew is also giving money to ten state organizations to lobby state television stations for more coverage of statewide races.[46]

• Another Pew effort to influence the press was a $1-million grant to the University of Maryland, which produced a report in July 1998 charging that newspapers were neglecting state politics. The report contended that 27 state capitals had fewer reporters covering them in 1998 than in 1996, and that only 14 states had more press coverage.[47]

• In the fall of 1996, a subcommittee of the Republican-controlled Pennsylvania state legislature denounced the Pew Charitable Trusts' health-care activities as "purchasers of public policy." It charged that the Trusts, in alliance with the Robert Wood Johnson Foundation, "are providing grants as 'seed money' to state, county, and local governmental bodies to develop new or to expand existing government programs, all without the informed consent of the General Assembly... It is one thing to seek change, it is quite another when changes in public policy are influenced by the offering of public money to state governmental institutions."[48]

In May of 1998, Rebecca Rimel appeared at a Planet Hollywood restaurant in Washington, D.C. for a news conference with rap singer Chuck D., associated with Rock the Vote, and former "Melrose Place" television star Andrew Shue, founder of the group Do Something. She announced that the Trusts would give both groups $4.7 million to get more young people to vote. These votes, Rimel explained, were "a health plan for our ailing democratic heart."[49]

Since the second edition of this book, the Pew Charitable Trusts has distanced itself even further from its founders. Rebecca Rimel has addressed the issue of donor intent on at least two occasions. In an August 2000 interview in *Philanthropy*, she claimed that J. Howard Pew "was a man of strong convictions and his successors on the board are following in his footsteps by having strong convictions." She claimed that "the only person on the board since its founding" (whom she did not name) said "we could not have known what he [Howard Pew] would or would not have done in current circumstances. But he was fiercely independent, he had very strong ideas and he believed that everything he did should be toward the public good and the public interest, and that it should prepare citizens to self-govern in the future. If you apply that standard, we are totally in sync with his intent and interests on individual program areas that were not even around when he was alive."[50]

Rimel expanded on these ideas in an April 2001 speech to the American Philosophical Society. "The law recognizes that circumstances change over time," Rimel said. It gives what lawyers call 'an affirmative duty' to find a way to continue to honor donor intent, and it assumes that honoring donor intent is a dynamic process. The Pew Trusts believe in our stewardship of our donors' intent. It is through our current work that we honor that intent."[51]

Under Rimel's rule, foundations honor donor intent by doing…well, whatever *they* feel like doing. It is hard to see how the Pew Trusts's feel-good communitarianism in any way honors the Pew family's commitment to limited government and traditional virtue.

The Pew Trusts took two further steps to distance itself from its founders. In July 2003, they announced that they would partially secede from the Glenmede Trust. The Glenmede Trust split into two parts—a nonprofit entity which continued to manage the $3.8 billion Pew Trusts endowment, and the original trust, which would continue to be a private bank for the Pew family and other wealthy customers. As of 2003, Glenmede had $13 billion in assets and served 1,300 customers, each of whom had to have at least $3 million in investments.[52]

In November 2003, Pew announced that it would transform itself from a grantmaking foundation into a nonprofit organization that would largely fund entities that it created. The Internal Revenue Service allowed such a change because nonprofits are supposed to obtain funds from a variety of sources, and the IRS declared that the seven trusts were, under the law, seven separate foundations.

The move frees Pew to spend as much as five percent of its budget on lobbying, and also allowed it to raise money for other organizations (as we will see in the discussion of the Barnes Foundation). Pew also no longer had to pay five percent of its assets out as grants each year. As a public charity, Pew also saves $4 million in excise taxes that most foundations have to pay.

Rebecca Rimel told the *Wall Street Journal* that it would "build a wall" between organizations it said were nonpartisan, including its polling activities, and more partisan advocacy groups. "We are going to be even clearer in the future that we value both" advocacy and nonpartisanship, Rimel said, "but they are separate."[53]

The "wall" however, seemed to be quite porous (if it existed at all.) Pew was increasingly interested in advocacy. Among recent activities:

• In 1999, Pew announced that it was going to spend as much as 40 percent of its budget on a "national cultural policy." It said it would establish a center in Washington that would conduct polls, hold conferences, and issue reports about the arts.

Historian Alice Goldfarb Marquis noted that such a policy was unnecessary, since the charitable tax deduction encouraged millions of Americans to donate money to arts groups each year, as well as allowing 18 million Americans to volunteer in arts organizations. "American culture is so rich," Marquis wrote, "precisely because it has no organizing framework."

The proposed Pew arts center was never created.[54]

Pew continued to pour tens of millions of dollars into the environment each year. "With its deep pockets and focus on aggressive political advocacy, Pew is not only the most important new player but also the most controversial among opponents in industry." *New York Times* reporter Douglas Jehl noted in 2001.

Jehl found both conservatives and liberals opposed to Pew's efforts to place the environmental movement under the command of Pew environmental director Joshua Reichert. "I don't think you make social change on the basis of paid staff in Washington and paid ads anywhere," Sierra Club executive director Carl Pope told Jehl.

Jehl reported that Rep. Helen Chenoweth-Hage (R-Idaho) said in a 2000 Congressional hearing that Pew's efforts to close the national forests to economic activity showed how communities near these forests "are being crushed by an inaccessible and faceless movement wielding great power and influence."[55]

Pew also poured millions into trying to influence the 2004 election. It donated $9 million to the New Voter Project, which said it would register 265,000 18-24 year old voters in Colorado, Iowa, Oregon, Wisconsin, New Mexico, and Nevada. Though the group was allegedly nonpartisan, the project was a joint venture between George Washington University and the Nader-created State Public Interest Research Groups, a nonprofit entity hostile to Republicans.

"Voting is an acquired habit," Rimel told the *Philadelphia Inquirer*. "Some people say that young people are distracted. Once they get a house and kids, they'll vote. So, in 10 or 15 years, you've got less than half of the people participating in what is arguably our most civic responsibility."[56]

Pew also spent millions pursuing campaign-finance reform. In 2005, *New York Post* reporter Ryan Sager discovered a 2004 videotape made by Sean Treglia, a Pew vice-president for many years, at a conference at the University of Southern California. In the tape, Treglia said that Pew had created fake grassroots organizations designed to persuade Congress that there was a national call for campaign-finance reform. According to Political Money Line, Pew spent $40.1 million between 1994-2004 on campaign finance reform grants.

"The target audience for all this activity was 535 people in Washington," Treglia said. "The idea was to create an impression that a mass movement was afoot—that everywhere they spoke, to academic institutions, in the business community, in religious groups, everywhere, people were talking about reform."[57]

In a letter to the *New York Post,* Rebecca Rimel said that Treglia had repudiated his charge that Pew was trying to hide its role in campaign-finance reform and "from the beginning, the Trusts' grants on campaign-finance reform were transparent and were intended to be."[58]

# CHAPTER II

# The Barnes Foundation

The problems of donor intent also exist in the art world. In many cases, donors create art collections and will them to museums with very specific instructions regarding how they should be maintained and expanded. Later, the donors' wishes are partly or totally violated.

Charles Lang Freer (1854-1919), a Detroit industrialist who made a fortune building railroad cars, retired at the age of 45 to collect Asian art. When he died, his collection went to the Smithsonian Institution along with an endowment and very detailed instructions on how the new Freer Gallery of Art was to operate. But as Benjamin Forgey reported in the *Washington Post*, the Smithsonian has in many cases ignored Freer's intentions. Although Freer insisted that the collection be seen in natural light, the Smithsonian installed artificial lighting during a 1980s renovation. Freer also insisted that no one except a small number of close friends be allowed to donate additional art to the gallery. The Smithsonian, however, spent years exploring ways to technically comply with this clause, such as buying objects for a dollar that were actually worth millions. In the 1970s, Freer officers "simply reinterpreted the will in a way that allowed gifts."[1]

In other ways, however, the Smithsonian has upheld Freer's will. As requested, it has obeyed the clause saying, "nothing else shall ever be exhibited with the collection," and has honored Freer's request to always keep his art in the building. In a codicil to Freer's will, Freer stated that the purpose of the Freer Gallery was to support "the study of civilization of the Far East, as the Regents of the Smithsonian Institution shall determine."[2] For years, some Smithsonian executives tried to broadly interpret this so that the Freer endowment could be spent on research projects only loosely connected to Asia. Eventually, however, Freer Gallery officials won the dispute, and the endowment is now used to maintain the Freer Gallery and to buy new pieces for the collection.

While the Freer case is common, a far more controversial case is the Barnes Foundation. This example shows that courts have, in fact, taken very specific instructions and declared them null and void, thus destroying donor intent.

### Albert C. Barnes: Entrepreneur and Art Collector

For many people, the creator of the Barnes Foundation, Albert Coombs Barnes (1872-1951), was an unpleasant man. Carl W. McCardle, whose four-part *Saturday Evening Post* profile was the longest article written about Barnes during the donor's lifetime, observed that Barnes "in his dealings with the public is a combination of Peck's Bad Boy and Donald Duck."[3]

"A love of fighting," A.H. Shaw noted in a 1928 *New Yorker* profile, "seems to have been the dominant characteristic of his entire career."[4]

"If Barnes had peacefully assembled his paintings, written his books, and directed the educational work of his Foundation," notes biographer Howard Greenfeld, "he would have been unqualifiedly respected and universally mourned at this death. Yet such was not the case, and he left behind him far more enemies than he did friends. The former despised and feared him; the latter worshipped him and remain, even today, stubbornly loyal to his memory."[5]

An essay Barnes wrote in 1945, " Sabotage of Public Education," indicates his general temperament. He condemned the Philadelphia public schools for

> poisoning the wells of public enlightenment by maintaining pseudo-modern educational projects that nullify everything which the leaders of modern scientific education have striven for and accomplished; in doing lip-service to spontaneity and liberty they condemn their deluded followers to frustration and futility... Exposed as mountebanks and educational illiterates, they refuse the public the explanations to which it is entitled and take refuge in silence, with their political barricades assuring them continued access to the public funds... The Board of Education's sponsorship of the puerile and pretentious chatter of Invitation to the Arts puts a fitting climax upon a long career of educational sabotage.[6]

In short, Barnes had strong views that made him many enemies. "He was an outsider fighting to get inside, an unpleasant man in a society that valued good manners, a self-made millionaire of little breeding in a city ruled by men of superior upbringing," Greenfeld writes. "Yet his personality and his outrageous behavior should not be allowed to overshadow his very real achievement: his collection."[7] Further, those who have violated Barnes' wishes seem to have had reasonable and sensible goals. Barnes did not want his paintings to be shown at other museums.

# CHAPTER II

He did not want his collection reproduced in color. Even conservative Supreme Court Justice Antonin Scalia has called the lawsuit that voided large parts of Barnes's will "one of the few productive lawsuits in modern times."[8]

Albert C. Barnes was a Philadelphia chemist and entrepreneur. In 1900, he formed a venture with Hermann Hille to create new pharmaceutical products. In 1902, Hille perfected Argyrol, a type of silver nitrate. Doctors knew that silver nitrate was a powerful and effective antiseptic, but also an extremely caustic compound that could easily cause burns, particularly when treating small children and infants. Hille's achievement was to create a variant of silver nitrate that was therapeutic and far less dangerous than existing forms of the compound.

Argyrol became very popular. "In America," Greenfeld notes, "its acceptance was so complete that many states passed laws requiring that a few drops of the solution be placed in the eyes of newborn infants to prevent infant blindness."[9] By 1910, Barnes was so wealthy that his only business concern was hunting down competitors who sold bogus versions of Argyrol. He began to immerse himself in three passions that would engage him for the rest of his life: philanthropy, radical politics, and art.

Politically, Barnes was a leftist-somewhat more radical than the typical New Deal Democrat. He was one of the early backers of the *New Republic* and supported the National Urban League. He also funded *The Masses* (a radical weekly) and aided Leon Trotsky in his years of exile from the Soviet Union. He was a friend and supporter of John Dewey and gave him the title of director of education at the Barnes Foundation. In 1941, when Bertrand Russell was fired by the City College of New York, Barnes hired him to lecture at the foundation. (He fired Russell a year later for reasons that seem to have been largely personal.)

Barnes's politics is important because it underscores what the Barnes case is *not* about. Unlike the cases of the Pew, MacArthur, and Ford foundations, the Barnes Foundation did not involve liberals violating the beliefs and wishes of pro-capitalist donors. Henry Hart, a former Barnes Foundation employee who in 1963 wrote an appreciative memoir, best summarizes Barnes's political views. Barnes, he said, "never wittingly contributed to a Communist cause, though he did contribute to things in which Communists had injected themselves, as, for example, the Sacco-Vanzetti case." According to Hart, Barnes was anti-Stalinist but not anti-Communist. He believed "a certain amount of government control was necessary, and he thought Roosevelt and his New Deal had prevented totalitarianism here [in the U.S.]. He believed in a mixed economy—some socialism, democratically arrived at, and some private enterprise."[10]

By 1910, Barnes had become a full-time art collector. He later explained that his passion for collecting was largely due to his own inability to master painting. Barnes completed over 200 canvases before realizing that his talents lay elsewhere. "I collected my own pictures when I didn't have money," he later said, "and when I had money I collected better ones."[11] Barnes was one of the first Americans to recognize the importance of French modernist art. He bought over 100 paintings by Cezanne, over 30 Picassos, 60 canvasses by Matisse, as well as others by Daumier, Manet, Monet, Modigliani, and fine examples of ancient art from Egypt, Africa, Persia, and China. By 1922, he had acquired so much that he felt it was time to formally organize his collection.

**Creation of the Barnes Foundation**

The Barnes Foundation, created in 1922, was intended to be different from other museums. It was not to be a place where the idle could derive some amusement by breezing through a collection. The paintings of the Barnes Foundation were to be *tools*. The museum was to be a giant textbook to teach Barnes' views of art appreciation.

Barnes explained his views in a 1923 article in *The New Republic*, "We believe that paintings, trees, or any objects representing genuine human values can be made more vital, more valuable if they are studied according to methods which it has been the great achievement of a few educators to put into such shape that they can be used by teaching organizations," Barnes wrote. "We hope to effect some working plan with colleges and universities in which the scientific approach to the study of our resources shall be made a part of the curriculum."[12]

Barnes discussed his ideas in five books. Two points are noteworthy. First, he believed that to understand a painting, one had to spend considerable time observing the original. Barnes fervently opposed studying art by means of reproductions. Second, he believed that only those should see his collection seriously interested in art. Among his many dislikes was using a collection to create a trendy gathering place. As clause 34 of the Barnes Foundation by-laws says,

## CHAPTER II

> It is... expressly stipulated by the Donor that at no time after the death of said Donor, shall there be held in any building or buildings any society functions commonly designated receptions, tea parties, dinners, banquets, dances, musicales or similar affairs, whether such functions be given by officials, Trustees, or employees of The Barnes Foundation or any other person or persons whatsoever, or whether such functions be private or public. It is further stipulated that any citizen of the Commonwealth of Pennsylvania who shall present to the courts a petition for injunction based on what reputable legal counsel consider is sufficient evidence that the above mentioned stipulation has been violated, shall have his total legal expenses paid by The Barnes Foundation.[13]

To view the Barnes Foundation collection during Barnes' lifetime, one had to obtain a card of admission. Without a self-addressed stamped envelope, one's letter was automatically rejected. Cynthia Flannery Stine, who was Barnes' secretary in the 1930s, said that the rules for admission were simple:

> If you wrote on fine stationery engraved with your estate, if your name lurked in the social register, if you belonged to outstanding clubs and schools, you were out. But if you lived in South Philadelphia, the scene of Dr. Barnes' emergence, if you wrote on cheap paper, misspelling words, and your name was Italian or Jewish, you had a nine-to-one chance of being accepted. At least you were given an interview in our office.[14]

James Michener, a student at Swarthmore College, learned about these rules in 1928 when he tried to visit the foundation. After being turned down three times, he acquired a Pittsburgh mailing address and wrote Barnes pretending to be an unemployed steelworker. Barnes enthusiastically accepted, and spent two hours showing him around. Then Barnes found out about the deception, and began a feud with Michener that lasted the rest of Barnes' life.

### Critic of the Art Establishment

In 1947, after Michener published *Tales from the South Pacific* and began a career as a novelist, Barnes routinely sent a chauffeur 50 miles to his house to deliver what Michener called "letters that were pure venom." Michener also told *Art News'* Milton Esterow that at the time, Barnes showed up at a lecture he was giving and spent the evening excoriating him, calling him "a damn fool" and "a lousy writer" who didn't know what he was talking about. "[He challenged me to a series of public debates-on anything," Michener said. "I must say I chickened out. He was too tough."[15]

Barnes's behavior towards Michener was typical of those he disliked. For the last 30 years of his life, when not acquiring more art, writing books, or running the foundation, Barnes engaged in vitriolic feuds with the Pennsylvania Academy of the Fine Arts, the Philadelphia Museum of Art, the art faculties of Haverford, Swarthmore, and Bryn Mawr colleges, Temple University, the University of Pennsylvania, numerous art critics and historians, and nearly all the newspapers and magazines that wrote about him. Cynthia Stine recalled that Barnes spent twenty minutes of each working day instructing her how to forge his signature so that he could deny writing a vituperative letter if he was ever challenged in court. She also routinely signed letters with the name "Peter Kelly," an imaginary secretary who "would fill his letters with stinging insults, usually at people who wanted to visit the collection."[16] Even Barnes's dog, Fidele-de-Port-Manech, conducted an extensive ghostwritten correspondence.

Carl W. McCardle gives illustrative examples of Barnes's temper. "The Barnes gallery," McCardle wrote, "is practically hermetically sealed to socialites." "Take your guest to the movies," he would thunder to a member of the upper class who wanted to see his paintings. "You can probably understand the movies." In addition, any rich collectors were also rejected. When art collector Walter F. Chrysler, Jr. asked to see the collection, a note sent by "Peter Kelly" said that Barnes "gave strict orders not to be disturbed during his present strenuous efforts to break the world's record for goldfish swallowing."[17]

Here, in its entirety, is a 1951 letter Barnes wrote to Sir Kenneth Clark, the eminent British art historian, who asked to see Barnes's paintings.

"Dear Clark:

"Your recent letter telling me of your proposed visit here prompts me to inform you that all participants in the current

# CHAPTER II

ballyhoos of the institution known as 'The House of Prostitution of Art and Education on the Parkway,' are barred from admission to the foundation's gallery.

Yours truly,<br>
Albert C. Barnes[18]

Barnes also engaged in a feud with the Lower Merion Township Commission. In 1927, the commissioners approved the construction of houses for low-income families in areas that Barnes thought were too close to his building. He loudly announced that he was going to convert his foundation to a "national negro education center" and donate all the paintings to the Metropolitan Museum. "I shall be an humble and unworthy follower of great people" like Leopold Stokowski and Mary Cassatt, Barnes said, "who leave Philadelphia to get a breath of fresh air and never come back."

After a heated meeting, the commissioners reminded Barnes that the owner of the adjacent property bought the land with no restrictions on its use. Barnes calmed down and agreed to stay.[19]

But by the late 1940s, this protracted warfare left Barnes unsure how his collection would be maintained after his death. In his original will, he declared that the University of Pennsylvania, upon the death of himself, his wife Laura, and the trustees he had appointed, would have the power to appoint more trustees who would take control. But according to Howard Greenfeld, in the late 1940s Barnes became distressed after the University of Pennsylvania had appointed Harold Stassen as president. Barnes had been dissatisfied with the university's earlier presidents and had a low opinion of the university's School of Fine Arts. Stassen initially promised to make changes in the arts school, but he did not make them fast enough to satisfy Barnes. By the summer of 1950, Barnes declared that Stassen still wore "the dunce cap that Tom Dewey had placed on him" and was "what psychologists term a 'mental delinquent,' variously known to laymen as "dumb bunny, false alarm, phony.""[20]

## The Barnes Foundation By-Laws

On August 18, 1950, Barnes received a letter from Horace Mann Bond, president of Lincoln University, a black school located 30 miles from the Barnes Foundation's headquarters in Merion, Pennsylvania. Bond offered Barnes a position as lecturer in art for the 1950-51 school year. The job would pay only $9.25 an hour for four to six lectures a year, Bond wrote, but would be "endowed with complete prerogatives of giving the President and his fellow faculty members Hell with no restrictions... The African people, from whom I have the honor of claiming descent, are people generally endowed with a loving, affectionate and grateful soul. I believe that you could help increase that fund of love and affection and arm it with greater intelligence and appreciation."[21]

Barnes quickly wrote back, saying he was "so overwhelmed with joy and admiration at the ease with which you disposed of the work and worry that face me in the future, that I danced the cancan." He offered to place his collection under Lincoln University's control, saying this would ensure that "when given the proper opportunity, the Negro demonstrates that his intellectual capacity is at least equal to that of the white man" and that "his endowment for aesthetic appreciation is even greater than that of the average white man."[22]

On October 17, 1950, Barnes amended paragraph 17 of the Barnes Foundation by-laws for the second and last time. After the death of Barnes and his wife, the Girard Trust bank was to fill the first vacancy on the five-person board. (After a merger, Mellon Bank assumed the Girard Trust's role.) The next four positions would be chosen "by election of persons nominated by Lincoln University, Chester County, Pennsylvania." Thereafter, new vacancies would be filled by the Girard Trust and Lincoln University acting jointly-"provided, however, anything to the contrary herein notwithstanding, that no Trustee shall be a member of the faculty or Board of Trustees or Directors of the University of Pennsylvania, Temple University, Bryn Mawr, Haverford or Swarthmore Colleges, or Pennsylvania Academy of the Fine Arts."[23]

Barnes had no further chance to change the by-laws, because on July 24, 1951, he died after a car crash. The terms of the by-laws then came into force. These are quoted at length to indicate why they were later disputed. After eight articles setting forth the structure of the Barnes Foundation, including its size, structure, and board membership, a ninth article described the "management of the corporation," and included the following paragraphs:

> 9. At the death of Donor, the collection shall be closed, and thereafter no change therein shall be made by the purchase, bequest, or otherwise obtaining of additional pictures, or other

works of art, or other objects of whatsoever description. Furthermore, after the death of Donor and his wife, no buildings, for any purpose whatsoever, shall be built or erected on any part of the property of Donor.

10. After Donor's death no picture belonging to the collection shall ever be loaned, sold, or otherwise disposed of except that if any picture passes into a state of actual decay so that it no longer is of any value it may be removed for that reason only from the collection.

13. All the paintings shall remain in exactly the places they are at the time of the death of Donor and his said wife... No individual, institution, academy, college or university shall use or employ the said administration building or its contents for any purpose other than the promotion of the advancement of education and the appreciation of the fine arts, and only in connection with the purposes of the Barnes Foundation as stated and implied in the covenants and agreements as set forth in various aspects in this Indenture and Agreement.[24]

27. During Donor's lifetime moneys available for investment or reinvestment, whether principal or income, may be invested in any good securities whether legal investments for Trustees or not; but after Donor's death, such moneys may only be invested by Donee in such obligations of the United States of America, obligations of the several States of the United States and obligations of municipal corporations and districts in the several states of the United States which are legal investments for savings banks under the laws of the state of New York.[25] (Barnes believed in investing in government securities as part of his political beliefs.)[26]

30. After the death of Donor and his said wife, the gallery and the arboretum shall be open five days of each week, except during the months of July and August of each year—and solely and exclusively for educational purposes—to students and instructors of institutions which conduct courses in art and art appreciation, which are approved by the Trustees of Donee. On

Saturday of each week, except during the months of July and August of each year, the gallery and the arboretum shall be open to the public between the hours of ten o'clock in the morning and four o'clock in the afternoon, under such rules and regulations as the Board of Trustees or Donee may make. It will be incumbent upon the Board of Trustees to make such rules and regulations as will ensure that the plain people, that is, men and women who gain their livelihood by daily toil in shops, factories, schools, stores and similar places, shall have free access to the art gallery and arboretum upon these days when the gallery and arboretum are to be open to the public, as hereintofore provided. On Sunday of each week during the entire year the gallery and the arboretum shall be closed to students and public alike.

34. At no times after the death of the Donor shall the art gallery be used for exhibitions of paintings or other works of art, or of any work whatsoever, that are not the property of The Barnes Foundation. At no time after the death of the Donor shall the art gallery be used for painting, drawing, or sculpturing by any person or persons, whether said persons be students or instructors of The Barnes Foundation, or from any other institution where students are instructed how to paint, draw, or sculpture. This means specifically that The Barnes Foundation is to be maintained perpetually for education in the appreciation of the fine arts and not as a school for instruction in painting, drawing, sculpturing or any other branch of art or craftsmanship. This restriction also prohibits the copying of any of the works of art of The Barnes Foundation by any person whatsoever.[27]

To ensure that his intent would be respected, Barnes inserted a tenth article in the by-laws on amendments, saying that five of the previous articles, including Article IX, "are unamendable and shall never be amended in any manner whatsoever."[28]

**Early Lawsuits**

In February 1952, six months after Barnes's death, the *Philadelphia Inquirer* began an assault on the Barnes will. Editorialist Harold J.

## CHAPTER II

Wiegand filed a suit in the Court of Common Pleas of Montgomery County, Pennsylvania, asking that the Barnes Foundation be open to the public more than one day a week. The *Inquirer* urged the court to overturn *Barnes Foundation v. Keely,* a 1934 Pennsylvania Supreme Court ruling that declared that the Barnes Foundation, because it had received a tax exemption–not as an art gallery, but as an educational institution–was entitled as a privately owned college or university to determine who could use its facilities.

In June 1952, the Court of Common Pleas dismissed the *Inquirer* case, saying that it had no jurisdiction and that only the state of Pennsylvania could set rules for how nonprofits should function.

Laura Barnes, in an August 1952 interview with the *Washington Post,* said she hoped the Barnes Foundation's admission restrictions would continue indefinitely. "The Barnes Foundation is an educational institution," Laura Barnes said. "The pictures are a part of the art school. Not a museum. It will remain that way. There is no reason to change our policy."[29]

In 1958, the state of Pennsylvania finally decided it had jurisdiction. It sued the Barnes Foundation, saying it had to show why it could restrict entrance to its collections.

The case moved through the Pennsylvania state courts. The Court of Common Pleas ruled in favor of the Barnes Foundation. On appeal, the Pennsylvania Supreme Court overturned the decision. But in ruling against the foundation, Justice Michael A. Musmanno, who wrote the decision, declared that the foundation had to be more open to the public because of clauses in its bylaws, which stated that the foundation would open its doors one additional day upon the death of Laura Barnes. The Commonwealth of Pennsylvania's petition, Justice Musmanno declared, called "upon the Barnes Foundation and its Trustees to show cause why they should not unsheathe the canvases to the public in accordance with the terms of the indenture and agreement entered into by Albert C. Barnes, the donor, and the Barnes Foundation, the donee.[30] In short, the court said it based its decision on its interpretation of clauses 29 and 30 of the by-laws. (But as Gilbert M. Cantor notes, the clauses could also be read as saying that the foundation could not be open to the public until after the death of Laura Barnes.)

In 1961, the Barnes Foundation agreed to open its galleries to 200 people two days a week, and would add a third afternoon after the death of Laura Barnes (who died in 1966). The foundation then announced that it would charge two dollars to pay for additional security. The state of Pennsylvania sued, and the Pennsylvania Supreme Court ruled that the Barnes Foundation could only charge a dollar.

Lois G. Forer a Pennsylvania Deputy Attorney General who helped successfully prosecute the 1961 cases, said in a 1964 article in *Horizon* that the state considered trying to remove four of the five Barnes trustees for incompetence, but decided against it. She added that "certain friends of the Foundation, including lawyers who should know better," proposed that the Barnes abandon its tax-exempt status and begin to pay property taxes in return for being left alone. But these Barnes supporters changed their mind after being told that the foundation might have to sell its art to pay 40 years' worth of property taxes.[31]

Aside from these suits, the affairs of the Barnes Foundation were exactly as Barnes would have wanted them. This is because the trustees, chiefly Violetta de Mazia, a close friend of Barnes, were very long-lived. When Howard Greenfeld surveyed the Barnes Foundation in 1986, he found that three of five members of the board were associates of Barnes; the fourth was a representative of Mellon Bank and the fifth a Lincoln University representative. "Clearly, time had stood still behind the Foundation's walls," Greenfeld concluded. "Yet change seems inevitable... When each of the next four trustees resigns, becomes incapacitated, or dies, he or she is to be replaced by persons nominated by Lincoln University. The Foundation's future is in their hands... When the time comes for them to exercise their responsibility, it can only be hoped that they will act in the best interests of art, education, and the public."[32]

**Ongoing Controversies**

In 1988, Violetta de Mazia died at age 89. Her $9-million estate went into a trust to support the Barnes Foundation. By 1990, two of the original trustees had also retired. Under the terms of Barnes' will, Lincoln University appointed replacements, ensuring that it had four seats on the Barnes board. For the first time in its history, people who did not know Barnes controlled the Barnes Foundation.

The most vocal of these was Richard Glanton, Lincoln University's general counsel. A Republican, Glanton served as a fundraiser for George Bush in the 1988 presidential campaign and also worked as an assistant to Pennsylvania Governor Richard Thornburgh. Glanton was appointed president of the Barnes Foundation in 1990 for a five-year

## CHAPTER II

term. What he saw was a foundation with assets (art) worth between $300 million and $3 billion, but with an endowment of only $10 million that provided $1 million annually for operating costs. (The $9 million De Mazia Trust was an independent charity not under Barnes Foundation control.) The Barnes Foundation building had also deteriorated over the years. In 1985, a steam explosion damaged nine paintings. The building's electrical system had not been changed since 1923.

The amount needed to renovate the Barnes Foundation was in dispute. Glanton claimed that up to $15 million was needed to renovate the building. Glanton's foes believed the damage was far less severe. "I just laughed when Glanton got in there and started screaming about how the Barnes was sinking," former Barnes trustee David Rawson told author John Anderson. "Not only was the Barnes solvent financially when Glanton 'inherited' it, the physical plant was in good shape. We'd replaced the roof. The place was watertight."[33]

Also disputed was whether Glanton's estimate was only for the foundation's galleries or included administration buildings not used for displaying art. No independent estimates exist. Glanton's goal, according to a 1993 interview by Carol Vogel, was to turn the Barnes Foundation into "a high-visibility institution with state-of-the-art facilities and the cachet of the Frick collection." Glanton told Vogel "the problems of the Barnes were so obvious Ray Charles could see them in a swamp at midnight."[34]

Glanton also wanted to have the Barnes Foundation affiliated with a major museum, such as the Philadelphia Museum of Art. Classes could be taught, but not according to Barnes' principles. (Glanton described Barnes' theories of art as "not art history" but "hokum."[35]) A few scholarships might be available to the needy, but these would be as expensive as tuition at major art schools. Paintings would be freely bought and sold. In short, the Barnes Foundation would be systematically purged of everything that Albert C. Barnes believed.

To achieve these goals, Glanton faced two major obstacles. The first was the foundation by-laws. The second was opposition from the De Mazia Trust and former students of Barnes. In February 1991, Glanton petitioned the Orphans Court of Montgomery County, Pennsylvania (which specializes in trusts and estates) to sell (or, as museums describe it, "de-accession") as many as fifteen paintings from the Barnes Foundation collection. Glanton argued that the low regard in which the Barnes Foundation was held necessitated a drastic step. "You know the pecking order and the way they fix their boards in terms of how they get support," he told *Vanity Fair's* David D'Arcy. "*They* [Barnes supporters] don't even have [enough] funds to have endowments that would throw off enough operating cash to get them through these hard fiscal times."[36]

The art world was in an uproar. "De-accessioning" is seen as a last resort, taken only when all other methods of fundraising have failed. Glanton's request also came when the global art market was in a recession. Further, it was unclear whether the Orphans Court would grant Glanton's request without calling for a full investigation of the Barnes Foundation's books.

**Breaking the Barnes Will**

In June 1991, Glanton announced that the de-accessioning plan would not proceed. Other violations of donor intent, however, have occurred. Glanton allowed the Barnes Foundation building to hold parties for a private school and for the Union League Club of Philadelphia. In June 1991, the foundation announced an agreement with Alfred A. Knopf to publish two books of art that would reproduce the foundation's collections in color in return for an advance of $700,000. Interestingly, in April 1991, the Samuel I. Newhouse, Jr. Foundation, whose wealth derives from publishing enterprises, including Alfred A. Knopf, donated $2 million to Lincoln University.

The Newhouse donation prompted the De Mazia Trust to petition the Orphans Court for standing in the Barnes Foundation controversies. Standing was granted, and in 1991 the trust sued, stating that Lincoln University had improperly diverted funds that should have been used for the Barnes Foundation, and that higher bids from other publishers were not considered. The Barnes Foundation filed a counter-suit, claiming that most of the assets of the De Mazia Trust, including all of the art Violetta de Mazia collected, were stolen from the Barnes Foundation, and that all the assets of the De Mazia Trust should be transferred to the Barnes Foundation.

Neither of these suits has been settled, and they are still causing bitterness on both sides. Richard Glanton told the *Washington Post* in May 1993 that attorneys for the De Mazia Trust were charging excessive legal fees in an effort to "loot" the trust's assets. "Mr. Glanton says whatever comes to his head," De Mazia Trust attorney Gordon Elkins told the *Post*. "It's not true, but that doesn't stop him. It's a kind of Joseph Goebbels approach."[37]

In 1992, the Barnes Foundation petitioned the Orphans Court to allow some of the foundation's paintings to be sent on tour. Judge Louis Stefan granted the request, but imposed severe restrictions on how the exhibition could be handled. The paintings were to be removed from the foundation walls only once, and only those in good condition could be removed. Before a single painting was removed, the foundation had to submit a new program of education, which the court had to approve. When the paintings returned to the foundation, they had to be put back in the exact spots where they had been. In making these restrictions, Stefan said that he had little tolerance for the efforts of the trustees to violate Barnes' intentions. The trustees' actions "give rise to the suspicion that [their] intentions... might be somewhat more ambitious than what their present request has indicated."[38]

In January 1995, the Barnes Foundation and the De Mazia Trust reached an out-of-court settlement in which the Foundation agreed to permanently offer art courses based on Barnes's views. It further agreed that the Trust is an independent organization over which it has no legal authority. In return, the Trust agreed to donate $2,750,000 over seven years to pay for the art courses. This settlement was rejected in July 1995 by Montgomery County Orphans Court Judge Stanley Ott, and litigation between the Trust and the Foundation continues.[39]

In November 1995, the Barnes Foundation reopened its galleries after being shut for 32 months. The around-the-world tour netted the foundation between $16 and $17.5 million (accounts differ on the precise amount raised), and $12 million was spent on the renovation. At first glance, nothing had changed. The renovators, employees of renowned architect Robert Venturi, restored the paintings to the positions they occupied before the tour began. Even the old thermostats were restored. The long-closed French quarry, which had cut the rock for the Barnes's steps, was reopened so that new rock could be cut.

But if the Barnes Foundation at the beginning of Richard Glanton's tenure was an educational institution with a gallery, the foundation had now become a museum. Included in the renovation was a museum shop, which sold a CD-ROM of the paintings. "The Barnes is no longer an intimate place," wrote *Philadelphia Inquirer* art critic Edward J. Sozanski. "It's more of a popular experience—that is to say, a tourist experience—and it will become more so."[40]

But even if the Barnes Foundation was a museum, it had never been zoned as one. This led Richard Glanton to yet another battle, this time with the Lower Merion Township Zoning Hearing Board—a battle that ultimately led to his downfall. Glanton announced at the time of the Barnes Foundation opening that he had grand ambitions. In an interview with the *Wall Street Journal,* he listed some of them: opening the foundation for six days a week (instead of the court-mandated three-and-a-half days), increasing the admission price from $5 to $10, building a new exhibition space on the Barnes Foundation grounds, and increasing museum attendance from 30,000 to 120,000. Without these measures, he threatened, the Barnes paintings would either go on a second world tour or the foundation would be forced to close.[41]

The courts, however, were reluctant to further violate the wishes of Albert Barnes. Only one further deviation from Barnes' wishes was permitted—the termination of the clause restricting fundraisers and parties on the Barnes grounds. In November 1995, the Pennsylvania Superior Court allowed a $1,000-a-plate fundraiser on the grounds, provided there was adequate security at the event. The Superior Court overturned Orphans Court Judge Ott, who ruled the event permissible only if the dinner guests were not allowed to tour the galleries afterward.[42]

The Pennsylvania Superior Court upheld its ruling in 1996, stating that fundraising events did not violate Barnes' seemingly explicit ban on them, so long as they were not "trivial." Superior Court Justice John T. J. Kelly, writing for the majority, stated that Barnes did not explicitly prohibit "on-site fund-raising functions" at the Barnes Foundation, but that Barnes' intentions were that he did not want his "gallery trivialized by the use of it as a mere rental hall for socialites...There is a decided difference," Justice Kelly wrote, "between fundraising functions which have as their purpose the preservation and enrichment of the assets which the Foundation is charged with protecting and a social affair which has as its purpose the inclusion of some and the exclusion of many."[43]

At the time of this victory, Glanton was in the middle of a battle with the zoning board. In December 1995, the board, citing overcrowding of township streets, ordered the Barnes Foundation to cut its hours to 2½ days a week and allow no more than 500 visitors a week. Glanton called the zoning board's decision a "frivolous action."[44] The board's decision was not enforced, and in July 1996, the Pennsylvania

# CHAPTER II

Superior Court allowed the Barnes Foundation to open in July and August for the first time, once again violating an explicit instruction of Albert Barnes. However, the court upheld Judge Ott's decision to limit admission to 3½ days a week.[45]

In February 1996, Glanton launched a counter-suit against the township commissioners and 17 nearby residents. He claimed that his civil rights were violated because the zoning board's request for a limit on the Barnes' hours was the result of racism, in as much as a majority of the Barnes board was made up of African-Americans. According to court documents, Glanton denounced Barnes Watch, an organization dedicated to supporting Albert Barnes' ideals, as "sort of like a vigilante Klan organization... a bunch of weird racists masquerading as being concerned about the Barnes." The township commissioners then counter-sued, claiming that Glanton had defamed them.[46]

Niara Sudarkasa, who voted with Glanton to sue the zoning board, later recalled to John Anderson that the dispute "didn't have anything to do with race. It had to do with Richard wanting a parking lot. That's all it was about. A parking lot that would generate money."[47]

In August 1997, the zoning board won a victory. Montgomery County Court Judge Bernard Moore said the Barnes Foundation had illegally transformed itself from an educational institution into a museum, and he ordered the foundation to limit its hours to 2½ days a week, with attendance at no more than 200 per day. Neighbors of the Barnes stood watch outside the museum with cameras and counters ensuring that the court's decision was enforced. Richard Glanton denounced the decision, and then flew to China to negotiate a tour of Barnes paintings in Shanghai.[48]

One month later, the Barnes Foundation's allegations of racism against the Lower Merion Township commissioners were thrown out of court. District Court Judge Anita B. Brody declared that there was "no evidence whatsoever" that the commissioners made the decision against Barnes because of race, and that "the vast majority of the Barnes' evidence has nothing to do with race, but merely details various stages of a run-of-the-mill land dispute." Earlier, Judge Brody dismissed the complaint against the neighbors, stating that they had a First Amendment right to voice their opinions.[49]

Still, the controversy would not die. Lower Merion Township commissioners sued to recover court costs, which they estimated at $1.5 million. The Barnes Foundation hired former Judge A. Leon

Higginbotham, Jr., a veteran civil rights activist, to defend it. In November 1997, the Montgomery County Court upheld the zoning board, and it ordered the board and foundation to negotiate an attendance figure acceptable to both sides. (This figure would be less than the 97,000 people who visited the Barnes Foundation in 1995-1996, but more than the average 1990-1992 attendance of 42,000.)[50]

Then, in February 1998, Richard Glanton abruptly resigned. Not surprisingly, tensions between Glanton and his board had been increasing. One trustee, Lincoln University president Niara Sudarkasa, fumed that she learned about a Barnes hiring decision from press reports, not from Glanton. Glanton claimed that another trustee, Mellon Bank executive Sherman White, was secretly working with township commissioners "to prove the township's point that I was out of control."[51]

Glanton's departure was hastened by the cost of the Barnes's lawsuits. According to *Philadelphia Inquirer* reporter Anne Barnard, tax records showed that the Barnes Foundation spent $1.6 million on legal fees between 1993 and 1996. Should the zoning board win its suit to recover court costs, the Barnes Foundation could be faced with a bill of $1.8 million. Another suit, was filed against the Foundation by Rome, capital of Italy. It charges that the Foundation agreed to make the city's famous Museo Capitolino a stop on the Barnes' world tour, and that Richard Glanton has breached the contract. (The city of Rome also entered documents into the court record charging that Glanton, while courting the Italians, also tried to solicit business for his law firm from Fiat and other potential clients.)[52]

While the Barnes Foundation eventually won the lawsuit against the city of Rome, the costs incurred by those who ignored Albert Barnes's wishes have been considerable. Not only is the Pennsylvania Attorney General's office looking into the Foundation's finances, but also the Foundation trustees have opened themselves up to close scrutiny. Two people have been named to replace Glanton. Kenneth A. Sadler, a North Carolina dentist and chairman of the Lincoln University board of trustees, was appointed president. Like Glanton, he has no professional training in arts administration. Another member of the Lincoln University board, former Arco Chemical executive Earle L. Bradford, Jr., was named acting chief administrative officer. They promise to be less confrontational and litigious, and Sadler has promised to mend relationships with "those who have traditionally been friends with the

## CHAPTER II

Barnes," including the De Mazia Trust and Barnes Watch. He added that it was his goal to "honor the wishes of the donor to the extent that it is possible in the modern world."[53]

After Glanton's departure, some analysts observed that Albert Barnes' ideas were not all bad ones. *Philadelphia Inquirer* art critic Edward J. Sozanski, for example, noted in a commentary that "it always seems to me that Barnes' achievement was underplayed. The media doted on his eccentricities," which included refusing admittance to people he didn't like, "but the boldness of his connoisseurship—and the passion for art that inspired it—wasn't sufficiently appreciated... One can only hope that Glanton's successors will pay closer attention to their moral obligation to the founder and be more sensitive to the need to preserve and protect this unique collection. The Barnes experience isn't just the paintings on the walls but the sense of the whole."[54]

It may be that Barnes's method of intensely looking at great art has merits that the trustees overlooked. "Are we going to provide a rich, lasting experience for a small group of people," barber Danni Melitsky told the *Washington Post,* "or are we going to trek these paintings around the world and allow a lot of people to look at them for three seconds? If you want to see the Sistine Chapel, you get on a plane and go to Italy. If scholars really are interested in the fantastic Cezannes, they can get their butts to Merion."[55]

"What the Barnes controversy is very much about," notes *Washington Times* art critic Eric Gibson, "is trusteeship. How responsibly are the officers of the Barnes living up to their obligations to perpetuate Albert Barnes' manifold legacy, a gift that is now a public trust? Are they really rescuing it for the future, or does 'saving' the Barnes now mean altering it beyond recognition?[56]

"The Barnes affair is one of the great scandals in American art museums," noted Smithsonian Institution assistant secretary Tom Freudenheim in a 1995 interview with *National Law Journal,* "and it sets a dangerous precedent. If a will isn't sacrosanct under the law, what is? The Fricks, Barnes, and Carnegies of the future are going to think very carefully before donating their masterpieces to our institutions and to our future generations. And that is a more dangerous situation than the public understands it to be."[57]

The Barnes Foundation continued to chip away at Barnes's intentions. In August 1998, the foundation received permission from Judge Ott to remain open during the months of July and August.

Acting Chief Officer Earle Bradford said that Barnes's fear that summer humidity would damage the paintings was now, with better air conditioning, unfounded.[58]

In 2001, the Third Circuit Court of Appeals ruled that the Barnes Foundation had to pay $125,000 in legal fees to five neighbors of Barnes whom Glanton accused of being racists. The court said there was no evidence that the neighbors were racists and ordered a lower court to determine if the Barnes lawsuit was made in bad faith.[59]

Niara Sudarkasa then filed a $7 million lawsuit against Richard Glanton, claiming that "Mr. Glanton was corrupted by his power—he used his power to reward his friends and punish his enemies," and had used his power to conduct a smear campaign. She said that Glanton leaked evidence to two Pennsylvania state senators alleging corruption on Sudarkasa's part. In August 2001, Common Pleas Judge Howland W. Abramson dismissed the suit after a four-week trial, saying that Sudarkasa, a public figure, offered no evidence that Glanton acted maliciously.[60]

The Barnes Foundation said that it was bleeding red ink. A 2000 Deloitte and Touche report said that the foundation needed $85 million in the long term and $15 million in the short term to become a stable organization. The foundation began to receive $500,000 grants from the J. Paul Getty Trust, the Pew Charitable Trusts, the Wilmington Trust, and the Henry Luce Foundation.[61]

## Bombshell

Then in September 2002, the Barnes Foundation dropped a bombshell. In order to preserve the foundation, they argued, Barnes's intentions had to be completely destroyed. They announced that they would file a suit in Montgomery County Orphans' Court allowing the foundation to move to downtown Philadelphia. They said that if the move took place, the Pew Charitable Trusts and the Lenfest Foundation would raise $150 million to ensure the Barnes Foundation's survival. Under the plan, the Barnes board of trustees would be expanded from five to 15 members—a move that would take control of the foundation away from Lincoln University. (A month later, the Annenberg Foundation signed on to the capital campaign.)[62]

Three Barnes Foundation students then sued to block the move. Lincoln University also filed suit to preserve its control of the foundation. The Barnes Foundation countered by saying that the

# CHAPTER II

students did not have standing and that the additional trustees were necessary to aid the foundation's fundraising efforts.[63]

The foundation's next move was to answer Lincoln University's charges. It said that having Lincoln control 80 percent of the trustees would ensure that the foundation would not be able to function. Foundation lawyers also claimed that Barnes planned to sever ties with Lincoln. In June 1951, Barnes refused to attend the Lincoln University commencement and did not establish formal academic ties between the foundation and the university. These actions, Barnes Foundation lawyers argued, were evidence that Barnes was planning to alter his will—an action they said he was unable to do because of his sudden death in a car crash a month later.[64]

At the same time, the De Mazia Trust asked to have standing in the case. The trust's lawyers said that they were not opposed to moving the foundation or expanding the board, but insisted that the foundation's educational programs be preserved.[65]

Lincoln then called upon its allies in the Pennsylvania State Legislature. In November 2002, a clause was inserted in a bill designed to aid spouses of 9/11 victims that said that members of the board of a nonprofit affiliated with a "state-related institution" could not increase or decrease the size of their board "without the prior written approval of the state-related institution." The bill passed the Pennsylvania House by a 195-1 margin but was not considered by the state senate.

The bill, Barnes Foundation attorney Carl Solano told the *Philadelphia Inquirer*, "was done in secret and voted on in the dead of night, when nobody knew what they were voting on." But the measure showed that Lincoln was a tough antagonist.[66]

In January 2003, newly elected Pennsylvania Governor Ed Rendell offered to act as a broker to settle the Barnes Foundation lawsuit before it came to trial. At the same time, NAACP Chairman Julian Bond, son of Horace Mann Bond, said that the efforts of the Pew, Lenfest, and Annenberg Foundation "could be construed as racially hostile, although I do not make such a charge."

Both sides declined Rendell's offer. Bernard Watson, chairman of the Barnes Foundation board, said that the expanded board would have an African-American majority, even if the new members would not be affiliated with Lincoln University.[67]

Judge Ott made his first rulings in February 2003. He said that Lincoln University would have standing in the case, but refused to grant standing to the Barnes Foundation students and the De Mazia Trust, whom he said would be represented by Pennsylvania Attorney General Mike Fisher.[68]

A month later, Judge Ott ruled that the Barnes Foundation had to make public a "forensic audit" of the foundation's finances between 1992 and 1997 that was conducted by Deloitte and Touche. Lincoln University lawyers requested the audit, Barnes Watch spokesman Nick Tinari said that the audit would show that the foundation was not in dire shape. "It has always been my contention," Tinari told the *Philadelphia Inquirer*, "that the financial problems at the foundation, including the most recent ones, are its own doings, are correctable, and should not cause the intent of Dr. Barnes to be thwarted."[69]

Judge Ott gave the Barnes Foundation a month to produce the audit. After the deadline, the foundation refused, saying that the report "contains candid discussions about former personnel... that might be embarrassing to those individuals if publicly disclosed." The foundation added that Richard Glanton "explicitly threatened" the accounting firm and the law firm that produced the audit "with suit if allegations investigated in connection with the report were made public."[70] Glanton, who had left Philadelphia to become a vice-president of the utility Exelon, subsequently wrote Judge Ott that "I did not and never opposed the audit. I have no object to its disclosure." He said in the letter that what he objected to was the Barnes Foundation being forced to spend $1 million on the audit, which he thought should be paid for by the state attorney general's office.[71]

Attorney General Fisher then stated which parts of Barnes's intentions he wished to preserve—that the art could not be moved from its original positions and could not be sold, that the foundation continue to provide educational programs, that the Barnes Foundation not merge into another institution, and that no Barnes Foundation trustee would be a professor or trustee of the University of Pennsylvania, Temple University, Bryn Mawr, Haverford, or Swarthmore Colleges, or the Pennsylvania Academy of the Fine Arts.

General Fisher expressed ambivalence about whether or not art that was in storage could be sold. As for Lincoln University's role, he told the *Philadelphia Inquirer* that "We have said to the attorney for the Barnes Foundation, 'Look, you need to reach out and figure out a way to preserve Lincoln's role in the operations of the Barnes.'"[72]

In June 2003, Bernard Watson said that the Pew, Lenfest, and Annenberg Foundations were threatening to withdraw their support

# CHAPTER II

because they feared they would be accused of a "white takeover" of the foundation if they were successful. He said that Rebecca Rimel was "more concerned" about the issue of racism than the heads of the other two foundations.[73]

The next move came with the release of the Deloitte and Touche audit in July 2003. Among the audit's findings:

• The Barnes Foundation board secretly voted to fire Richard Glanton in 1993, but reversed their decision.

• The Foundation received $16 million from the world tour of the Barnes paintings and $3.2 million from sales of associated merchandise. But despite this cash flow, the foundation posted a deficit every year from 1993 to 1998.

• In 1994, Glanton went to Charles Frank, Mellon Bank's trustee on the foundation board and allegedly told Frank if he would "stop the fighting" among board trustees, he would give Frank certain financial information and allow the bank to control $2.6 million in revenues from the world tour. Glanton told the *Philadelphia Inquirer* that this allegation was false and that Mellon would have controlled the money anyway.

• Glanton hired a partner at his law firm, Thomas Massaro, to oversee reconstruction of the Barnes gallery, without telling the board that Massaro was a partner. Massaro billed the foundation $391,644 between 1995-98 for his services.

• Glanton hired another partner at his law firm, Eugene Cliett, to provide printing, computer, and telephone services to the Barnes Foundation without telling the board that Cliett was his law partner. Cliett billed the foundation $292,455 between 1996-97.

• In 1996, Glanton allowed two women to live rent free at a house the foundation owned in Merion Township. After neighbors complained of loud parties, the Merion Township Board said the house was no longer tax-exempt and billed the foundation $4,400 in property taxes. After four months, the women moved out, having saved themselves $4,000 in rent. The foundation subsequently sold the house.

• In 1997, at a time the audit said when "Glanton had reason to believe he might be replaced as president," Glanton spent $22,000 of foundation money redoing the foundation's introductory brochure, largely to replace a Barnes quotation on the brochure's front cover with one by Glanton.[74]

The Barnes Foundation argued that the audit's findings showed that Lincoln University was an incompetent steward of the foundation's assets. "We don't understand,' said foundation lawyer Carl Solano, "how Lincoln can claim that it had no responsibility for what happened in the 1990s when the people who ran the foundation were the same people who simultaneously were running Lincoln as its trustees, president, and legal counsel."

Lincoln University president Ivory Nelson responded that Lincoln's control of the foundation was indirect. "Remember, Liucoln's role is simply to nominate," he told the *Philadelphia Inquirer*. "Its role is not for management and oversight." He added that when the university discovered the abuses, it took action to make sure that the abuses didn't happen again.[75]

In September 2003, the outside donors said they would withdraw their support if Lincoln retained control of the Barnes. Rebecca Rimel said that Pew had made no decision to withdraw funding. H.G. "Gerry" Lenfest said "We felt it was fruitless to continue if Lincoln was not going to give up their control of the Barnes board."[76]

Bernard Watson threatened that if the outside charities withdrew their offer, the Barnes Foundation could go bankrupt, "Given our financial situation, given the unlikely situation where we're going to get the kind of support that we need, we're going into bankruptcy, and it's that simple," Watson told the *Philadelphia Inquirer*. "We go into bankruptcy, at which point the attorney general of the Commonwealth of Pennsylvania takes over, and it's up to him what happens to the Barnes after that."[77]

Two weeks after these gloomy pronouncements, Lincoln University and the Barnes Foundation reached a compromise. It agreed to allow expansion of the foundation board to fifteen members, of which it would appoint five, one more than it currently had.

At the same time Lincoln University made this concession, Gov. Ed Rendell said that he would ask the Pennsylvania state legislature to give the university $50 million for a science and technology center and for one more building. Gov Rendell also said that the state would help the university in a $100 million capital campaign. Both Gov. Rendell and university officials denied that there was any quid pro quo between Lincoln University's decision to settle the lawsuit and the financial aid. (Lincoln, although a private university, was "state-related," meaning it was under partial state control. Gov. Rendell nominated two members of the Lincoln board.)[78]

In another move, *Los Angeles Times* art critic Christopher Knight published an article in his newspaper arguing that the J. Paul Getty Trust buy the Barnes Foundation and leave it in Merion. The Getty refused. "Unequivocally we support the plan" to move the collection, Getty president Barry Munitz told the *Philadelphia Inquirer*. "We have no interest in breaking up the collection. We have no interest in disturbing the educational philosophy" of the foundation.[79]

The three Barnes Foundation students—Sue S. Hood, William Phillips, and Harvey A. Wanik—then asked Judge Ott to grant them standing, saying that since Attorney General Fisher supported the move, no one now represented the students' interest. In November 2003, Judge Ott allowed the students to be "friends of the court," meaning they had a limited power to seek information from the foundation, but couldn't participated in the discovery process or appeal Judge Ott's rulings. Their lawyer was also limited to asking questions about the foundation's educational program.[80]

Meanwhile, the Pew Charitable Trusts was completing its conversion into a public charity. As one condition of the conversion, the IRS requires public charities to raise funds from outside organizations. In filings with the IRS, Pew lawyers said that the Barnes Foundation capital campaign was the "best example" of Pew's "ability to attract outside funding" and was "a prime example of the valuable role" that Pew would play as a public charity.

John Anderson, author of *Art Held Hostage*, an investigative history of the Barnes Foundation battles, noted that if Pew controlled the $150 million endowment, it could control the foundation, making its effort more like a hostile takeover of the Barnes Foundation than a bailout. "In controlling the money," Anderson charged, "Pew would have de facto control over the Barnes Foundation itself, with a powerful role in determining the future character and direction of the Barnes. In such circumstances, would the interests of Pew coincide with those of Dr. Barnes?"

Rebecca Rimel, in an interview with the *Philadelphia Inquirer*, said that "the operative word is 'could'... There is no decision made about what role we are going to play, assuming a positive outcome of the court decision." In a second interview, she said that Pew would "administer" the $150 million, but Pew program officers would examine Barnes Foundation invoices and pay what was needed. This, she argued, was short of Pew actively controlling the Barnes Foundation.[81]

In December 2003, Judge Ott convened a hearing on the case. Bernard Watson testified that he had tried to get other donors interested in funding the Barnes, but only the offer from Pew, Lenfest, and Annenberg allowed the Barnes to keep its independence. Under questioning from the students' lawyer, Watson admitted that the foundation had never considered other options for raising money, such as selling Ker-Feal, the Barnes estate, selling art that wasn't on display, or raising the admission fee. Barnes Foundation director Kimberly Camp, questioned by Judge Ott, said that the foundation had never considered another tour because such a move would ensure that some of the artwork would "not be part of the collection." She said a tour would be a graver violation of donor intent than moving the museum.[82]

The hearing concluded with testimony from Rebecca Rimel. She said that should Judge Ott rule that the Barnes Foundation should not move, the Pew Charitable Trusts would cut off support to the foundation. Pew had paid the Barnes Foundation's legal bills and operating expenses since 2002. Rimel said that Pew's funding of the Barnes Foundation was highly unusual for Pew, but was done because "the need was so great and the opportunity was so compelling."[83]

Judge Ott made a ruling in January 2004. He allowed the expansion of the Barnes Foundation board to 15 members. But he deferred a decision on moving the museum until the Barnes Foundation presented more evidence that such a move was necessary. "The fact-finding in this case has been seriously hamstrung by the total absence of hard numbers in evaluating these proposals," Judge Ott said

"Other than the offers for the land surrounding Ker-Feal," Judge Ott ruled, "we have not heard even a wild estimate of the value of the items owned by the foundation but not on display in the gallery in Merion. Nevertheless, the possibility of selling some or all of these holdings has been floated as the only lifeboat in the entire sea. Since the outside charities are footing the foundation's legal bills in these hearings, we accept their single-option theory as the product of zealous advocacy."

The judge noted that the Barnes Foundation indenture "does not specifically state that the gallery must be maintained in Merion or cease to exist. Nevertheless, it is difficult to dismiss Dr. Barnes' choice of venue as a minor detail."

Judge Ott also denounced Attorney General Fisher for declaring that he supported the foundation's move before the hearing was held. "The course of action chosen by the Office of the Attorney General prevented the court from seeing a balanced, objective presentation of the

## CHAPTER II

situation, and constituted an abdication of that office's responsibility," Judge Ott declared.[84]

While the Barnes Foundation gathered its evidence, its neighbors on Latches Lane in Merion quietly started a campaign to let it be known that they in fact wanted the foundation to stay. Judge Ott, as part of his ruling, said that "Lower Merion Township certainly bears some of the responsibility for the financial crisis, The foundation's attempt to raise revenues by increased public access to the gallery was met with hostility, bordering on hysteria, from some of the owners of the adjacent houses." Moreover, some of the neighbors were still suing the foundation over being repaid for legal fees for the civil rights lawsuit.

Neighbor Walter H. Herman spent $400 to create a series of "Burma Shave" style signs that read:

No matter what
The papers say
The neighbors want
The Barnes to stay.

"We have been characterized as unrelentingly hostile to the Barnes," Herman told the *Philadelphia Inquirer.* "It's absolutely untrue. We do not want the Barnes to leave. Being called hostile doesn't help our cause, so we decided to take a more jocular approach."[85]

In September 2004, Judge Ott convened a second hearing. The Barnes Foundation presented as witnesses real estate appraisers Glen Perry and William Wood II, who testified that the 4,532 pieces of art that wasn't on display and the Ker-Feal property was worth $24.7 million—$5 million for the real estate, $19 million for the art. The students presented an appraisal by art dealer Richard Feigen that said that the art was worth $32.8 million and the property $10 million.[86]

The next day, Barnes Foundation finance committee chair Stephen J. Harmelin said that the foundation's annual deficit was "$1 million, plus, or minus," and admitted that this deficit would be covered by a $25 million endowment, which the students contended could be met without moving the foundation. Barnes Foundation attorney Ralph Wellington countered that if the foundation stayed in Merion, "donors would drop away" if the foundation lost the court case or had to sell art.[87]

The court then heard from Marie C. Malaro, former Smithsonian associate general counsel, who was called as a witness by the students. Malaro said that because the Barnes Foundation was still legally an educational institution and not a museum, the prohibitions against museums selling their art did not apply to it "I believe that... what Dr. Barnes wanted was for his foundation to perpetuate his particular unique method of teaching art appreciation in a school format. That was made very clear in the indenture." She added that the proposed new downtown museum "will overwhelm, or at least put in the background, Dr. Barnes' purpose."

Barnes Foundation archivist Barbara Beaucar pointed to a 1923 letter Barnes wrote to his lawyer saying that "I want the gallery to be a public one after my death." Judge Ott, however, quoted from a 1941 letter from Barnes to Winterthur Museum director Henry du Pont, saying that many people wanted to come to the foundation because they were "curiosity seekers." "It is because of this that we have formulated strict regulations concerning admission to our gallery," Barnes wrote.[88]

Lower Merion Township Commissioner Joseph Manko then announced he was going to try to allow the Barnes Foundation to build an access road, which would allow visitors to come to the foundation without tying up traffic on Latches Lane. Manko said that Gov. Rendell was a "good listener" when presented with the idea.[89] Manko and another commissioner, James Ettelson, said they would work with the Barnes Foundation to solve their parking problems if they stayed.

Paul Kelly Jr,. director of the Paul E. Kelly Foundation, announced that his foundation would give $100,000 to the Barnes Foundation over a two-year period if they didn't move. He said he made the offer in the hopes that other donors would oppose the move. "Barnes was obviously an unusual man," Kelly told the *Philadelphia Inquirer*. "But I don't think it is required that the trust indenture be totally thrown out, and that is the effect of it moving downtown."[90]

The hearing then concluded. In December 2004, Judge Ott made his ruling. The Barnes Foundation had triumphed. Barnes's indenture was destroyed. Judge Ott said that because the students couldn't show that the foundation could raise enough money from selling the non-displayed art and the Ker-Feal property, "we find that the foundation showed clearly and convincingly the need to deviate from the terms of Dr. Barnes' indenture."

"By many interested observers, permitting the gallery to move to Philadelphia will be viewed as an outrageous violation of the donor's intent," Judge Ott wrote. He said the foundation introduced letters by Barnes suggesting that he thought that, after his death, the foundation

CHAPTER II

should become important. "To the court's thinking, these clues make the decision—that there is no viable alternative—easily reconcilable with the law of charitable trusts. When we add this revelation to the foundation's absolute guarantee that Dr. Barnes' primary mission—the formal education programs—will be preserved and, indeed, enhanced as a result of these changes, we can sanction this bold new venture with a clear conscience."

He warned, however, that if the foundation failed to meet the revenue projections it forecast, the foundation could be in court again. "If the admissions do not meet expectations, or any of the other components of the Deloitte model do not reach their targets, something will have to give."[91]

It remained unclear, however, if the restrictions in the Barnes Foundation indenture limiting hours, barring fundraising events, selling art that it wasn't exhibiting, or hosting exhibitions of art that it didn't own were still in place. Judge Ott amended his original decision to say that all those restrictions were gone as well.[92]

Because students Sue Hood, William Phillips, and Harvey Wanik were not granted standing, they couldn't appeal Judge Ott's decision. But another student, Jay Raymond, asked to appeal the decision. In March 2005, the Pennsylvania Superior Court said that it would allow Raymond to appeal Judge Ott's decision. Raymond said that the proposed move was "such a huge change" to Barnes's intentions "that it just should not be allowed, and certainly it should not go unchallenged."[93]

The Pew, Lenfest, and Annenberg Foundations then announced they would suspend their payments until the appeal was settled. The Barnes Foundation announced it was once again in a precarious financial condition, and doubled the admission fee to $10. It persuaded the Supreme Court to hear the case on an expedited schedule (known as a "King's Bench petition").

The Pennsylvania Superior Court, in April 2005, declined to hear the appeal on the grounds that Judge Ott had denied Raymond standing in February 2003, and Raymond did not appeal Judge Ott's decision within 30 days, as required by Pennsylvania Rule of Appellate Procedure 903. "We find that Mr. Raymond's failure to attain intervenor status before the orphans' court foreclosed his ability to file a cognizable appeal relative to the court's final decree," declared Pennsylvania Justice Thomas G. Saylor.[94]

There is one final revelation about the Barnes Foundation legal drama. In October 2006 *Los Angeles Times* reporter Christopher Knight discovered that in October 2002 the Pennsylvania state legislature secretly earmarked $107 million to aid the Barnes. This was after the Pew, Annenberg, and Lenfest foundations offered their bailout plan but before the start of the legal battles between the Barnes Foundation and Lincoln University. The earmarks were part of the 2001-02 Pennsylvania state budget, and included $7 million for "restoration, stabilization, and site enhancements for the Barnes Foundation" and $100 million for "design and construction of a museum facility" for the foundation.

The earmarks were never mentioned at any point during the trial or in any news stories about the Barnes Foundation. Judge Ott, responding to a letter "written by a Barnes Foundation neighbor who had discovered" the hidden appropriation, said the letter "was to my knowledge, the first time I'd seen or heard" about the $107 million. Representatives from the Barnes Foundation or the Pew, Annenberg, or Lenfest foundations did not comment on Knight's revelation.[95]

**Barnes in 2006**

The foundation continued to raise money. In May 2006, the foundation announced that its $150 million fundraising drive had been met. Donors of over $10 million included $30 million from the Annenberg Foundation, $25 million from the Commonwealth of Pennsylvania, $20 million from the Pew Charitable Trusts, $15 million from the Lenfest Foundation, and $10 million from the Newbauer Family and William Penn Foundations.[96]

Kimberly Camp resigned, and was replaced by Derek Gilman, director of the Pennsylvania Academy of the Fine Arts. As of August 2006, the demolition of the juvenile detention center on which the Barnes Foundation hoped to build its new home was not scheduled to be completed until August 2007. No decisions had been made on which architect would build the museum's new home or when construction was scheduled to begin.[97]

The Barnes Foundation case is a severe blow to the cause of donor intent. Albert C. Barnes could not have been more explicit in what he wanted. But the foundation was now under the control of people he likely would have despised—the Pew Charitable Trusts, well known for their cavalier disregard of donor intent, the Lenfest Foundation, whose founder was a major patron of the Philadelphia Museum of Art,

# CHAPTER II

and the Annenberg Foundation, whose founder was one of Barnes' principal foes.

"Doesn't this decision," Julian Bond told the *Chronicle of Philanthropy*, "say to every donor that no matter how strong your intentions are someone with more money and better lawyers can come along some years later and change the gift?"[98]

Leslie Lenkowsky, an Indiana University public affairs professor, wrote that Judge Ott's ruling was a dangerous precedent. The decision, he wrote, "cannot help but encourage courts to act more assertively to alter donations that trustees or political officials, such as state attorneys general, regard as antiquated or problematic. Since clear standards of when such intervention might be justified or what remedies might be warranted are often difficult to determine (such as in the Barnes case), the potential for overdoing it is great. The result will be not just a great deal of second-guessing about how money set aside for particular charitable purposes ought to be spent, but also greater caution on the part of donors about making unusual or politically controversial bequests."[99]

Thomas Freudenheim added that the Barnes decision should provide a warning for donors seeking to build their own museums that the likelihood that these museums would honor posthumous donor requests was nil. "I'm all for supporting our museums—so go ahead, be generous," Freudenheim wrote. "But if you really love what you've collected and want to find a good home for it, you should probably face reality: there is no good home. And you might find that, when you're ready, selling what you own while you're around (along with the joy of playing cat-and-mouse with competing auction houses, getting your name on a sales catalog and having a front-row seat at the auction) can be just as exciting as collecting was. And, in any case, you won't be fooling yourself."[100]

Drexel University historian Robert Zaller holds hopes that the destruction of the Barnes Foundation can be stopped before the museum is forced to move. "No deed, no trust, no donor is ever completely proof against changing circumstances," he writes. "That is why the law of trust provides for prudent adjustment to such changes. The Barnes Foundation wasn't perfectly provided against all contingencies, more than any other child of time, and it was certainly not immune to the abuse of fools. But the trust need not have been betrayed. And we, the community, need not accept that betrayal in our name."[101]

# The Buck Trust and
# Marin Community Foundation

The Buck Trust case is the most obscure of the seven discussed in this chapter.[1] It is the only one that involves a regional foundation rather than a national one. On the surface, it was concluded in a way that upheld donor intent. After a lengthy battle described by newspapers as "the Super Bowl of Probate," the courts ruled that the fortune of Beryl Buck, a long-time resident of Marin County, California, should be used in the way she intended to help the people of that county.

But the Buck Trust case is not that simple. Two lessons can be learned from it. First, it clearly shows the doctrines that foes of donor intent use. Second, the case was a Pyrrhic victory for supporters of donor intent. The trust's money is now largely used in ways favored by those who wanted to break the will. The only restriction is that those funds are limited to charities and nonprofits in Marin County.

**The Estate of Beryl Buck**

Aaron Wildavsky, a political scientist at the University of California at Berkeley, noted that the Buck case has deep implications for nonprofits: "Does inconvenience satisfy the general rule that bequests may be set aside if they cannot be fulfilled?"

> What mattered more, however, was the ideological-cum-philosophical question: Did foundation policy include a commitment to carry out public policy defined as achieving greater equality of condition or should foundation policy respect the will of the benefactor and the social and economic systems that made this largesse possible...? At stake was the legitimacy of using money derived from the private sector of society to oppose capitalism.[2]

The wealth of the Buck estate came from oil. In 1870, the Buck family settled in California to begin farming. In 1911, Frank Buck, Beryl Buck's father-in-law, bought 30,000 acres of land in Kern County, California, which had some oil wells. He founded the Belridge Oil Company, a private corporation, to handle the family's oil business. His son, Leonard Buck II, who died in 1953, held a large portion of Belridge Oil shares, but his primary interest was medicine. He spent his career at

## CHAPTER II

the University of California at San Francisco, where he organized the university's museum of pathology. When he died, his entire estate, including the Belridge Oil shares, was willed to his widow, Beryl. This gave her a seven-percent interest in Belridge Oil.

By all accounts, Beryl Buck (1896-1975) was a private woman who preferred to do charitable work quietly. "Mrs. Buck was a generous person," Judge Homer Thompson concluded in his decision on the Buck Trust case. "She made many charitable gifts during her lifetime. For example, she gave gifts of money, food and/or clothing to people who had worked for her and people she knew who suffered from catastrophic illness. Mrs. Buck preferred to make her charitable gifts anonymously. She especially wanted to help persons who had done what they could to help themselves, but because of illness or accident, needed assistance."[3]

Beryl Buck's nephew, Lee Hamilton, told the *Los Angeles Times* that his aunt was particularly worried about middle-class people who had few resources to fall back on when misfortune struck. "One thing that she always stressed with me was charity for the middle-class people that had catastrophic diseases and disorders and accidents. A man would be making good money, but for some reason someone in the family had high medical bills, and they would have to slowly sell off his assets, and then he'd end up on welfare."[4] Likewise, in a memorandum to her attorney, John E. Cook, Beryl Buck responded to one of the drafts of her will that Cook had prepared, stating that the language restricting donations to Mann County "isn't as specific as I think it should be for Marin County only, and for middle-class people for illnesses, rehabilitation so they won't lose their homes, automobiles, et cetera, which they have saved for all their lives."[5]

Beryl Buck lived in Marin County from 1938 until her death. The county changed considerably during that time. When she settled there, it was largely farmland; when she died, it was one of America's wealthiest counties. But her interest in improving the county remained constant.

In 1961, John E. Cook went to the San Francisco Foundation (SFF), a community foundation, to see if it was willing to manage what was then called the Leonard W. Buck Trust. Beryl Buck asked that the trust's distributions be limited to Marin County, and the foundation agreed to the restriction. On July 11, 1961, foundation president John May wrote to Beryl Buck, saying that "I can assure you that the Foundation will do its best to administer the Leonard W. Buck Foundation in accordance with your wishes."[6]

Five versions of Beryl Buck's will were drafted between 1961 and 1973. Each contained a clause limiting donations to Mann County. No one from the foundation informed Mrs. Buck or her attorney of any intention to change or challenge this clause. On June 25, 1973, Beryl Buck executed her fifth and final will. The second clause of the tenth article contained this provision:

> The trustees shall have investment, management, and custody of the assets to be known as The Leonard and Beryl Buck Foundation, to be held by a separate fund subject to distribution through The San Francisco Foundation. They shall be governed by the rules, regulations, resolutions, and declarations governing The San Francisco Foundation as now or here after existing: provided always that such rules, regulations, resolutions, and declarations are not inconsistent with the provisions of decedent's will and any decree of final distribution directing that the distribution from The Leonard and Beryl Buck Foundation shall always be held and used for exclusively nonprofit, charitable, religious, or educational purposes in providing care for the needy in Marin County, California, and for other nonprofit charitable, religious or educational purposes in Marin County, California."[7]

By accepting these terms, the foundation agreed that the Buck Trust would be limited to Marin County, and that this limitation would have precedence over any of the foundation's own rules and regulations.

In Beryl Buck's last years, the worth of her estate grew as the Belridge Oil shares became more valuable in the wake of the 1973 oil embargo. Descendants of its two founders largely owned Belridge Oil. Since its stock was rarely traded over-the-counter, the exact value of the company was not known. The courts concluded, however, that Beryl Buck knew the worth of her shares was increasing. In a conversation with Rev. John Evans, a long-time friend, she said that Belridge Oil's Kern County properties were "the largest untapped oil reserves in the United States." She told another friend that the stock should not be sold because "it was a gold mine and it would be for future generations."[8]

# CHAPTER II

Beryl Buck died on May 30, 1975. The worth of her estate was finally determined in December 1979, when Belridge Oil was bought by Shell Oil for $3.65 billion or $3,664 a share. This made Beryl Buck's seven percent worth $253 million. The San Francisco Foundation became the third largest community foundation in the country, with total assets of over $280 million. In the same month, the foundation signed a preliminary decree, stating that it would honor Beryl Buck's restrictions on the distribution of funds. It also agreed to Buck's stipulations in March 1980, when the courts published a final decree awarding the administration of the Buck Trust to the San Francisco Foundation.

As late as 1983, the San Francisco Foundation still publicly stated that it would honor Beryl Buck's wishes. "We feel a deep responsibility for spending Mrs. Buck's money the way she wanted it spent," board member Robert C. Harris told *The Nation's* Peg Brickley and Fred Powledge. Harris added that the trust would be honored until "the day... comes that we fill every rut in the roads in Marin County."[9] Privately, however, the foundation was plotting to break the will.

## The Foundation Moves to Break the Will

In determining donor intent, courts use a rule known as *cy pres*, taken from the French term *cy pres comme possible*- "as close as possible." When it is no longer possible to honor a donor's wishes exactly, courts try to honor them as closely as possible. In deciding whether a donor's original intent can be fulfilled, courts first seek to determine if the donor's wishes are illegal, impracticable, or impossible. If they are, the will is modified.

Some employees of the San Francisco Foundation apparently knew about *cy pres*. In an internal memo dated July 26, 1979 and addressed to foundation counsel Robert C. Harris, Wayne Lamprey, the foundation's legal counsel, argued that "the San Francisco Foundation will in all [likelihood] never be able to establish that expenditures for charitable purposes in Marin County are impossible,"[10] since even an area as wealthy as Marin County has many people in need of charity. But it might be shown that the Buck Trust was inexpedient, or that Beryl Buck did not know how large her estate would be, and that therefore she would have wanted the funds to be used elsewhere.

Lamprey cited as evidence *Hoyt v. Bliss*, a 1919 Connecticut case in which a trust was established for a single student. The court ruled that if the trust's income was large enough to support a second student, then this change in the trust should occur, since the donor did not know how large the trust would be. To support a single student in "extravagance or wastefulness" was not what the donor intended."[11] "Like the trustor in *Hoyt*, it could be argued," Lamprey wrote, that "Mrs. Buck did not anticipate that trust income would exceed the amount reasonably required to accomplish the trust purpose." Since Marin County was wealthy, the funds needed to help the poor there were far less than the amount of the Buck Trust, so the best way to honor Beryl Buck's wishes was to have a court overturn the Mann County restriction.

On November 10, 1979, while the Buck will was still being probated, the San Francisco Foundation distribution committee met to discuss changing the will. In June and July 1980, three months after the probate court's final decree, the committee again discussed breaking the will. That July, it "agreed to follow the letter of the will until [the foundation had] enough experience to determine that this is not feasible." As foundation president Martin Paley later testified, the agreement to honor the Buck Trust was "not a forever commitment."[12]

The Buck Trust increased the San Francisco Foundation's endowment tenfold. This entirely changed the nature of the foundation. One distribution committee member said at an April 1983 meeting, "we must figure out more creative ways for the SFF to retain its integrity in the presence of a 'thousand pound gorilla' sitting in our midst. Buck has been a great opportunity and a great dilemma."

In May 1983, the San Francisco Foundation launched a formal effort to break the will. On May 24, Martin Paley wrote a memorandum saying that

> it is my judgment that the present method of organization and management of The San Francisco Foundation does not easily accommodate the long-term pursuit of full expenditure of Buck monies in Marin County. I believe this because I see an increasing strain placed on policies, procedures and personnel of the organization by maintaining two rather disparate standards of operation between Marin and the rest of the Bay Area. The Foundation therefore is faced with one of two choices—either redesign the structure and program of the San Francisco Foundation in order to accommodate the Marin responsibility with less strain to the institution or modify the

## CHAPTER II

nature of the Buck Trust to conform to and become compatible with the values and procedures of the Foundation as a whole.[13]

The foundation chose the latter course, and spent the last half of 1983 preparing its lawsuit. On December 13, the distribution committee voted 4-2 to file suit to break Beryl Buck's will. The two votes opposing the suit were from Marin County residents.

The San Francisco Foundation seems to have consulted few people before deciding to break the will. Recipients of Buck Trust grants were only told of the lawsuit on January 28, 1981one day before it was filed. Even Judy Edgar, the foundation's grants officer for Marin County, was told only a week before. The foundation also had few allies. One group that did offer support was Public Advocates, a San Francisco public-interest law firm that believed the Buck Trust funds would be better spent on low-cost housing and social services. (As early as 1980, Public Advocates employees were exploring ways to break the Buck Trust.)[14]

### "Effective" Philanthropy

In a December 22, 1983 memorandum to California Attorney General John Van de Kamp, the San Francisco Foundation outlined its plan. It had "consulted with a number of nationally recognized experts in various aspects of philanthropy" who were "substantially unanimous" in their view that the Buck Trust should be broken. But the foundation cited only two experts: John Gardner, former president of the Carnegie Corporation, and John Simon, a Yale Law School professor who also directed Yale's Program on Non-Profit Organizations.

Simon was an advocate of "strategic" or "effective" philanthropy. In a petition filed with the Marin County Superior Court in February 1984, he argued that historically, all foundations begin with local concerns; as their endowments grow, however, they expand or should expand to include national issues. "In its infancy, a foundation's charitable program may be narrowly constructed, with severe limits on the size and shape of the beneficiary community. But as the resources grow, the giving program reaches out beyond its parochial origins to address a more populous and diverse slice of humanity." The Ford Foundation, he said, began with Henry Ford's efforts to help Detroit, but later expanded to improve the country. "Charity may begin at home, but large-scale charity does not stay there."[15] Restricting the Buck Trust to Marin County "seems to violate principles of fairness and distributive justice," given that federal and state tax exemptions enabled the trust's endowment to grow.[16]

But as Robert B. Buck, Beryl Buck's grandnephew, noted, using "distributive justice" as a standard for judging donor intent would have two harmful consequences. First, it would create "reluctance on the part of persons wishing to make a charitable bequest, simply because few if any individuals wish to have their wishes second-guessed by those who presume to know better how to spend the donor's charitable dollars." Second, "breaking Beryl Buck's Will could only result in an avalanche of litigation, since the result would be ample precedent for an attack on any charitable institution and its trustees wherever and whenever it is perceived by some that the use of the charitable funds is not the 'best use' of these funds."[17]

For two years, the parties in the suit argued in pre-trial negotiations. At least twenty settlements were proposed, and all were rejected, including one by Public Advocates lawyer Sid Wolinsky. This would have divided the Buck Trust into two funds: one for Marin County and the remainder for the San Francisco Bay area. Martin Paley became extremely unpopular in Marin County; billboards were erected to denounce him. One dry cleaner collected 30,000 signatures for a petition demanding that the Buck Trust be upheld, and also distributed 6,000 bumper stickers that said, "The Buck Stops Here."[18]

Paley publicly argued that if Beryl Buck knew how much she was worth, she would have altered her will. He told the *Chronicle of Higher Education* in 1985 that his goal was not to destroy Buck's intentions "but rather to enforce her primary goals of making a meaningful, productive contribution to charity and creating a significant memorial to her husband. We believe that had Mrs. Buck known of the true value of her trust, she would not have limited the use of its income so narrowly."[19]

On January 2, 1986, California Attorney General John Van de Kamp announced that he would oppose the San Francisco Foundation. In a memorandum, he said that the lawsuit was "premature" in that the foundation had arbitrarily restricted the Buck Trust funds by barring "religious grants, grants for medical research and other scientific research, endowments, literary publications, government funded programs and funding of deficits for ongoing charitable projects." Further, the foundation was using "new and untested concepts of

## CHAPTER II

'relative need' or 'inefficient philanthropy,'" seeking to replace time-honored means of modifying trusts (i.e., determining whether the donor's wishes were illegal, impossible, or impracticable). He also suggested that the foundation might be removed as administrator of the trust, and contended that it should be "surcharged" for the lawsuit's growing legal bills.[20]

If "distributive justice" was to be the new standard of donor intent, California Deputy Attorney General Carole Kornblum noted, "there would be no reason that the trustees and directors of other charities could not sit back and say, 'There are starving people in Africa, why don't we change things?'" Should the San Francisco Foundation prevail, "you destroy the certainty that exists under trust law now, and that law is designed to encourage people to leave money to charities."[21]

**The Trial**

On February 3, 1986, the case of *Estate of Beryl H. Buck, Deceased* began in Mann County Probate Court. Marin County, the California Attorney General, the Buck Trust's lawyer and bank, and a group of Marin County charities opposed the San Francisco Foundation, Public Advocates, and 46 San Francisco area charities. From the beginning, the foundation was forced to retreat. Two days into the trial, Judge Homer Thompson ordered the release of 60 documents. These showed that the foundation had begun considering ways to break the trust ten days after it signed an initial decree to receive the funds, and that it had spent $230,000 in trust assets publicizing its efforts. A 1983 memorandum by Martin Paley noted that the foundation "presently has little difficulty in responding to an abundance of qualified grant proposals" from Marin County charities.[22]

A month into the trial, Judge Thompson ruled that the foundation could not compare the "efficiency" of grants in Marin County with grants outside the county. In other words, the charitable needs of the San Francisco area were not pertinent to the case; only Marin County's needs would be considered. Thompson also ruled that if the foundation were to argue that the Buck Trust restrictions were impracticable because of the foundation's own policy for distributing funds, the foundation's opponents could use this to argue that the foundation had done a poor job and should be removed as the trust's administrator. The foundation's attorney, Stephen Bomse, pleaded with the judge, arguing that evidence of the needs of people outside Marin County was necessary to show why the foundation acted as it did. "If we are wrong," Bomse said, "we really do not have a case to offer the court."[23]

Judge Thompson denied Bomse's request, but agreed to allow a one-week recess. Out of court negotiations began, and the foundation agreed to allow 80 percent of the Buck Trust funds to remain in Marin County. This offer was accepted by Marin County, but rejected by the Buck Trust and the California Attorney General. In late April, Thompson made two more rulings. He refused to set a standard for applying *cy pres,* and he declared that much of the testimony by expert witnesses about the "relative need" of various counties, including all the testimony of John Simon, was irrelevant to the question of whether Buck Trust funds were being spent wisely.

The foundation appealed these rulings, asking that the case be split in half, one part setting the *cy pres* standard for the case, the other addressing whether the foundation was qualified to manage the Buck Trust. Both a district court and the California Supreme Court upheld Thompson's ruling. The foundation and its allies were devastated. "This is Vietnam for us," Public Advocates' Sid Wolinsky told the *San Francisco Chronicle* in early May. "[W]e spent months brainstorming this case, and never in our wildest imagination did we dream that testimony comparing Marin County to other counties would be ruled inadmissible."[24]

The foundation also pursued a risky strategy that backfired. In order to prove that the Marin County restriction was impracticable, San Francisco Foundation program officers repeatedly testified that they weren't able to find useful ways to spend the Buck Trust money in Marin County, and therefore made bad grants to county organizations. "Marin's lawyers delighted in the tactic," wrote *Foundation News'* Roger M. Williams, "which made the foundation look like a bunch of bumblers; foundation staff, on the other hand, loathed it."

"For all of us, this was the single most offensive aspect of the whole case," a former San Francisco Foundation staff member told Williams. "We knew it would backfire, and anyway, we didn't believe it. 'Go out and tell the world what a lousy grantmaker you are.'"[25]

As the trial continued, the foundation further retreated. Beryl Buck's attorney, John Cook, testified that "I am responsible for having brought the foundation into the picture, and I am very ashamed." He added that if he had known that the foundation would try to break the trust, "I would never ever have used the foundation, and I don't think anybody else would, either. I think that's a shocking thing, to destroy the intention of the testator [donor]."[26]

# CHAPTER II

By mid-June, it was clear that the San Francisco Foundation would lose. In a speech before the Commonwealth Club, Martin Paley told the audience,

> To borrow a phrase from a popular movie, "I'm mad as hell, and I'm not going to take it any more..." I'm mad because, for trying to do the right and proper thing, we have been besmirched as "grave robbers" and accused of trying to break the will of an elderly widow... We thought it proper to exercise restraint in what we expected to be a dignified legal procedure... Our reward for this has been continued demagogic attacks, most recently as a Dickensian villain who "takes his little ward and kicks him down and throws him in the snow."[27]

Two weeks later, the foundation announced that it would end the case and cease to be the administrator of the Buck Trust.

## A Mixed Victory for Donor Intent

After a month's negotiations (chiefly over who would pay the case's legal bills), Judge Thompson made his ruling. Initially, it seemed that *Estate of Buck* would be a major victory for supporters of donor intent. Thompson ruled that the San Francisco Foundation had shown an inability to fairly administer the Buck Trust, and ordered that a new foundation, to be known as the Marin Community Foundation (MCF), be created to spend the Buck Trust funds. He also ruled that "the Petitioners failed to prove that it was impracticable, permanently or otherwise, to spend all of the annual income from the Buck Trust in accordance with the terms of the [Trust]. Neither 'inefficiency' nor 'ineffective philanthropy' constitute impracticability, nor does either constitute an appropriate standard for the application of *cy pres*."[28] Martin Paley resigned as president of the foundation. As of 1993, the foundation's endowment was $265 million–about a third of what it would have been with the Buck Trust.

But Judge Thompson did not give a clear-cut victory for supporters of donor intent. He required that the Marin Community Foundation spend part of its funds (an amount that would decrease from 25 percent of total grantmaking in 1987 to 20 percent in 1993) on "major projects" that "shall be of national and international importance and significance, the benefits from which will inure not only to Marin

County but all mankind."²⁹ By ordering the creation of three new nonprofit organizations–the Buck Center for Research on Aging, the Beryl Buck Institute for Education, and the Marin Institute for the Prevention of Alcohol and Other Drug Abuse Problems—Thompson technically adhered to Beryl Buck's wishes, since the organizations would be headquartered in Marin County. But their creation was also a response to the San Francisco Foundation's argument that the Buck Trust could be better used to address national rather than local problems. There is little evidence that Beryl Buck was interested in using her estate to study drug abuse, gerontology, or any other national problem.

In a 1987 *University of San Francisco Law Review* article, Yale law professor John Simon expressed dissatisfaction with the verdict. While continuing to support the San Francisco Foundation's position, he believed the court's decision to create national organizations headquartered in Marin County was misguided, since there was no evidence that Beryl Buck favored such organizations. The language of the Buck Trust will, he said, "is not the language a testator would use if she wished to support a national or international grant program merely headquartered in Marin County... Under the terms of Mrs. Buck's will, therefore, it is, to put it mildly, very difficult to justify a national-international 'major projects' scheme."³⁰

Moreover, the three court-mandated nonprofits were to receive some $8 million in Buck Trust funds a year, some of which has arguably been used lavishly. Many Marin County residents criticized plans of the Buck Center for Research on Aging to build a 500-acre headquarters designed by renowned architect I.M. Pei. "They're spending far too much money," retired judge Harold Brown told the *San Jose Mercury News*. Brown, brother of former California Governor Pat Brown and uncle of former California Governor Jerry Brown, charged that the Buck Center was "building over 100 condominiums and a swimming pool and tennis courts and recreation areas, all for the researchers. That will run into many millions. With people going homeless and hungry and the jail overcrowded, there are hundreds of other needs here for this money."³¹

The Marin Community Foundation spent its first few years organizing meetings to decide what to do with the Buck funds. But it often chose to continue grants that were made by the San Francisco Foundation. Environmental groups have received funds even though Beryl Buck was evidently unconcerned with environmental issues.

However, the Marin Community Foundation, unlike the San Francisco Foundation, has given money to religious organizations. Still, many of these groups have used the funds for esoteric purposes. The National Conference of Christians and Jews used a grant "to support the Green Circle program which helps young children (grades Kindergarten through 6th) to build their self-esteem. understand and appreciate cultural and racial differences, and develop peaceful conflict resolution skills."[32]

In June 1990, the Marin Community Foundation's first president, Douglas X. Patino, resigned over disputes about whether the Marin County Board of Supervisors could intervene in the affairs of the foundation. Stephen Dobbs, former head of the Koret Foundation, who was still president as of 1997, succeeded Patino. The Marin Community Foundation does fulfill Beryl Buck's wishes by spending money in Marin County. But there is little evidence that it supports causes she would have favored. Supporters of donor intent won the battle over the Buck Trust, but lost the war over how the trust's funds should be spent.

By 1996, the Buck Trust's assets had risen to $748 million, and the Marin Community Foundation (which has a staff of 35) had distributed $22.3 million from the trust's assets to various Marin County programs. Among these, the three court-mandated nonprofits created by the Buck Trust settlement—the Buck Center for Research on Aging, the Beryl Buck Institute for Education, and the Marin Institute-received 20 percent of the income generated by the trust's assets, or $6.3 million. Among recipients of Buck Trust funds were the cities of San Rafael and Novato, the United Nations Association ("for support of storytelling programs in Marin public schools based on the 50th anniversary of UNICEF"), the National Conference of Christians and Jews, the Spectrum Center for Lesbian, Gay, and Bisexual Concerns ("for a one-time technical assistance to develop an evaluation tool"), the Earth Island Institute, the Marin Audubon Society, the National Audubon Society, the Natural Resources Defense Council, the World Without War Council, and the POINT Foundation, publishers of the *Whole Earth Review*.[33]

In 2002, the controversy about Beryl Buck's rule made a brief re-appearance. A Latino group called the Greenlining Institute demanded that the Marin County Foundation redistribute $150 million of Buck Trust money to poor Latinos in the city of San Francisco. Their efforts persuaded the San Francisco Board of Supervisors, who unanimously passed a resolution demanding that the Marin Community Foundation create "a regional plan to effectively address the needs of the poor in the Bay Area."

At issue was the clause of Beryl Buck's will that said the Buck Trust should be used for "providing care for the needy in Marin County." The Greenlining Institute claimed that the clause meant that the trust should be used exclusively for the poor, and that the Marin Community Foundation was improperly diverting money to grants for the "environmental elite."

Marin Community Foundation president Thomas Peters told the *San Francisco Chronicle* that Judge Thompson's interpretation of the will was that "needy" meant all people in Marin County with needs, not just the poor. "Easily 75 percent of the money we granted over the past year could be classified as pointed towards families where economic, social, and linguistic needs were paramount."[34]

The San Francisco Board of Supervisors never pursued its resolution, and the issue quietly died.

The Marin Community Foundation was so well established that in 2004 it moved into fancy new offices. It continued to spend money on poor people and arts organizations, and began to put much of its resources into land trusts to preserve the remaining farmland in Marin County.

The three nonprofits created as a result of Judge Thompson's decision continued to grow. The Buck Center for Research on Aging renamed itself the Buck Institute for Age Research. In 2006, the institute started its first capital campaign, and announced that it was eager to get grants from other foundations.

CHAPTER II

# The Robertson Foundation

The battle between the children of Charles and Marie Robertson, heirs to the A&P grocery fortune, and Princeton University over control of the Robertson Foundation could be the most important donor intent case of this decade. As of July 2006, *Robertson v. Princeton* has not yet come to trial, and the case has been repeatedly postponed over the past two years. But Princeton University has already spent more on this case than on any other one in the university's venerable history. This spending is understandable since the foundation's wealth amounts to as much as six percent of Princeton's endowment. Moreover, it's clear that if Princeton wins the case, it would be a severe blow to donor intent.

At stake are these questions. Should the Robertson Foundation be independent of Princeton, or should the foundation be absorbed into Princeton's endowment? Should the foundation's grants be used exclusively to benefit the Woodrow Wilson School to train students for careers in public service? Or can the foundation's fortune be used for anything that benefits Princeton?

Charles Robertson (1905-81), a Princeton alumnus of the class of 1926, wanted to use his wealth to help his alma mater. In 1934, he married Marie Hartford Hoffman Reed, whose grandfather, George Huntington Hartford, founded the A&P supermarket chain.

In 1961, Charles and Marie Robertson created the Robertson Foundation and endowed it with 700,000 shares of A & P stock, worth $35 million. Clause three of the foundation's certificate of incorporation says the organization would have the following purposes:

"(a) To establish or maintain and support, at Princeton University, and as part of the Woodrow Wilson School, a Graduate School, where men and women dedicated to public service may prepare themselves for careers in government service, with particular emphasis on the education of such persons for careers in those areas of the Federal Government that are concerned with international relations and affairs;"

"(b) To establish and maintain scholarships or fellowships, which will provide full, or partial support to students to each Graduate School, whether such students are candidates for degrees, special students, or part-time students;"

"(c) To provide collateral and auxiliary services, plans and programs in furtherance of the object and purpose above set forth, including but without limitation, internship programs, plans for public service assignments of faculty or administrative personnel, mid-career study help, and programs for foreign students or officials training."[2]

After stating that "no substantial part of the corporation's activities shall be carrying on propaganda, or otherwise attempting, to influence legislation," the incorporation certificate concludes by stating that the Robertson Foundation could only be dissolved during the lifetime of Charles or Marie Robertson by their written permission, and then, within fourteen years after the death of either founder, by the consent of three of the Robertson children. Thereafter, unanimous consent of the trustees was needed. In the event of dissolution, the foundation's endowment would be "for investment purposes, be made a part of the general endowment fund but which otherwise shall be considered and administered as a separate and distinct endowment fund to be known as the 'Robertson Fund' and to be used by Princeton University to further the object and purpose above set forth."[3]

Documents introduced into the trial show further evidence of Charles Robertson's intentions. The earliest note is dated March 8, 1960. "Consider a small committee to undertake a study of the need for a training school for government employees—1 to 2 year course—*no frills*—rotating faculty periods of government employment—study abroad—12 months—year around work and study—building—practical emphasis on bold approach to a new curriculum and faculty. The B.F. to finance the costs of this study."

One week later, on March 15, 1960, Robertson made further notes on what he called "Project X." "Consider a fully endowed small government training school at graduate level—part of Woodrow Wilson School—for candidates for govt departments—State, Commerce, Labor, Interior, Budget, Welfare etc., etc.

Provision for degrees

"for financial assistance to students

"professors salaries +

"maintenance of bldg. & possibly a *small well equipped bldg*".[4]

On June 10, 1960, Robertson wrote to Princeton president Robert F. Goheen, in a letter, which is the oldest evidence that Robertson wanted to limit his grant to students training for positions in international affairs. "As I indicated in confidence to you at the National," Robertson wrote, "we may decide in 1961 as to arrange our financial affairs as to be able to assist in a very substantial manner a program or programs in educational areas which might not otherwise attract significant support. Our confidence and our anonymity I know will be

## CHAPTER II

respected. Our interest in the Graduate Program of the Woodrow Wilson School goes back several years. Its purpose to provide advanced professional training for policy making and administrative positions in government fills an ever growing need. May I suggest that some time between the middle of August and your return to active duty, you, Dr. Patterson, Marie and I sit down together and discuss those areas of the Woodrow Wilson School Graduate program you feel it might be desirable to enlarge or to review provided the necessary financial assistance might be provided."[5]

In December 1960, Robertson held meetings in Washington, and subsequently wrote an *aide-memoire* about what took place. The only participants identified in the discussions are Gen. Andrew Goodpaster, a former NATO commander who would serve as a Robertson Foundation trustee from 1961-2002, a Mr. Hoskins, director of the Foreign Service Institute, and Allen Dulles, who served as director of the Central Intelligence Agency in the Eisenhower and Kennedy administrations.

In these discussions, Robertson stated that the director of the Woodrow Wilson School administering Robertson's programs must have "a wide ranging experience in the public service in Washington. He must be a really top flight man with a really good mind, well liked, well known and trusted in Washington. He should be able to move easily in the top echelons in Washington."

"He will necessarily stress the importance of creating a market for his output. He will make it his business to keep advised of the availability of 'exempt' jobs (as opposed to civil service jobs on routine Foreign Service assignments) under keymen (sic). He will know who is seeking an apprentice or an assistant and what type of special training this man must have had. He will know 'whom to recommend to whom.' His graduates will not be lost in Washington's 'grinding mill'."

Robertson quoted Gen. Goodpaster as saying that the positions Woodrow Wilson School graduates would assume would be comparable to Supreme Court justices' law clerks or newly appointed doctors who served residencies with surgeons after receiving their M.D.s.

"These men will assume the burdens assigned and will work like hell," Gen. Goodpaster said. "The C.I.A. for instance would be a good bet for these men—Dulles has plenty of money, plenty of exempt positions and a real need for fine minds."

The comments Dulles made are more cryptic, except to say that "confidentially he is not impressed with the W.W. School" and "our concept of the new school is 'thrilling.' He would be delighted to be of service in launching the new school."⁶

One week later, on December 22, 1960, Robertson received a letter from his lawyer, Eugene Goodwillie, later to serve as a Robertson Foundation trustee for many years. Goodwillie was apparently the first person to suggest that the foundation have seven trustees of which Princeton would pick four. He also stated that the foundation should have the objective "to overcome the shortage of trained men qualified to hold responsible positions in government departments and agencies concerned with foreign affairs

Goodwillie also asked questions about what the foundation should do.

1. "Is there really a shortage of trained men?
2. Specifically in what departments or agencies?
3. If 20 to 40 highly trained men come out of the W.W. School each year—how would they go about getting into government service?
    a. Could they be absorbed into important jobs
    b. What pay would they get
    c. Opportunity for advancement
    d. Role of politics in the top jobs
4. Do we have, or are we likely to get a 'career foreign service comparable to the British F.O. [Foreign Office]'
5. Are these jobs sufficiently attractive to hold a reasonable proportion of these men (say 2/3) in government service for life, or would a large proportion be drained off into private industry after a few years."

Under a subsection entitled "Students," Goodwillie asked: "What, if anything, could be done to ensure that a substantial proportion of students would enter government service?"⁷

Goodwillie's questions were good ones, and the problems of the Robertson Foundation begin with the fact that these questions were never satisfactorily answered. The next item in the file is a letter from Brian P. Leeb, chairman of the Princeton University Fund, which handled alumni fundraising, to president Goheen dated January 6, 1961. Leeb enclosed a sheet of notes written by Robertson, which said that "the Robertson Fund to maintain and preserve its separate and special identity through the years—its funds to be separate from the University."⁸

## CHAPTER II

Why did Robertson insist that his foundation be a nonprofit controlled by Princeton but legally independent of Princeton? Gen. Andrew Goodpaster provides the best answer in a 2002 deposition. Gen. Goodpaster stated that the foundation has the structure it has because it was Charles Robertson's "observation, and I might say mine as well, that on occasion gifts were made to universities, and they were not applied in the way intended by the giver, and he and his wife really wanted to be sure that this gift, which is of magnificent size, would be applied in the way that they envisaged, so rather than make it outright because of that concern of giving assurance that the intent would be fulfilled, he wanted to stay in considerable degree of contact with just what was done with the money."[9]

In a 1979 letter to his son William, Charles Robertson explained, "the reason for the creation of the Robertson Foundation, as a separate entity from Princeton University, was the need for family and independent guidance as to the management and expenditure of Foundation income and assets. The founders felt that for the Foundation to achieve its stated objectives, family and outside, independent elements must be closely meshed with all phases of the management and spending policies of the Foundation. Moreover, they must enforce the official documents."[10]

Princeton University president Robert F. Goheen, on accepting the gift, said the money would be used for an "objective to develop, in the Woodrow Wilson School, post-graduate programs of instruction that will augment the flow of well-prepared people into positions of public responsibility and set new patterns of excellence throughout the nation for the training of men for the public service, with particular attention to international and foreign affairs."[11]

One of the grounds of dispute between the Robertson family and Princeton is whether or not the "public service" President Goheen referred to is the same as "government service." Princeton's position has been that if Woodrow Wilson School graduates pursue careers in nonprofits, then they are pursuing careers in "public service" and are therefore fulfilling Charles Robertson's intent. The Robertson family disagrees, saying that only Woodrow Wilson alumni who pursue careers in the federal government are doing what the Robertson Foundation wants.

The $35 million gift was the largest donation Princeton had received at the time, and remained the biggest Princeton donation until

1995. But the Robertsons refused to claim any credit for the gift. They insisted on anonymity, to the extent of keeping the Robertson Foundation out of any reference works on foundations. Princeton announced only that the donor was "Foundation X."

"The gift," the *New York Times* reported, "is the largest in Princeton's 215-year history and is believed to be the largest anonymous donation to American higher education… Princeton is expected to set new patterns in the approach by American universities to the professional training of the policy-making echelons of government."[12]

But the anonymous nature of the gift led to rampant speculation on campus about the identity of the Woodrow Wilson School's mysterious benefactor. According to the *New York Times*, some thought the CIA was behind it all.

In 1973, after the death of Marie Robertson, the Robertson family publicly acknowledged their generosity. One of the Robertson children (who would not give his first name) told the *New York Times* that the reason for the initial anonymity was "entirely the family's idea, and the children abided by the desire for no publicity. They [Charles and Marie Robertson] are very, very quiet people, very reticent. Publicity is anathema to both of them."

He added that "the pressure on the school to reveal the source of the donation income grew" and that after the death of Marie Robertson, Charles Robertson finally decided to make the gift public. "The family wanted to emphasize the importance of the school and not the family," the son added, "But the public demanded to know who the hell's money it was, even though it was none of their damned business."[13]

Because of the Robertson family's desire to avoid the limelight, the evidence for Charles and Marie Robertson's intentions rests on Charles Robertson's letters introduced into the trial as evidence. The earliest is from Charles Robertson to his son William dated July 3, 1962.

"Possessed of a large fortune, in the making of which we had no part whatsoever, the proud and devoted parents of a wonderful young family and ever mindful of our countless blessings we for years had searched for a cause, a project, so that we might serve to strengthen the Government of the United States and, in so doing, to assist people everywhere who sought freedom with justice," Charles Robertson wrote. "In due course and after a diligent search we, solely through our own initiative, decided to finance through a foundation a school in which outstanding college graduates truly dedicated to the service of the

## CHAPTER II

public would be educated to assume the responsibilities of important positions in those areas of the Federal Government concerned with international affairs."

"The Robertson Foundation was created in 1961 as a vehicle for underwriting the initial costs of establishing and operating, through the Trustees of Princeton University, the new Woodrow Wilson School of Public and International Affairs," Charles Robertson continued. After explaining that he expected his children to actively participate in the foundation, he added that "we are all prone to take for granted the gifts of freedom and of justice we as Americans enjoy forgetting that these great privileges simply do not just happen and flourish—bestowed to us by a benign and generous Providence. Men by the millions have fought for freedom and men by the uncounted thousands have died that you and Mother and I, along with our fellow countrymen might live securely and happily in this free country."

"It may well be that your life and the lives of those who follow you will be enriched by reason of your and of their identity with this project which was conceived with the express and clearly defined purpose of strengthening our government and our country," Robertson concluded. "As many times as you travel abroad you, like Mother and I, will return with the firm and lasting motivation that 'this is my own my native land'—cherish it and protect it."[14]

Charles and Marie Robertson expanded on this idea in a 1962 letter to the directors of the Banbury Fund, the Robertson family's personal foundation. "If substantial numbers of persons trained in the School do not go into government service, or do not remain in government service, or, if by reasons of politics, or bureaucracy, or any other reason, the recipients of the training provided by the school are unable to achieve positions of major responsibility in the government, then no matter how excellent their training may have been, the basic purpose of the School is not being achieved."[15]

"Success to Charlie," Gen. Goodpaster said in his deposition, "would be providing a large group of graduates to the government…to support the conduct of foreign policy and international policy, security policy and the life. That to him would have been the real measure of success."[16]

As the years went by, the unusual form of the Robertson Foundation was legally clarified. In forms submitted to the IRS in 1970, Charles Robertson stated that "the Foundation was organized exclusively for the benefit of, to perform the functions of, and to carry out the purposes of Princeton University…the Robertson Foundation is controlled by Princeton University. The university made it clear from the outset that it would not undertake the long-term commitment involved in the project (e.g., faculty contracts, student fellowships) unless it had effective control of the foundation." The vehicle by which the university would control the foundation, Robertson continued, would by having four of the seven seats on the foundation's board (with the Robertson family having the remaining three).[17]

In November 1970, the IRS responded that the Robertson Foundation was not a private foundation, but was a 509 (a) (3) non-profit organization. Princeton has claimed that this ruling showed that the Robertson Foundation is a supporting organization of Princeton; the Robertson family disagrees.

One of the questions the Mercer County Superior Court will determine is this: if the Robertson Foundation is legally independent of Princeton, but is "controlled" by Princeton, what actions would the Robertsons have to do to force a court to nullify Princeton's control? Can the relationship between the university and the foundation be severed without dissolving the foundation and using the money to fund the Princeton endowment?

## A History of Dissatisfaction

There is substantial evidence that Charles Robertson was dissatisfied with the number of Woodrow Wilson School graduates hired by the federal government. In 1963 Robertson wrote to Woodrow Wilson School Dean Gardner Patterson. "I have glanced over the list of recent graduates, particularly the list of the class of '63," Robertson wrote. "Of the 17 graduates 3 are preparing to enter law school and but 6 into federal service. I must confess to a feeling of acute disappointment. It was with this class in which we entered the scene at Princeton and for which Marie and I have entertained the highest hopes. The last thing in the world we would like to contemplate would be for the Woodrow Wilson School to act as a stepping stone or springboard for potential Harvard Law School graduates regardless of whether they indicate some idea of [a] later political career. Roughly 1/3 of these graduates are listed as interested in public service in the Federal Government. You and Murver assured us that this will not happen again but I am not at all clear as how you propose to change the admissions program so that you will have reasonable assurance that your students will enter Federal public service."[18]

# CHAPTER II

In 1971, a memorandum from Woodrow Wilson School dean John Lewis to Princeton President William Bowen stated that "with 45 million in the till to work with it should be possible to guide annually into the main stream of the Federal Government three or four dozen highly motivated...young Americans *(if not one hundred)*".[19]

This lofty goal was never met. A letter from Charles Robertson to Princeton University president William Bowen dated November 18, 1972 shows that the benefactor was dissatisfied with how Princeton was spending the Robertson money. By then the Robertson Foundation endowment had grown to $50 million, ensuring $1.5 million for support of the Woodrow Wilson School. Robertson noted that in 1972, the school had 47 students who were graduated with masters in public affairs (MPA) degrees. Of these, the federal government hired 10, and four became Foreign Service Officers. Similar graduation rates had taken place in 1971.

"In 1971 and again in 1972 the School conferred MPA degrees on ten candidates each year who were able to secure jobs in the Federal Government—irrespective of careers concerned with international relations. Would I be very far off target remarking that the amount spent by the University to educate each MPA candidate exceeds by a very wide margin the cost of educating any M.D., L.L. B., Ph.D. in this or any other country? And would I be guilty of gross exaggeration were I to remark that the cost (total annual income divided by the number of MPA's entering the Federal Government service) is, to express it with true British understatement, truly astronomical?"

"And what are my suggestions?" Robertson added. "Simply to turn this School around and start over again with the avowed purpose of living up to the terms and conditions of the donor's gift and the acceptance of the University of this gift with these terms and conditions in good faith. The time has come to face up to the obvious fact that the School has never come within shouting distance of achieving the goal and I personally doubt that it ever will as long as it continues on its present course."[20] Robertson requested that the university place someone in Washington to convince mid-level civil servants that it would be in their best interest to advance their careers by obtaining Woodrow Wilson School MPAs.

President Bowen responded in a December 1, 1972 letter: "I think it is important that we review carefully both out experience to date with the mid-career program and possibilities for the future, I must say, however, that I personally have strong reservations about the wisdom of putting anything approaching complete emphasis on the mid-career element of the School's program.

"Feeling as close to you as I do," President Bowen added, "I hope you won't mind, Charlie, if I go on to say that my most deeply felt reaction to your letter was one of real sadness at your continuing discouragement. I really think that you are being somewhat unfair both to the School and to yourself. We have problems to be sure, but we have also accomplished a great deal, and you deserve to take more satisfaction from the very real progress that has been made."

The Robertson family charges that for the next thirty years, Princeton gradually drifted away from Charles and Marie Robertson's intentions. In 1972, for example, Dean Lewis wrote to President Bowen in a confidential memo that "what bothers me" about the Robertson Foundation 'is the unspoken premise that, with respect to any American institution dealing in public affairs, the highest per se loyalty automatically must be to the U.S. Government... [That] is not a philosophical premise to which the Woodrow Wilson School, as an agent of general public-affairs enlightenment, really can be bound. I guess I hope the issue does not explicitly surface... But if it were to do so, the University should resist a blind commitment to nation-state parochialism."[21]

A 1973 memo from Princeton's Provost, Sheldon Hackney, to President Bowen said that the Robertson Foundation funds violated academic freedom. "Eventually, in the very long run, it would be a good thing if the Foundation itself were to be dissolved and the funds given to the University earmarked for the same purposes for which they are currently being used....We must make it clear that the School's autonomy and its independence of judgment are not impaired by the existence of the Foundation board...I assume you share the sense of discomfort that John [Lewis] and I have about the existence of the Robertson Foundation as a separate entity with control over its own investment decisions...and with an ill-defined degree of oversight of the school's decisions."[22]

The dispute between the Robertson family and Princeton continued quietly behind the scenes for the next thirty years. On the surface, all was serene. A profile of the Woodrow Wilson School published in the *New York Times* late in 2001 found that the school had, in the 2001-02 school year, had 65 students in its MPA program, an additional 30 in a Ph.D. program, and 20 mid-career civil students studying at Princeton for one year. The school had 2,463 alumni in the labor force; of which 19 percent worked for nongovernmental

## CHAPTER II

organizations, 18 percent worked for the federal government, and eight percent worked for foreign governments. The school's most famous federal government alumnus was Anthony Lake, who served as one of President Clinton's national security advisers.

As of 2001, the Robertson Foundation endowment was $550 million. The foundation's funds paid for scholarships that provided up to half the cost of Princeton's annual tuition of $26,000. And many Woodrow Wilson School classes met in Robertson Hall.

"My parents wanted to make a significant gesture of philanthropy," William Robertson told the *Times*, "and I think they wanted to address the current state of world affairs, which included the Cold War and the threat from the Soviet Union."[23]

### Robertson v. Princeton

Seven months later, in July 2002, four of William Robertson's children and a cousin[24] launched their lawsuit against Princeton. The initial charge in the complaint was that the university was illicitly commingling Robertson Foundation money with the university's endowment and using foundation funds for activities that had nothing to do with training students for careers in civil service. One charge was that in 1991 the school had taken $13 million from the foundation's endowment and used the funds for various construction projects, including Wallace Hall, used in part by the sociology department.

The Robertson family particularly objected to a university plan to have PRINCO, which managed Princeton investments, also manage the Robertson Foundation endowment. They noted that such a move directly violated Charles Robertson's intentions. In a 1979 letter to his son William, Charles Robertson stated that "the securities portfolio" of the Robertson Foundation "should not be commingled with the Princeton University Endowment Fund as long as Robertson family members or their representatives serve on the Foundation Board of Trustees. Family representatives should take an interest in the management of the portfolio and should be sure that the Foundation controls its own assets. If for any reason, Family members permit either commingling or University control over the portfolio they have the right to reinstate control and management responsibility to the Foundation at any time in accordance with the Bylaws and Certificate of Incorporation."[25]

The Robertson family charged that Princeton had shifted $54 million of the endowment away from the foundation's endowment

*Undermining Donor Intent*

manager, Essex Street Investments, and placed it in the control of a PRINCO subsidiary—even though Essex Street had achieved greater returns on its investments than had PRINCO.

Princeton University President Shirley A. Tilghman told the *New York Times* that the Robertson Foundation's "funds are in fact only allowed to be used for the benefit of Princeton University. They [the Robertson family] cannot take it out of university control without the vote of the foundation board, and the university appoints four of its trustees."[26]

In November 2002 Princeton requested that the lawsuit be dismissed. They said that only Robertson Foundation trustees had the standing to sue. Thus, according to Princeton, of the five Robertson family members who were plaintiffs, only William Robertson and his cousin, Robert Halligan, had standing to sue. But Princeton's view was that since both these trustees had been on the Robertson Foundation board for over 20 years, they actively participated in and either approved or acquiesced in many of the actions challenged by the lawsuit and on repeated occasions expressed their support and admiration for the Woodrow Wilson School and its leadership."[27]

Princeton's lawyer, Douglas Eakeley, told the *Daily Princetonian* "there has been one board meeting since the complaint was filed and there was consensus reached on a number of issues. President Tilghman said that it was "time to let the legal action run its course" and hoped that the appointment of a new Wilson School dean would result in "an opportunity for an entirely new beginning with the Robertsons."[28]

In February 2003, the Robertsons responded by adding new charges. They said that Princeton University internal memos obtained during discovery showed that the foundation board was not given current financial information, ensuring that "the Foundation was accorded no real-time oversight of the spending decisions made by Princeton." They added that they had obtained evidence that Woodrow Wilson School officials complained to the university that the foundation was charged excessive overhead by Princeton. Finally, they produced internal memos to claim that Princeton officials were "quietly contemptuous" of Robertson family complaints about the foundation's funds being used to build Wallace Hall.[29]

Princeton responded in a filing of March 2003 that they and the trustees they appointed to the Robertson Foundation did not misuse the foundation's endowment. "The University Trustees have done their utmost to respond to the family trustees' requests for information,

CHAPTER II

suggestions for changes in operating procedures and expressions of concern about the Foundation's mission," the university said.[30]

In June 2003, Princeton asked Judge Neil Shuster to dismiss the lawsuit, saying the matter was an internal conflict between the Robertson Foundation's university-appointed trustees and the family trustees. They also claimed that the Robertson family had no right to sue in the Robertson Foundation's name.[31]

On September 8, 2003, Judge Shuster dismissed Princeton's filing and set a tentative trial date of October 2005. By this time, the Robertson Foundation case had become national news, with major pieces about the case in *National Review* and the *Washington Post*. John J. Miller, writing in *National Review*, unearthed new details. He reported that the Robertson family now claimed that thanks to Essex Street management, the Robertson Foundation's endowment was $150 million larger than it would have been if PRINCO had administered the funds. Miller also wrote about an internal 1997 email from Michael Rothschild, dean of the Woodrow Wilson School, to Princeton president Harold Shapiro, about the Wallace Hall construction project and Princeton's request that the Robertson Foundation cover any gaps in the construction cost if Princeton failed to raise $25 million. William Robertson, according to the email, "is unhappy" about the Wallace Hall project "and if we use large amounts of Robertson money to pay for the building he will be more so."[32]

For the *Washington Post*, Robertson said for the first time that the ultimate goal of the lawsuit would be to sever all ties between Princeton and the Robertson Foundation.

"Princeton has known for decades that the goal of our foundation is to send students into federal government, and they've ignored us. Princeton has abused the largest charitable gift in the history of American higher education and that's embarrassing. They will lose the money."[33]

Faced with this upping of the stakes by the Robertsons, at a Robertson Foundation board of trustees meeting, the four university-appointed trustees outvoted the three Robertson family members and said that PRINCO would now manage the Robertson Foundation endowment. The Robertson family issued a statement saying that "the University's intentions are perfectly clear: grab the money." Princeton lawyer Douglas Eakeley told the *Daily Princetonian* "the university-designated trustees acted as they did because they felt it was in their fiduciary interest to do so." He claimed that PRINCO had won in a competition over nine other investment management companies.³⁴

William Robertson then wrote an op-ed for the *Christian Science Monitor* stating that his family's lawsuit against Princeton was not unusual. Other donors also had sued the recipients of their generosity for the return of misused gifts. He noted that the New York State Attorney General had ordered New York City's St. Luke's-Roosevelt Hospital to return $5 million of a $10 million bequest after finding that the hospital had not used the money for alcoholism-treatment programs. Another lawsuit by the heirs of patron Sybil Harrington charged that the Metropolitan Opera had failed to spend Harrington's $5 million bequest on traditional opera, as she had instructed.

"Nonprofit organizations need to be governed by the highest ethical standards," Robertson wrote. "When they accept donations for a specific purpose, that's how the money should be used."³⁵

The Robertson family's next action, in July 2004, was to amend its suit to request punitive damages from Princeton on the grounds that the university had defrauded not only the Robertson Foundation, but also other donors. "Princeton has a pattern and practice of violating donors' intentions and improperly spending restricted gifts in ways that benefit the university's own general fund," the Robertson family lawyers wrote in a brief that charged that the university had misspent at least $100 million of Robertson Foundation money. They said the university should alter the charter of the Robertson Foundation so that the Robertson family would appoint all trustees and restore with interest any misused money.

As evidence, the family cited an audit done by former Princeton development official Jessie Washington of Princeton's School of Religious Life, in which the employee wrote that "funding allocations are not in alignment with their intended purpose; i.e., the donors' wishes have been ignored; money for religious life has been knowingly withheld."

Princeton responded in a statement that the Robertson family claims were "unsubstantiated and misleading" and that the allegation that donors interested in supporting religion at Princeton were defrauded "was thoroughly investigated and determined to involve no wrongdoing."³⁶

The *Daily Princetonian* subsequently found out that Washington was asked to audit restricted funds to the Office of Religious Life by

## CHAPTER II

Princeton vice-president for campus life Janet Dickerson. Washington found "inadequate information systems, poor business processes and questionable actions" by Princeton in the use of these restricted funds.

"I started to see problems by just standing at the photocopying machine and putting documents in order," Washington said. "It was like a psychological double-take. Am I seeing what I'm seeing?"

University officials refused to discuss Washington's audit because it had become part of the Robertson Foundation lawsuit. But Robertson family attorney Seth Lapidow admitted that no one else had come forward to support Washington's allegations that Princeton routinely abused donor intent.[37]

The Robertson family lawyers also charged that the foundation's money was being used to pay for graduate school fellowships in sociology, political science, and economics, and that the foundation was billed for faculty salaries in Princeton's Office of Population Research and the Center for International Studies.

"We feel the money should be used to pay teachers to teach and encourage students to go into government service," Robertson family lawyer Seth Lapidow told the *Daily Princetonian*. "Princeton has lost sight of that vision."

Princeton lawyer Douglas Eakeley said the foundation money used for departments outside the Wilson School was necessary to strengthen interdisciplinary studies between them and the Wilson School. "There are various elements that go into having a vibrant program in public and international affairs," Eakeley said, including interdisciplinary programs.[38]

In October 2004, Judge Shuster accepted the amendments. If Princeton was found guilty of fraud, the university could be held for punitive damages should the Robertson family win. Douglas Eakeley told the *New Jersey Law Journal* that the new charges "only add to the decibel level. They just make it harder for Shirley Tilghman to assist the foundation and make it harder to effect a reconciliation."[39]

By November 2004, the Robertson suit had become the most expensive legal case. Princeton said it had spent $2 million defending itself, while the Banbury Fund committed $5 million. The Robertson family had four lawyers on the case; Princeton had two partners and two senior associates. Over 40 depositions were recorded, with 25 left to go. Three former Princeton presidents had been deposed; President Goheen's deposition had taken six days due to his age.

The Robertson Foundation board still regularly met while the lawsuit was taking place. "The closed-door meetings" of the Robertson

Foundation trustees, reported the Newark *Star-Ledger's* Kelly Heyboer, "according to both sides, are tense and swarming with lawyers."[40]

Princeton filed the next salvo in February 2005. It asked Judge Shuster to declare that the Robertson Foundation funds could not be transferred to another university, that PRINCO should be able to manage the Princeton endowment, and that the university could spend capital gains and interest from the Robertson Foundation endowment. It also declared that the Robertson family trustees were "attempting to hold the foundation and the Woodrow Wilson School hostage" and that the Robertson family was engaging in a "gratuitous, baseless public relations campaign" which would harm both "the potential pool of student applicants [and] the receptiveness of funding agencies to Woodrow Wilson School grant applications."

Princeton general counsel Peter McDonough told the *Daily Princetonian* that these rulings were necessary to make sure the board did its job supervising routine matters at the Woodrow Wilson School. "Board members have had to continue to be responsive to the needs of the foundation," he said, "and it's very difficult to do that in real time while these very fundamental issues are in dispute and are affecting the ability of the foundation to be managed."

Princeton also introduced a letter by Robert Goheen written early in the 1960s when the Robertson Foundation was applying for tax-exempt status. "From the very inception of the proposal," the letter stated, "the prospective donor has understood and agreed that the University must have the responsibility for the direction, maintenance, and operation of the School in all its aspects…Thus, there is no question that the gift is for the sole use of Princeton University."

Robertson family lawyer Frank Cialone said that Goheen's declaration did not in any way inhibit the Robertson family from suing to sever the bond between Princeton and the foundation. "Nothing that Dr. Goheen says here supports the notion that the University's actions are beyond judicial review."[41]

In June, the Robertson family again sought to amend their complaint, stating that they had obtained evidence during discovery that the university had diverted $100 million from the Robertson Foundation endowment to programs that shouldn't have been funded with foundation money. The amendment charged that "the pattern and practice of diverting donations from their intended purpose" was "systemic" at the university.[42]

## CHAPTER II

The 2005-2006 school year began with the resignation of the Robertson Foundation's auditor, Grant Thornton LLP. The Robertson family wanted an independent audit of the Robertson Foundation books, and did not want to use the university's accountants, Deloitte Touche Tomatsu.

"We are aware of a sharp division of opinion among the parties relating to the Foundation's accounting for certain transactions, investment management, internal controls, and allegations of fraud," Grant Thornton said in its resignation letter. "Based on these matters and the substantial uncertainty surrounding their ultimate resolution, we have made the professional judgment to resign as auditors of the Foundation for the year ended June 30, 2004."

William Robertson told the *Daily Princetonian* that for an "auditor to resign suggests that the client was just not cooperating or was concealing considerable information from them."

"Mr. Robertson should know better than to suggest that we were not complying with the auditor," Douglas Eakeley responded. "There's no basis for that statement."

Alyesha Day, an accounting expert at the University of Chicago business school, speculated "especially in the post Sarbanes-Oxley regime, the liability of auditors has gone up." She thought Grant Thornton would not want to involve itself in an enterprise where members of the board sued each other.[43]

The Robertson family's next move was in December 2005, where it released a Zogby poll about donor intent. The poll reported the following:

- Fifty-three percent of Americans surveyed said they would "definitely stop giving" if a charity "used your donation for a specific purpose and you know they ignored your request." An additional 36 percent said that they would "probably stop giving" if a charity misused their donations.
- When asked if a charity should return a donation "if they used your money for a purpose other than the one for which it was given," 36 percent surveyed said that the charity should definitely return the money and an additional 23 percent said that the charity should probably return the money.
- The survey asked if charities who misuse donations 'should be held legally or criminally liable for acting in a fraudulent matter." Forty-seven percent said that the charity should be held legally

and criminally liable, while 24 percent said that the nonprofit should just be held legally liable and three percent said the organization should be criminally liable. Only 18 percent said that the charity should not be held legally or criminally liable.
- When asked, "how important do you think showing respect for a donor's wishes is to the ethical governance of nonprofit charitable organizations," 83 percent of those surveyed said it was very important and 15 percent said it was somewhat important.[44]

In January 2006, Princeton resubmitted its request to Judge Shuster that he rule that Princeton "is and will continue to be the sole beneficiary of the Robertson Foundation," that the university can continue to choose four of the foundation's seven trustees, that the foundation can spend capital gains from its endowment, and that the foundation's decision to retain PRINCO as investment advisers "represented a good faith exercise of its independent business judgment."

"It seems clear that these three issues can and should be resolved as a matter of law on the basis of the undisputed facts," Douglas Eakeley said.[45]

"Princeton's notion for summary judgment," Robertson family attorney Ronald Malone said in a statement," like its position throughout this controversy, betrays an attitude of arrogance and profound disrespect for commitments made to long-deceased donors."[46]

A front-page investigative piece in the *Wall Street Journal* in February 2006 substantially enhanced the Robertson family cause. "*Robertson v. Princeton,*" noted reporters John Hechinger and Daniel Golden, "may be the most important case higher education has faced over the question of honoring the wishes of a donor."

According to Hechinger and Golden, the Robertson family has spent $10 million on the suit, resulting in over 170,000 pages of depositions, including from four former Princeton presidents. Princeton, they estimated, had spent $12 million defending itself.

The *Wall Street Journal* reporters charged that Jessie Washington's audit had unearthed one major and one minor violation of donor intent. Washington found a 1988 donation of $5,000 from alumna Lois Thompson, stating that the funds should be used to "maintain and preserve" the organ in the university chapel. She found writing on the sheet used to record the donation stating that the money should be used

# CHAPTER II

"to relieve general funds" and "Dept. is not to know." She also said that when she told Steven Gill, now the Princeton budget director, about Thompson's misused donation, Gill said, "don't tell the *New York Times*." (Douglas Eakeley said that the notation meant that Princeton was going to reallocate general funds that had been used to maintain the organ and that Gill was joking.)

Princeton, Washington contended, also misused a $1 million donation made by the Danforth Foundation in 1959 to strengthen "religious work" on campus. Over the years, the donation had grown to $18.5 million. She reported that in fiscal year 2003, only $6,000 of the Danforth grant was used to support religion, but $650,000 intended to support scholarships for students studying religion was used instead for general funds.

The *Journal* article also made public a 1993 investigation of the Woodrow Wilson School by a team led by former Federal Reserve chairman Paul Volcker, who was teaching at Princeton at the time. The Volcker report found that the faculty was engaged "more and more in theoretical abstractions further and further removed from public policy" and that Robertson Foundation funds were used in ways "hard to relate to the mission" of the Woodrow Wilson School.

Hechinger and Golden also reported that in 2002, in the early stages of *Robertson v. Princeton*, Princeton university secretary Thomas M. Wright sent an email to President Tilghman stating that the foundation was spending $750,000 for student tuition for courses that weren't part of the Wilson School curriculum and for general purposes and that this spending would "greatly upset" the Robertson family and that the university should act "fast" to disclose it. Princeton failed to disclose this diversion of funds but told the *Journal* that this failure to disclose was "inappropriate" and wouldn't happen again.

Finally, the *Journal* was the first to report the analysis of the Robertson Foundation's books by Michael McGuire, a PricewaterhouseCoopers accountant who formerly was the Harvard Medical School's finance director. McGuire, hired by the Robertson family, issued a report in which he declared that $207 million of the $330 million the Robertson Foundation spent between 1996-2003 was "diverted" improperly, and that only $26 million of the $330 million was used for classroom instruction. He found that Princeton double-billed the foundation for building and equipment expenses by first charging the foundation for construction of a building, and then charging the foundation a second time when the building or the equipment depreciated. "In effect," said Hechinger and Golden, "the foundation was like a consumer who pays for a car once with cash upfront and then again on the installment plan."[47]

Princeton responded to the *Wall Street Journal* article in several ways. It said Hechinger and Golden's reporting on the hundreds of thousands of pages of documents obtained during discovery was "selective," although it did not say how anyone could write about such a huge amount of material without being selective. It also said the Danforth Foundation gift was, despite Washington's allegations, properly used for "academic and non-academic programs of a religious nature."[48]

As for the misused $750,000, Princeton responded to an article about this that appeared in the *Trenton Times*. "These funds," said Princeton vice-president Robert K. Durkee, "were not diverted to outside uses and she had no role in how they were reported."[49]

In February, Princeton announced that it would create a new Woodrow Wilson School fellowship called "Charles and Marie Robertson Scholars in the Nation's Service," which would be funded with $10 million of Robertson Foundation money. The fellowship would give five students grants for summer internships in their junior and senior years, and then place the students in $50,000 a year jobs for two-year tours of duty in the federal government, to be followed by a return to Princeton for a masters' degree program. The nonprofit group Partnership for Public Service would be hired to help place scholars in federal agencies, and if no openings were available, Princeton would pay the scholars' salaries.

At a press conference flanked by famous Woodrow Wilson School alumni, including New York Attorney General Eliot Spitzer, New Jersey state senate minority leader Leonard Lance, and Mike McCurry, President Clinton's press secretary, Woodrow Wilson School dean Anne-Marie Slaughter said that the Robertson Scholarship program "is a direct response to the critical need in this country to attract students to careers in the federal government."[50]

Robert K. Durkee told the *Wall Street Journal* that the Robertson Scholars program had been in development before the Robertson family launched its lawsuit and that the creation of the scholarship program was "not at all" related to the lawsuit.

In March 2006 Princeton filed a brief with the New Jersey Superior Court stating that it had "undercharged" the Robertson Foundation by

# CHAPTER II

$235 million over the years by not charging the foundation for programs that existed at the Woodrow Wilson School before 1961. Princeton now said it had erred for only charging the Robertson Foundation for programs created with the foundation's money.

Princeton also said William Robertson should be thrown off the Robertson Foundation board, and that "by his actions and words Mr. Robertson has demonstrated that he is no longer qualified to serve as a Trustee of the Robertson Foundation." It also said William Robertson had approved all Robertson Foundation grants prior to the beginning of the lawsuit in 2002.

Robertson told the *Daily Princetonian* that one reason for the family's lawsuit was Princeton's cover-up of the misallocation of Robertson Foundation funds during many of his years as a trustee. "I had been in the dark as to what we know now. Princeton has been keeping secrets from us. A main part of our allegation is that they've been covering up information for a long time."[52]

In July 2006 Princeton admitted that it had diverted $782,375 out of the Robertson Foundation for other programs. In March 2007 Princeton announced that it reimbursed that amount to the foundation. But the university also said it had spent $3.1 million in general funds on Robertson Foundation programs. The Robertson family responded that the partial disclosure was really a failed cover-up.

As of July 2006, a trial date for *Robertson v. Princeton* had not been set.[53]

# CHAPTER III
# Preserving Donor Intent

The stories of foundations are as varied as the methods used to create them. Some foundations continue unchanged from generation to generation; others change radically as soon as their founders die.

The debate over donor intent is largely ideological. Usually, capitalists who create great fortunes tend to be conservative or libertarian. Those who inherit their wealth, including most foundation executives and heirs to estates, tend to be liberal or socialist. The transformation of philanthropy from an avocation to a profession has also increased the likelihood that donor intent will be violated. Quite simply, there are many people in the nonprofit world who look down on donors who want some say in how their money is used.

Some foundations, however, continue to spend money in ways their founders intended. This chapter examines four such foundations, which provide important lessons in how donor intent can best he preserved.

## The JM Foundation

The JM Foundation, created in 1924 and based in New York City, is a family foundation with assets of $22 million, and is controlled by the grandson of its founder. Biographer John Briggs shows in his recent book, *The Face of a Family*, how the foundation has managed to uphold the intent of its founder.

In 1857, inventor Gail Borden perfected the process of canning condensed milk, allowing this product for the first time to be transported long distances without spoiling. (In the days before pasteurization, most milk was locally produced and quickly consumed.) Borden had opened a milk-condensation plant in Connecticut, but capital for operating the facility was hard to acquire because the country was in the midst of the Panic of 1857. Creditors often sued Borden, and the scarcity of funds forced several closures of his plant.

One day, Borden left his plant "not knowing where to go or what to do," notes his biographer, Clarence R. Wharton. "[H]e took the train for New York on a vain hunt for something or somebody and crowded his tall, wistful figure into a railway seat. It was one of those accidents which determine great issues in life."[1] Borden met Jeremiah Milbank

CHAPTER III

(1818-1884), a New York banker looking for new investments. Milbank became convinced that Borden's factory could be profitable, and invested $50,000 in return for a 50 percent interest in the venture; a year later, he invested another $50,000. (As Briggs notes, this would be equivalent to $2 million today.)

During the Civil War, both Borden and Milbank made huge fortunes selling canned milk to the victorious Union forces. Milbank used his share to start an investment banking firm and the Chicago, Milwaukee & St. Paul Railroad, one of the nation's first cross-country routes.[2] When he died in 1884, he left an enormous estate. This was equally divided between his two children, Joseph Milbank (1838-1914) and Elizabeth Milbank Anderson (1850-1921), each of whom also received 25 percent of the stock in Borden's company, known then as the New York Condensed Milk Company. (It was renamed the Borden Company in 1919.)

**The Milbanks: Pioneers in Philanthropy**

Both Joseph Milbank and Elizabeth Milbank Anderson were philanthropists. Joseph Milbank continued to run the family's investment banking firm, which grew substantially after he sold his share of the Borden stock. Elizabeth Milbank Anderson used much of her fortune, as did many late Victorian philanthropists, to directly help the poor. Her millions provided free lunches to public school children (a project later assumed by government), public baths for tenement dwellers, and the like. With Joseph Milbank she created a "People's Palace" in Jersey City, New Jersey, where the poor could enjoy sports and entertainment at minimal cost.[3] Her most lasting philanthropic achievement, however, was the creation of the Milbank Memorial Fund in 1905. Started with an endowment of $3 million, it has become one of the nation's leading philanthropies devoted to medical and scientific research.

By the time the second Jeremiah Milbank was born in 1887, the family had a firm tradition of philanthropy. The younger Jeremiah was educated at private schools, and later went to Yale University, where he was graduated in 1909. He married and began working in his father's invest-ment banking firm. After Joseph Milbank's sudden death in 1914, Jeremiah Milbank became president of J. Milbank & Company, and continued a long career until his death in 1972.[4]

In 1917, Jeremiah Milbank became concerned about the problems of those with disabilities. John Briggs says that the roots of this interest are unclear, but that Milbank began to worry about the many men with disabilities he saw begging on New York streets. A survey he commissioned found that most of these men were ready and eager to work if some way could be found to accommodate their handicaps.[5]

In 1917, Milbank gave the Red Cross $50,000, as well as a building, to establish an institute to provide training for men with disabilities. When the Red Cross Institute for Crippled and Disabled Men opened later that year, Milbank ensured that his name was nowhere on the building. Milbank made sure he was only the vice-chairman of the new institute, even though he was the principal funder.[6]

For the rest of his life, Milbank's main philanthropic concern was helping those with disabilities. In 1924, he created The JM Foundation. The largest recipient of JM Foundation grants has been the International Center for the Disabled (ICD), originally called the Institute for the Crippled and Disabled. During his life, Milbank gave the organization $36 million.

Milbank didn't just write checks. He delighted in an annual excursion from New York up the Hudson to Indian Point, where disabled people could have some summer fun. In 1929, for example, 600 disabled people had lunch and competed in contests, including rowing, running, a potato race, and baseball. "Orchestral selections" were played for people not strong enough to compete.[7]

Milbank's interest in helping those with disabilities changed as needs changed. In the late 1920s, he began a campaign to eradicate diphtheria, a scourge of the young. Due in part to his efforts, this debilitating disease was largely eradicated by 1930. In 1928, he joined other prominent Americans to form the International Committee for the Study of Infantile Paralysis, a clearinghouse for information on ways to treat and prevent polio. He gave $1.6 million that year to help establish the committee, and added millions more until Jonas Salk's polio vaccine became widely available in the mid-1950s. "The war against disease in all its forms," Milbank wrote in 1928, "presents a stirring challenge and maintains a keen and never-failing interest. One of its satisfactions is that the battle line never retreats and, while progress may prove slow, each again is held and forms the base for further advance."[8]

**Conservation Efforts**

In the late 1930s, Milbank developed an interest in conservation. In 1939, he purchased 28,000 acres of land in Jasper County, South

# CHAPTER III

Carolina for a farm and vacation home. Although the farm, called Turkey Hill Plantation, was run as a profit-making venture, Milbank wished to preserve part of the land for future generations. In his only book, *Turkey Hill Plantation* (1966), he wrote that 10,000 acres were set aside as a recreation reserve for shooting, hunting, and other sports. To ensure high-quality hunting, Milbank protected the entire farm. The plantation, he wrote, "provides not only protection for game, but cover and feed as well, to sustain and perpetuate types of wildlife that range many, many miles beyond our property. Therefore I think that, in essence, it represents a 28,000 acre refuge for South Carolina's whole coastal plain."[9]

But Milbank's interest in conservation went further. Three thousand acres of the plantation were set aside as a game sanctuary, and leased without charge to the South Carolina Wildlife Resources Department. All Turkey Hill employees were designated unpaid South Carolina game wardens, and given full powers to arrest poachers. Milbank was thus an innovator in using private funds to preserve and protect natural resources.

## Milbank's Political Career

Milbank was also active in the Republican Party. In the 1928 presidential campaign, he served as a fundraiser for Republican candidate Herbert Hoover. He found that traditional Republicans thought Hoover too liberal, as he opposed strikebreaking and supported labor's right to create unions. Milbank announced that the Republican Party would accept no contributions over $25,000, and tried to broaden the party's financial base by accepting thousands of small contributions from first-time donors. He was so successful in this effort that the Republican Party emerged from the race with a surplus in its bank accounts.

Hoover asked Milbank to work for him. As Briggs notes, "there were many who assumed that the office of secretary of the treasury could be his for the asking." But Milbank declined all government posts, saying, "The one thing I want to do is to keep out of Washington."[10] After serving again as a fundraiser in the 1932 presidential contest, he abandoned active involvement in politics.

Because Milbank rarely commented on public policy, his political beliefs cannot be precisely known. But he was a loyal Republican throughout his life, and retained his friendship with Herbert Hoover. In 1964, he gave $250,000 to the Hoover Institution on War, Revolution and Peace. In 1968, Richard Nixon wrote him to seek advice on a vice-presidential running mate. Milbank responded that his pick would be Ronald Reagan. "I believe that Governor Reagan of California would add the greatest strength to your ticket as a campaigner for the election. His position on the issues is consistent with yours and therefore would be enunciated with great clarity. His recognition factor is undoubtedly the greatest among the various possibilities, and his television appeal I believe is very strong."[11]

## Principles of Giving

Milbank had strong views on how foundations should be run. In the 1960s, he formulated five principles of grantmaking that forcefully show how he wanted his money used:

• Grants should be made to organizations working to prevent illness. According to John Briggs, Milbank "drew no distinction between illness in the physical sense, which could cripple or kill, and illness in the social sense, which deprived children from poor backgrounds of a fair chance in life."[12]

Before beginning a new project, experts should be consulted and the best advice gathered. The goals of the project should be determined, and grant recipients should not be allowed to deviate from them. As Briggs notes, this principle later became known as "management by objectives."

• Innovation in the social sciences should be the responsibility of the private sector. Although Milbank believed that government had some responsibilities in meeting human needs and alleviating suffering, he devoted his life to private initiatives as the preferred alternative to government programs.[13]

• Since intentions of the creators of great foundations are often diluted over time, the "long, strong thread of family involvement [is] the only way of ensuring consistency of purpose."[14] Milbank sought to ensure that his children and grandchildren understood his views and were motivated to continue The JM Foundation in a way he would approve.

• Gifts should be made as anonymously as possible. Milbank never sought publicity or fame for his philanthropy, nor saw it as a way to acquire power. He believed giving was simply the right way to live. He never asked that any buildings or institutions be named after him, and always asked to be treasurer of the organizations he founded or favored, as this was a fairly inconspicuous position.

# CHAPTER III

Milbank's reticence extended to his personal life. Few journalists knew that Milbank was one of the wealthiest Americans of his time. When *Fortune* profiled the Milbanks in a 1959 article (the only one to appear in Milbank's lifetime), the anonymous author noted that the family was so quiet about its wealth that the magazine missed counting them in another survey. "The Milbank family of New York controls what is probably the least publicized of the 'mature' great fortunes of America," it observed. "It is a tribute to the Milbanks' dislike of publicity, and their skill in avoiding it, that so little is known about them."[15] Jeremiah Milbank's collaborator in the Turkey Hill Plantation book, Grace Fox Perry, summed up the Milbanks' reticence: "Avoidance of publicity is an inherent tradition in the Milbank family."[16]

## Continuing a Tradition

Milbank's clearly articulated principles have largely been followed by his successor as president of The JM Foundation, Jeremiah Milbank, Jr. The younger Jeremiah's views are best expressed in a 1984 article he wrote for *Leaders* magazine. He believes that corporations should not give in order to redistribute wealth, nor to provide social services, but to provide themselves with "an opportunity to invest in a program or an enterprise offering a long-range benefit that will strengthen and enhance the overall growth and development of that corporation within a free society."[17] He believes that corporate grants to organizations that seek to motivate troubled urban youth to work hard, for example, help ensure that businesses will have committed future employees.

Jeremiah Milbank, Jr. urges philanthropists to keep their staffs small and to limit grantmaking to groups that fit corporate objectives. The leader of a corporate foundation, he believes, should be someone with both an extensive business background and experience in local community service organizations. While such people are admittedly rare, finding them is necessary if businesses are to avoid giving to groups that oppose free enterprise as well as to groups that are ineffective in aiding the distressed.

Many of The JM Foundation's recent grants have gone to organizations that have long been favored. In 1991, the foundation disbursed $2,286,410. The biggest beneficiary was the International Center for the Disabled, which received $250,000 for its 75th Anniversary Campaign, $55,000 for a new program to rehabilitate stroke victims, and $75,000 for the National Search for Excellence Awards in

Vocational Rehabilitation, which gives three $20,000 prizes annually to programs helping those with disabilities. The second largest recipient was the Boys and Girls Clubs of America, which received $255,000 to expand efforts to aid low-income youth. The elder Jeremiah Milbank was treasurer of the Boys Clubs of America for 25 years, and Jeremiah Milbank, Jr. has served as president.

One major change in The JM Foundation's giving has been a rise in the number of grants to market-oriented public-policy organizations. These include the Heritage Foundation, Madison Center for Educational Affairs, National Center for Neighborhood Enterprise, and Manhattan Institute for Policy Research. While such grants are not known to have been made in Jeremiah Milbank, Sr.'s day—indeed, few conservative or libertarian organizations existed during his lifetime—such gifts seem clearly consistent with the elder Milbank's beliefs and intentions.

The JM Foundation is a successful example of donor intent for two reasons: Jeremiah Milbank, Sr. made his charitable intentions explicit, and his family has honored those intentions. Such fidelity is rare in the history of foundations. If the creators of foundations routinely made their wishes clear, and if the children of philanthropists honored those wishes, many of the problems of donor intent could be avoided.

## The Lynde and Harry Bradley Foundation

The Lynde and Harry Bradley Foundation, founded in 1946 and reorganized in 1985, is a large Milwaukee-based foundation with few family members on its board. Nonetheless, as biographer John Gurda shows in his book, *The Bradley Legacy: Lynde and Harry Bradley Their Company, and Their Foundation,* the Bradley Foundation, like The JM Foundation, has managed to uphold donor intent.

Lynde Bradley (1878-1942) came from a family interested in invention. Bradley's mother and father both held patents, and Bradley himself acquired his first patent at age 16. While growing up in Milwaukee, Bradley experimented with electricity, built Milwaukee's first X-ray machine, and made headsets that allowed people to listen to live concerts over the telephone.

Because of the family's financial problems, Lynde Bradley was forced to begin a career before finishing high school. While working on his

# CHAPTER III

X-ray device, he met Stanton Allen, a physician interested in using X-rays in medicine. When an effort to start an X-ray business failed, Bradley decided to create a company to build rheostats-devices that ensure a steady flow of electric current to electromechanical products.

## The Allen-Bradley Company

In 1901, Allen and Bradley formed a partnership, creating what would become the Allen-Bradley Company. Allen provided $1,000 in capital as well as workspace and moral support, while Bradley supplied inventive know-how. The business expanded steadily, and employees were hired. Among the first was Lynde Bradley's brother, Harry Bradley (1880-1965), and Fred Loock, an engineer who was to work for the Allen-Bradley Company for 57 years.

In 1916, the Bradleys acquired Allen's share of the business, thus making the Allen-Bradley Company a privately held firm with most shares owned by the Bradley brothers. With the boom in radio sales in the 1920s, millions of hobbyists bought Bradleystat capacitors and resistors to make their home-built radios work better. When mass-produced radios became common in the late 1920s, Bradley units "became standard components in factory-built radios, and manufacturers bought tons of them."[1] Thousands more of these were used in Singer sewing machines.

The Allen-Bradley Company limped through the Great Depression and survived a major strike in 1939. During World War II, however, the firm prospered, as Allen-Bradley resistors were needed in walkie-talkies, radar, and aircraft. Allen-Bradley electromechanical controls were also used to improve machine tools in defense plants. In 1940, Allen-Bradley Company sales were $4.2 million; by 1945, they had increased to $15.4 million.

## Creation of the Foundation

By the mid-1940s, ownership of the Allen-Bradley Company had become complex. Lynde Bradley died in 1942, leaving a will that appeared to transfer his shares in the company to Harry Bradley, thus making him sole owner of the firm. Lynde Bradley also wanted to use his estate to create a foundation, but it took three years for his will to be probated. The settlement occurred largely through the efforts of Harvey Peters, a Milwaukee tax lawyer who had the Bradleys as "practically his only client."[2]

In December 1945, an agreement was reached. Under the probate of Bradley's will, Lynde Bradley's wife, Caroline, claimed the traditional "widow's third" of the Allen-Bradley shares (17 percent of the total Allen-Bradley stock.) The rest of the shares went to Harry Bradley, who transferred most of this to five trusts whose beneficiaries included his wife, three children, and Margaret Loock, wife of Fred Loock. (Peters established the fifth trust in Margaret Loock's name for fear that its income might be taxable if Fred Loock were the beneficiary.) In 1951, Caroline Bradley created three additional trusts from her share of the company, the beneficiaries of which were herself, her nephew, and her niece. Together, these eight trusts controlled nearly all the Allen-Bradley stock.

Lynde Bradley began to consider the idea of creating a foundation in 1941, when his lawyers persuaded him that this would allow inheritance taxes to be substantially cut. But he died before definite plans could be organized. Further, the creation of the Bradley Trusts nullified an original plan to endow a foundation with Bradley's portion of the Allen-Bradley shares. Instead, the Allen-Bradley Company regularly gave part of its profits to what would become the Lynde Bradley Foundation. The foundation's endowment climbed from $500,000 in 1946 to $1 million in 1951, and reached almost $4 million in 1960. In 1958, the Lynde Bradley Foundation was renamed the Allen-Bradley Foundation to signify its role as the philanthropic arm of the Allen-Bradley Company.

**Champions of Free Enterprise**

Biographer John Gurda notes that Lynde Bradley was so uninterested in politics that only one relevant remark by him is known to exist—a cryptic quote in a 1935 Allen-Bradley Company newsletter: "the blight of politics will rest upon us, as upon all others."[3] However, both Harry Bradley and Fred Loock, who succeeded Harry Bradley as company president in 1945, were vocal champions of free enterprise. Their views, says Gurda, were simple: "any force that sought to restrict the free market or the free individual was anathema. The pair directed their fire, accordingly, at what they considered the two major threats to freedom: the federal government and world Communism."[4]

Fred Loock wrote in a memorandum to employees in 1952,

# CHAPTER III

> At the rate our government is spending and we are paying—it won't be long before all money in excess of bare living will be taken away from us in Taxes. ...[E]xcept for the bureaucrats, you and I and every one else will become "slaves of the state"—a title no one should be proud of. It will be the end of "Free Americans." Fact is that we in this country are much farther along on the road to complete socialism than most of us are aware...[5]

Both Harry Bradley and Fred Loock used their wealth to advance conservative causes. Bradley was an early backer of National Review, and sought unsuccessfully to buy both Newsweek and the Milwaukee Sentinel. Both he and Loock also gave to such conservative presidential candidates as Robert Taft and Barry Goldwater. In 1964, Loock bought thousands of copies of *A Texan Looks at Lyndon; A Choice, Not an Echo;* and *None Dare Call It Treason* for the Allen-Bradley sales force, telling them that these books "ought to be required reading at the present time."[6]

Bradley was also a major supporter of the Christian Anti-Communist Crusade, whose founder, Frederick Schwarz, was a regular visitor to the Allen-Bradley plant, where he would often receive hefty donations. In 1957, the Allen-Bradley Company bought two pages in dozens of major dailies to reprint Schwarz's testimony on Communism before the House Un-American Activities Committee. At the end of the ads, the company announced that it "was trying to sell you nothing except the importance of holding fast to your American freedoms, including the freedom to live, the freedom to worship your God, and the freedom to work as you choose, which freedoms are still here in America, but have disappeared in much of the world."[7]

Bradley and Loock also withheld Allen-Bradley funds from causes they opposed. In 1964, Loock withdrew $100,000 worth of advertising from the *Saturday Evening Post* after it criticized Barry Goldwater in an editorial. When Allen-Bradley's New York bank hosted a luncheon in 1959 for Soviet diplomat Anastas Mikoyan, Bradley promptly withdrew company funds from the bank and blasted Mikoyan as a "Soviet murderer." According to Gurda, a Russian visitor to the Allen-Bradley plant in the 1950s reportedly "turned white" when he saw Harry Bradley's library, which included such works as *The Black Deeds of the Kremlin, Communist-Socialist Propaganda in the American Schools,* and *McCarthyism: The Fight for America.*[8]

An appreciative obituary in the August 24, 1965 issue of *National Review* described Harry Bradley as

> a phenomenon. He was professionally shy, and soft-spoken, and among the most adamant of men, who, if he believed in anything, was absolutely immovable... But his extraordinary generosity, much of it anonymous, to schools and hospitals and art galleries, made him a civic institution, and his death, even at his advanced age, deprived Milwaukee of one of its freshest and most resourceful sources of commercial and spiritual energy.[9]

Bradley drew a firm line between what he gave personally through the Allen-Bradley Company and what he gave through the Allen-Bradley Foundation. The foundation, while occasionally giving to conservative causes, was not primarily an outlet for supporting activists. "Conservative groups like the Christian Anti-Communist Crusade, the Manion Forum, and the Committee for Constitutional Government could generally count on a friendly response" from the foundation, Gurda writes. "Support for the right wing, however, constituted only a fractional percentage of the Foundation's total contributions. Harry Bradley and his colleagues had a strong interest in public policy but, from a philanthropic viewpoint, they considered public service more important."[10]

The Allen-Bradley Foundation's primary aim was simple: to support worthy projects in Milwaukee and Wisconsin. Harry Bradley wished to give some of the Allen-Bradley Company profits to the city that helped make him wealthy. In a 1977 interview, Harry Bradley's wife, Reg, told Gurda that her husband's "love was Milwaukee, you know, and Allen-Bradley. That's all he cared about. He never cared about going anywhere, doing anything, meeting anyone else. It was just centered right there, with all the people he cared so much about."[11]

The Allen-Bradley Foundation made grants in three areas: education, youth work, and health care. Each year a $5,000 check went to all the private colleges in Wisconsin, even though Bradley worried that they might be supporting "communistic and socialistic ideas." In the 1960s, the schools received $10,000 checks. St. Luke's Hospital and the Milwaukee Boys Club also received major contributions.

An additional insight into Allen-Bradley's giving comes from Harvey Peters, the lawyer who created the Bradley Trusts in 1945. According to Gurda, Peters was not a natural philanthropist: "his reluctance to part with money was legendary, and his fears of a 'financial catastrophe' were so acute that he once persuaded the [Allen-Bradley] company to start a corporate gold reserve."[12] Nonetheless, Peters was active in the Allen-Bradley Foundation from 1954 until the 1970s. A book he wrote, *America: Coming Bankruptcy: How the Government Is Wrecking Your Dollar* (1973), includes a chapter critical of nonprofits.

Peters worried that the growth of nonprofits would, in the long run, damage the American economy in two ways. First, since nonprofits were unrestrained by the profit motive, they had little incentive to keep costs low, and could spend more for labor then their for-profit competitors. "If the employer that produces goods and services wants to survive," Peters warned, "he must meet the competition of the nonprofit sector in striving to get, and keep capable employees. This can only mean that the employer producing goods and services has had to incur higher costs and, of course, this has increased the prices for goods and services that the consumer has had to pay."[13]

Second, Peters believed that nonprofits were spending too much money on administration and unnecessary frills. The charity that once was happy to get used furniture for its low-rent offices in a bad neighborhood now had a fancy office in a new high-rise:

> As uncontrolled monopolies, supported by tax-deductible dollars, nonprofit organizations have reflected the general American prosperity philosophy in that they have become quite materialistic. They have acquired costly real estate, they have built rather elaborate structures for office facilities, and they have considerably expanded their staffs of employees and administrators. There are even instances where a particular organization has actually accomplished the purpose for which it had been organized, and the organization promptly undertook new ventures rather than dismiss its staff and discontinue accepting contributions.[14]

Thus, the intent of Harry Bradley and his associates in their giving was as follows: benefit Milwaukee and the state of Wisconsin. Aid people who champion free enterprise. And ensure that administrative costs are as low as possible.

## Reorganization of the Foundation

In 1985, the eight Bradley Trusts sold the Allen-Bradley Company to Rockwell International for $ 1.65 billion. Six of the trusts either benefited their original recipients or those recipients' legatees. The largest beneficiary was Harry Bradley's daughter, Jane Bradley Pettit, who received $600 million.

When Caroline Bradley and Margaret Loock died, they willed that the Allen-Bradley Foundation inherit their trusts. These two trusts, however, controlled 22 percent of the Allen-Bradley stock, and Harvey Peters worried that this amount could violate tax laws restricting the amount of stock a foundation can hold in one company.

In 1977, the Allen-Bradley Company bought Caroline Bradley's stock for $5.8 million, but decided it could not afford to pay $23 million for the shares held by the Margaret Loock Trust. Because this trust had not been bought out, the Allen-Bradley Foundation's assets jumped from $14 million to over $290 million in 1985. The foundation promptly reorganized, renaming itself the Lynde and Harry Bradley Foundation and moving out of the Allen-Bradley plant to larger space in downtown Milwaukee.

The Bradley Foundation's executives, led by Milwaukee industrialist W.H. Brady and I. Andrew "Tiny" Rader, a long-time Allen-Bradley Company president, began a nationwide search for a president for the foundation. They selected Michael Joyce, who at the time was executive director of the John M. Olin Foundation. In 1985, he became executive director of the Bradley Foundation: in 1988, he became president with "Tiny" Rader assuming the post of chairman. Rader stayed on as chairman until 2000, when he retired and was succeeded by Allen M. Taylor.[15]

## Honoring Tradition

In 2004, assets of the Lynde and Harry Bradley Foundation totaled $665 million. Sarah Doll Barder, a niece of Lynde Bradley, has willed 70 percent of her trust to the foundation upon her death—an act that Gurda believes will add $100 million to the foundation's wealth.

In its grantmaking, the Bradley Foundation continues to emphasize Harvey Peters's business-like practices. It has fewer than 20 full-time employees, and administrative costs are kept to a minimum. "Applicants with bloated budgets for staff and office," Gurda writes, "generally go away empty-handed."[16] The foundation's guidelines state that no grants

## CHAPTER III

will be made to pay salaries for fundraisers, and that requests for funds to construct new buildings will only be considered if they have "a special interest to the work of the Foundation."[17]

The foundation is best known for its concern with public policy. The Heritage Foundation, a free-market think tank, has had Bradley Scholars-visiting writers who spend up to a year conducting research and writing books and articles. There have been Bradley Fellows at the market-oriented American Enterprise Institute (its former fellow is sociologist Charles Murray), the City University of New York, the Duke University Marine Laboratory, Claremont McKenna College, the universities of Chicago, Notre Dame, Rochester, Toronto, Virginia, and California at Berkeley and Los Angeles, as well as Boston, Carnegie-Mellon, George Mason, Johns Hopkins, New York, Princeton, Stanford, Texas A & M, Washington (in St. Louis), and Yale universities. Harvard University has Bradley Fellows in its economics department, Graduate School of Education, Russian Research Center, and Kennedy School of Government.

The Bradley Foundation is particularly interested in education reforms that promote parental choice. In 2004 it made major grants to the Phoenix, Arizona-based Alliance for School Choice ($45,000), Black Alliance for Educational Options ($300,000), the Boston group Building Excellent Schools ($190,000), Marquette University's Institute for the Transformation of Learning ($250,000), School Choice Wisconsin ($150,000), the Heartland Institute in Chicago ($125,000), and the Thomas B. Fordham Foundation ($95,000). It gave $2.9 million to PAVE, Partners Advancing Values in Education, which provides private scholarships to poor families, and it made grants to the Marva Collins School in Wisconsin and the Big Shoulders fund in Chicago.

Milwaukee's ballet, art museum, historical society, library, orchestra, and local theaters also receive large gifts. Even the city of Milwaukee received a grant to improve its police force. One major change has been the direct awarding of grants to nonprofits, rather than funding the United Way and an umbrella organization that support Milwaukee nonprofits devoted to the arts.[18]

In 1993, the Bradley Foundation announced that it would move away from scholarly research towards more support of "new citizenship" programs to encourage citizens to help make their communities better places to live. As an example, foundation president Michael Joyce told *National Journal* that he might fund programs that would provide toll-free numbers for parents who wanted to protest the sexual content of classroom materials.[19]

The Lynde and Harry Bradley Foundation is a successful example of donor intent in that it spends its funds in ways that Harry Bradley and Fred Loock would have approved and refrains from supporting causes they would have opposed. Foundation president Michael Joyce has called donor intent the "North Star of Philanthropy." "You don't stand for elections, so there is no political check," he told the Philanthropy Roundtable, a national association of individual, corporate, and foundation donors. "There's no market, [so philanthropy] has to have some North Star, and that North Star is donor intent."[20]

Among the Bradley Foundation's past activities:

• It donated $50,000 to support the Baraboo, Wisconsin, Great Circus Parade.[21]

• It supported school choice by giving a grant to the Institute for Contemporary Studies to hire Daniel McGroarty, a former speechwriter for George Bush, to write *Break These Chains* (Prima, 1996), a history of the fight for school choice in Milwaukee.[22]

• It continued to be a major backer of private vouchers in Milwaukee, supporting Partners Advancing Values in Education (PAVE) with $2.9 million in 2004. The Bradley Foundation's grants are matched by contributions from other charities, corporations, and individuals in Milwaukee.[23]

• It established the National Commission on Philanthropy and Civic Renewal to launch a major examination of philanthropy and recognize "civic entrepreneurs" who practice effective charity. The commission's report is *Giving Better, Giving Smarter: Renewing Philanthropy in America* (Washington, D.C.: National Commission on Philanthropy and Civic Renewal, 1997).

While Joyce's respect for the beliefs of Harry Bradley and Fred Loock helps explain the foundation's fidelity to its creators, Bradley and Loock also took steps to ensure that their successors would be firm advocates of free enterprise. As in the case of Jeremiah Milbank and The JM Foundation, donor intent is best preserved when donors clearly state how they want their fortunes used and when heirs to estates strive to honor those wishes.

The Bradley Foundation continues to be a leading patron of conservative causes. Evidence of its effectiveness comes when Eric Alterman, a columnist for *The Nation*, paid tribute to the foundation's

CHAPTER III

support of such noted authors as Charles Murray and Marvin Olasky. He cited Michael Joyce's estimate that the Bradley Foundation had supported the publication of over 400 books between 1985-1999 and had also provided support for Encounter Books, a new conservative book publisher.

While calling these books "ideologically revanchist," he noted that "while many of the most promising intellectual talents of the left have eschewed the 'real' world of public discourse for the cloistered confines of narrow academic concerns, the right has been taking its message to 'the people' in the form of bestselling book after bestselling book." Unlike liberals, Alterman admitted, conservatives "wrote books directed at a mass audience and received funding and support from conservative sources that understood the fundamental importance of the battle of ideas."[24]

"Where the traditional, well-established and more liberal lions of the foundation world such as the Ford Foundation and the Carnegie Corporation of New York were once seen as the trendsetters," *National Journal*'s Shawn Zeller reported in 2003, "today it is the conservative grantmakers—the Bradley Foundation, the David H. Koch Charitable Foundation, the John M. Olin Foundation, the Sarah Scaife Foundation, and others—that are creating a buzz."[25]

The Bradley Foundation also has been active in supporting inner-city groups in Milwaukee that encourage poor people to become self-reliant. In 2002 President Bush, in a visit to Milwaukee, praised the Bradley Foundation for promoting compassionate conservatism. "The Bradley Foundation has always been willing to seek different solutions," President Bush said. "They've been willing to challenge the status quo."[26]

The foundation has continued to introduce new programs. In 2003, it launched the Bradley Center for Philanthropy and Civic Renewal at the Hudson Institute. The center funds and publishes books and monographs (including my book *Great Philanthropic Mistakes*) and holds conferences on philanthropic issues.[27] In 2003, the foundation established the Bradley Prizes, four annual awards that could be considered the conservative counterpart to the MacArthur Fellows Program.[28]

Michael Joyce resigned as Bradley Foundation president in 2001 to head a new nonprofit designed to support funding of faith-based nonprofits. Joyce died in 2006; his death was marked by numerous tributes recognizing his importance as a grantmaker.[29]

Joyce's successor, Michael S. Grebe, was previously chairman of Foley & Lardner, a large law firm in Milwaukee. In a 2003 interview in *Philanthropy*, Grebe stressed the importance of donor intent.

"We are guided by donor intent," Grebe said. "We are fortunate to have a well-documented historical record of the philanthropy of the Bradley brothers, who created the wealth that funded this foundation. So even though they have not been with us for several decades, we have a good understanding of their philanthropic principles."[30]

## The Duke Endowment

The Duke Endowment is a major counter-example to the stories of foundations created by the heroic entrepreneurs of the late 19th century. James Buchanan "Buck" Duke (1856-1925), like John D. Rockefeller and Andrew Carnegie, was considered a "robber baron" in his day. Like Rockefeller, he created a huge corporation that was declared illegal by the Supreme Court. His creation of the Duke Endowment in 1924 with a gift of $40 million was surpassed at the time only by the gifts of Carnegie and Rockefeller.

Yet while the Carnegie Corporation and the Rockefeller Foundation have long since abandoned the philosophies of their founders, the Duke Endowment still gives grants according to the wishes of James B. Duke. Though it is currently the 13th largest foundation in America, it makes little news. It was not mentioned in the *New York Times, Washington Post, Wall Street Journal, Boston Globe, Atlanta Constitution, Christian Science Monitor,* or *USA Today* between 1985 and early 1994. But in its quiet way, it continues to do what Duke wanted to help the people of North and South Carolina by providing good hospitals, sound universities, and strong churches.

Like the foundation he created, James Duke did not court publicity, and most of his papers were destroyed after his death. He is known to have written only one article, and he gave few interviews. "I don't talk," he once said. "I work."[1] But from the interviews he gave, the recollections of his associates, and the indenture creating the Duke Endowment, his beliefs and intentions are clear and well defined.

### The Duke Fortune

The Duke fortune began to be created by James Duke's father, Washington Duke, after the Civil War. Washington Duke returned to his farm near Durham, North Carolina with little more than a fifty-cent piece in his pocket and a dream of starting a tobacco company. In 1866, he formed W. Duke, Sons, & Company to sell chewing tobacco. In 1878, the business became a partnership when James Duke and his brother Benjamin Duke (1854-1929) entered the company.

James Duke built the family enterprise into a big business. This occurred for two reasons. First, he shifted resources from chewing tobacco to cigarettes. He was the first to realize the potential of the cigarette-rolling machine, patented by James Bonsack in 1881. Before then, cigarettes were rolled individually by hand. Duke's competitors tried the Bonsack machine but rejected it, believing that consumers preferred hand-rolled to machine-made cigarettes. But Duke realized that Bonsack's invention could transform cigarettes from a handcrafted to a mass-produced item. By supporting Bonsack and using his machines extensively, Duke was able to cut the cost of cigarette production from 80¢ to 30¢ per thousand. Like most great capitalists of the 19th century, Duke increased his profits by offering a wider range of goods at steadily falling prices.

Second, Duke was one of the first American manufacturers to realize the importance of national advertising. In 1883, he shipped 380,000 chairs with Cameo cigarette labels emblazoned on their backs to cigar stores—a highly unusual move at the time. He also invented the cigarette box, ensuring that his company's cigarettes *were* less likely to be damaged during shipping than competitors' products, which were simply wrapped in paper. "James Duke was the leading innovator in the American cigarette industry during the 1880's," notes historian Patrick G. Porter. "He made entrepreneurial contributions in marketing, in purchasing, and in production which were the driving force for change."[2]

By 1890, these innovations allowed Duke to buy out many of his competitors and form the American Tobacco Company, which came to dominate the steadily expanding U.S. cigarette market and also held a major position in the more competitive cigar industry. The trustbusters in the Theodore Roosevelt Administration began attacking American Tobacco's near-monopoly. In 1908, a circuit court ruled that American Tobacco was an illegal trust under the terms of the Sherman Antitrust Act. In making its ruling, however, the court admitted that despite the company's dominant position, it did not arbitrarily raise prices or suppress competition. "There is an absence of persuasive evidence that by unfair competition or improper practices independent dealers have been dragooned into giving up their individual enterprises and selling out to the principal defendant," the court's majority declared.[3]

In 1911, the Supreme Court, shortly after ordering the dissolution of John D. Rockefeller's Standard Oil Company, ordered the American Tobacco Company divided into several parts, of which the most important were Liggett and Myers, P. Lorillard, R.J. Reynolds, and a vastly reduced American Tobacco. For a few years, Duke ran British-American Tobacco, one of the world's first multinational corporations.[4] But around 1915, he abandoned the tobacco trade and began a career as a utility executive.

Duke was one of the first Americans to realize that water power could be harnessed to produce large amounts of electricity. He created the Southern Power System to turn energy from the rivers flowing from the Appalachian Mountains into electricity.[5] Renamed the Duke Power Company after his death, this firm is still the electric utility for the western part of North Carolina.

**A Tradition of Philanthropy**

From 1915 onwards, Duke increasingly turned his attention to philanthropy. The Duke family, as devout Methodists, thought it their Christian duty to help the less fortunate. But until the creation of the Duke Endowment, Benjamin Duke, not James Duke, was better known for his philanthropic endeavors. This was a deliberate division of labor in the Duke family; Ben Duke dealt with charities while "Buck" Duke ran the family business.

Historian Robert F. Durden cites an 1893 letter that elucidates Benjamin Duke's charitable interests:

> "I want to talk to you about money matters," Ben Duke wrote to his brother, telling him that he contributed $7,500 to Trinity College and $4,016 to other charities and churches, which included "contributions to the poor fund of the town during the severe weather last winter, amounts given to the pastor of our church for the poor during the year which he used in doctoring the sick, burying the dead &c &c (all of which he rendered itemized statement of) Oxford Orphans Asylum, current expenses of our church of every kind. Colored School at Kittretl N.C. $500. Worn out Preachers of the N.C. Conference $500. To poor churches over the state &c &c...

# CHAPTER III

Of course, this does not count money that I have given kin people."[6]

"The amounts of money mentioned were yet small," Durden writes, "but there would be a striking continuity of purpose between the small-scale gifts of the 1890's, the larger donations of the 1900's, and the immense bequests of the 1920's."[7] In fact, nearly the Duke Endowment supports every organization and cause mentioned in Benjamin Duke's letter today. The only major addition has been hospitals. In creating the foundation, James Duke largely continued family traditions of philanthropy that spanned two generations and thirty years.

One area not mentioned in Benjamin Duke's letter was politics. Though named after Democratic President James Buchanan, James Duke like most members of his family, was a Republican. His fiercest foes in the press were editorialists at the *Raleigh News and Observer*, then (and now) a staunchly liberal Democratic newspaper. Some of Duke's political views are known. In a 1915 article in the *North American Review*, he attacked anti-business policies such as high tariffs that severely hindered export-oriented American firms in world markets. "Is it possible," he wrote, "that public men are more intent on the punishment of successful business men [sic], and preventing the accumulation of large personal fortunes, then on achieving a condition of helpfulness to all?"[8]

In 1922, Clarence Barron, founder of *Barron's*, interviewed Duke. Barron did not publish the interview, but preserved notes for a book that was never completed. In the interview, Duke supported a consumption tax, saying it would provide incentives to increase capital, which would ensure that America "would dominate and make prices for the whole world."[9] He also supported Henry Ford's idea of using capital to build job-creating enterprises rather than saving capital in banks. "You don't get rich by loaning out money," he said, "a country gets rich by paying wages to labor, maintaining large outputs, large consumption, and large markets."[10] More evidence of Duke's political views comes from a 1924 interview with the *New York Times* on the occasion of the Duke Endowment's creation. Duke said he was "unalterably opposed" to the League of Nations, but beyond that, the reporter said, "Mr. Duke would not talk for publication on political matters."[11]

The clearest indication of Duke's attitude towards politics comes from his 1915 *North American Review* article. "Public office," Duke wrote, "requires talents that the business-builder has not time nor environment to cultivate."[12] This view was one Duke clearly expressed throughout his career. Unlike Andrew Carnegie, Duke did not use his fortune to affect the issues of the day. And unlike Henry Ford, he did not toy with the idea of running for president. He was not active in politics, and neither is the Duke Endowment.

The Duke family's giving grew as their businesses prospered. From 1893 onwards, the chief recipient of their charity was Trinity College. Like most Southern colleges of the time, Trinity had a small endowment and was struggling. In 1892, Washington Duke gave the school enough to move 60 miles to Durham. By 1902, Benjamin Duke chaired the school's executive committee. He told a friend that Trinity "has reached that point of capacity and efficiency to warrant the claim that it is the best institution of learning in the South."[13] By 1909, Benjamin Duke's annual donation was $20,000.[14]

In 1905, Washington Duke died. Much of his fortune had been dispersed before his death, with Trinity College receiving $500,000 during his lifetime. He left $20,000 to the North Carolina Methodist Church, half to support mission work and half for "worn-out preachers." The two North Carolina branches of the African Methodist Church each received $5,000. A hospital in Durham also received $5,000, and two local orphanages received $3,000 each. Washington Duke's benefactions are noteworthy because his charitable interests—Trinity College, black institutions, orphanages, hospitals, Methodist churches—were, and are, ultimately the interests of the Duke Endowment. "The benefactions made in Washington Duke's will," historian Robert Durden notes, "not only recapitulated the dominant pattern of the family's philanthropy from the late 1880's on but also foreshadowed the pattern of the much larger giving that would be done by B.N. Duke and J.B. Duke in the twentieth century."[15]

**Trinity College**

When William Preston Few became president of Trinity College in 1910, gifts by the Duke family substantially increased. Few was an empire-building president who would not rest until the school was first rate. From his first days at Trinity College, he believed James Duke would likely provide the money needed to bring national recognition to the school.

# CHAPTER III

Historians disagree about when Few began courting Duke, but the most likely time is between 1914 and 1916. Until 1911, Duke was preoccupied with American Tobacco. After the Supreme Court divided the company, Duke was spending so much time in London overseeing British-American Tobacco that some speculated he was trying to become a British citizen. When World War I began, Duke returned to the United States. By 1916, he was usually in North Carolina developing Southern Power.

According to biographer Robert Woody, Few realized that Duke would not give to the school if Few appeared to have an insatiable appetite for money. "I do not want to feel that you have thrown us overboard," Few wrote to Duke in 1914. "But I do want you to feel that we will incur no added financial responsibilities without the approval before hand [sic] of your Brother and yourself; and that any further contributions are to be free will offerings made because you feel like making them and not because they are expected of you."[16]

Few picked the right moment to beseech Duke. By 1915, Duke had amassed a fortune, and even after the dissolution of American Tobacco, he was financially comfortable. At age 56, he finally had an heir in his first and only child, Doris Duke (1912-1993). But by becoming a father at such a late age, there was little chance he would have more heirs. His interest in the Southern Power System required him to spend far more time in the Carolinas. And there was the long-standing tradition of family charity to consider, begun by Washington Duke and largely continued by Benjamin Duke.

In an unpublished memoir, Few wrote that in 1916 James Duke "first spoke definitely to me concerning his purpose to give away during his lifetime a large part of his fortune."[17] Few knew that Duke would give much of this fortune to Trinity College, a gift that would fulfill Few's goal of transforming the school from a small liberal-arts college into a major university. But until Few could cajole Duke into making the gift, he could only flatter his most important donor. When Duke gave a $100,000 gift around 1918, Few wrote that "I sincerely believe that the work planted here by the Duke family will stand out in the long years of the future as an unequalled contribution in Southern civilization to liberalism, to right thinking, and to the great moral causes of mankind."[18]

The economic burdens resulting from the end of World War I in 1918 increased pressure on Few to convince Duke to make up his mind.

Postwar inflation reduced the value of salaries at Trinity College, and the flood of returning veterans strained the school's dormitories. Tuition income remained low, since the college during this period charged only $50 a year, and even waived the amount for children of preachers, anyone who planned to become a minister, and anyone pleading financial hardship. Moreover, around this time Benjamin Duke, the family philanthropist, had a near-fatal illness. While he recovered (and outlived his brother by four years), the episode reminded Few and his associates of the Duke family's advancing years.

In 1918, James Duke became a member of the Trinity College board of trustees. In February 1919, Few wrote to Duke proposing "that you create a separate corporation, perhaps to be called the James B. Duke Foundation or Fund, as you might prefer."[19] Few suggested that a seven-member Duke Foundation board of trustees also comprise Trinity College's Executive Committee, responsible for the school's finances. But because the proposed foundation would be independent of Trinity College, "you could direct the business and manage the property of the new Foundation, and you could determine the allotments to be made each year. During your period of service you could determine all questions of policy, and then I am sure you could safely depend on the character of the men who survive and succeed you to carry on."[20]

Few then wrote to Clinton Toms, a former school superintendent who later became president of Liggett and Myers. As a close friend of both Few and the Duke family, Toms was to play a crucial role in negotiations that would create the Duke Endowment. Few urged Toms to nudge Duke toward creating a foundation. "I believe if you will give him an opportunity, he will talk to you on the subject," Few wrote. "We must do our level best now to impress upon him the needs of the College... The time is upon us when we must go forward or take a second place."[21]

As Robert Durden notes, this pressure was not initially effective. "James B. Duke, for his part, probably felt annoyed that his brother, Few, Toms, and other friends of Trinity College would not leave him alone to proceed at his own pace in pursuit of his long-range goals."[22] According to Robert Woody, whenever Few's presence was announced, Duke would grumble, "here comes the hundred-million-dollar-man."[23] In December 1919, Duke agreed to give $100,000 to Trinity College provided that no more than $20,000 would be spent each year over a five-year period. Duke then returned to the Southern Power System,

CHAPTER III

which was engaged in an on-going battle with the North Carolina legislature over what rates the utility could charge.

**The Creation of Duke University**

In the winter of 1920-1921, Few had a serious illness, and during a long period of recuperation, Durden reports, he conceived the idea of a "Duke University"—a school that would include Trinity College as well as a medical school, a vastly expanded law school, and an engineering program. It was Few, not Duke, who decided that the university would be named after its chief donor, since there were already three other colleges in the U.S. named Trinity College, as well as San Antonio's Trinity University. "There were both in North America and in Great Britain many colleges, some independent and some parts of universities, with the name Trinity," Few wrote, "and it seemed to me therefore to have too little individuality to be attached to a great university... Mr. Duke has some times [sic] been blamed for insisting that the institution be named Duke University. It is for this reason that I am here going to some pains to make it plain that this was not his suggestion but mine."[24]

In the spring of 1921, Few sent a document to Duke proposing the transformation of Trinity College.

> I wish to see Trinity College, the law school & other schools expanded into a fully developed university organization. It has been suggested to me that this expanded institution be named Duke University as a memorial to my father whose gifts made possible the building of Trinity College in Durham, and I approve this suggestion. I desire this university to include Trinity College, a coordinate College for Women, a Law School, a School of Business Administration, a School of Engineering (emphasizing chemical & electrical engineering), a Graduate School of Arts & Sciences, and, when adequate funds are available, a Medical School. I desire this enlarged institution to be operated under the present charter with only such changes, if any changes at all, as the enlargement may require. To this university that is to be thus organized I will give _____ millions of dollars. I agree to pay in within _____ years _____ millions in cash or good securities.[25]

Duke did not fill in the blanks in this document. But Robert Durden notes evidence suggesting that Duke agreed to most of Few's plans at this time. Few told the Trinity College board of trustees in June 1921 that the school might well become a university soon, and also told close friends about "great plans which I think will in due course be completely realized."[26]

In 1923, Duke completed his legal battle with the North Carolina legislature. Southern Power was able to raise its rates enough to provide the dividends Duke felt necessary to ensure the company's stability. Duke then turned his attention to creating his foundation. He continued secret negotiations with Few, and also began looking at the medical needs of the Carolinas. Duke asked his secretary, Alexander Sands, to conduct a survey of how much medical care was available to North and South Carolina residents. Sands concluded that more hospitals were needed in rural areas, and that a foundation would be very useful if it acted as a central clearinghouse for hospitals, providing information on hospital organization and structure, as well as expert nurses and technicians who could train local residents in health procedures.

While there is abundant evidence of Duke's intentions towards Trinity College, there is less about why he became interested in hospitals. Biographer John K. Winkler suggests that Duke was trying to imitate the philanthropy of John D. Rockefeller. But historian James F. Gifford, Jr., whose account of Duke's interest in medicine is the most authoritative, argues that Duke's wish to build hospitals was consistent with other portions of the endowment, since his goal as an entrepreneur and philanthropist was the same: to help supply the needs of average residents in North and South Carolina. As a capitalist, he built a great power company to ensure that Carolinians would receive a constant supply of low-cost electricity. As a philanthropist, he wanted to ensure that his customers could easily see doctors. "Without good doctors," he once said, his customers "cannot live."[27]

Duke spent most of 1924 working on his foundation. According to Gifford, this included "consultation with officials of the Rockefeller foundations"[28] about the organization of the Duke Endowment, though it is unclear what advice was provided. Duke also authorized the architects who built his New York City mansion and part of his Somerville, New Jersey estate to work with Few in deciding what style of architecture would be used for the university. Duke's estate was near Princeton University, and he admired the Tudor Gothic buildings erected there when Woodrow Wilson was president of the institution. After visiting about a dozen colleges and universities, Few decided that Duke University would be built in Tudor Gothic style. "It is but the sober truth," Few wrote to Benjamin Duke on September 9, 1924, "to say that when these buildings as now planned are put on the grounds we will have here the most harmonious, imposing, and altogether beautiful educational plant in America."[29]

**The Creation of the Duke Endowment**

Duke's lawyer, William R. Perkins, completed work on the indenture for the Duke Endowment in late 1924. On December 1, Duke called a secret meeting of seven top business associates in Charlotte, North Carolina. They were presented with a draft of the indenture for the Duke Endowment, and spent four days from 8:30 in the morning until 10 at night reviewing it. Apparently, very little was changed, according to Norman Cocke, a senior Southern Power executive who attended all the sessions. Duke, Cocke recalled decades later, "was a positive man, and when he made a positive assertion very few people controverted"[30]

This acquiescence, however, may have had other causes. In his memoir, Few, who attended some of the sessions, said the planning had to be cut short because someone had leaked the indenture to the press. "We tried to isolate ourselves completely but in spite of all we could do there was a leak and the full text of the Indenture had to be hurried to the press of the country," he wrote. "For two or three years prior to December, 1924 we had had great difficulty in keeping from the public premature information about our plans."[31]

On December 11, 1924, the Duke Endowment was formally created. After determining that the endowment was perpetual and was to be governed by up to fifteen trustees, mostly residents of North or South Carolina, the fourth clause of the indenture authorized spending $6 million

> in establishing at a location selected by them within the State of North Carolina an institution of learning to be known as Duke University... However, should the name of Trinity College, located at Durham, North Carolina, a body politic and incorporate, within three months from the date hereof (or such further time as the trustees hereof may allow) be changed to

Duke University, then, in lieu of the foregoing provisions of this division "FOURTH" of this Indenture, as a memorial to his father, Washington Duke, who spent his life in Durham and whose gifts, together with those of Benjamin N. Duke, the brother of the party of the first part, and of other members of the Duke family, have so largely contributed toward making Trinity College at that place, he directs that the trustees shall expend of the corpus of this trust as soon as may reasonably may be a sum not exceeding Six Million Dollars in expanding and extending said University..."[32]

This clause is often misinterpreted to mean that Duke forced Trinity College to change its name as a monument to himself—or even, according to some rumors, that he tried to "buy" Yale or Princeton, and having failed, settled on "purchasing" Trinity College. But it was Few, not Duke, who wanted the institution to become Duke University, and as the clause clearly states, the school is named after James Duke's father. While the university does feature a prominent statue of James Duke, there is no evidence that Duke wanted this to be erected.

**Recipients of the Duke Endowment**
The fifth clause of the Duke Endowment indenture establishes who is to receive funds. Twenty percent of the disbursements were to be added to the foundation's capital until the total available reached $40 million. The recipients are as follows:

• Thirty-two percent of the disbursements are to go to Duke University "to be utilized by its Board of Trustees in defraying its administration and operating expenses, increasing and improving its facilities and equipment, the erection and enlargement of buildings and the acquisition of additional acreage for it, adding to its endowment, or in such other manner for it as the Board of Trustees of said institution may from time to time deem to be to its best interests.'[32] If Duke University was spending its funds in a way the endowment felt inappropriate, the endowment retained the power to deny a grant in any given year.

• Thirty-two percent of the disbursements are for nonprofit hospitals in North and South Carolina, either for construction or subsidization at a rate of one dollar per bed per day for patients too poor to pay for their care.

- Five percent is for Davidson College, a Presbyterian-affiliated institution in Davidson, North Carolina.
- Five percent is for Furman University, a Baptist-affiliated institution in Greenville, South Carolina.
- Four percent is for Johnson C. Smith University, an African-American institution in Charlotte, North Carolina.
- Ten percent is for nonprofit organizations "for the benefit of white or colored whole or half orphans within the states of North Carolina and/or South Carolina." The trustees are to have "uncontrolled discretion" in making grants as along as the funds go to "such organizations, institutions, agencies, and/or societies exclusively for the benefit of such orphans."[34]
- Two percent is for "the care and maintenance of needy and deserving superannuated preachers and needy and deserving widows and orphans of deceased preachers" who were Methodists who served in North Carolina."[35]
- Six percent is for building rural Methodist churches in North Carolina, provided that they are in towns that do not have populations over 1,500. Another four percent is for maintaining these churches.

The seventh section of the indenture establishes Duke's donor intent. Duke began by describing his waterpower projects in the Carolinas. By harnessing this power, he wrote, "which would otherwise run in waste to the sea and not remain and increase as a forest, both gives impetus to industrial life and provides a safe and enduring investment for capital. My ambition is that the revenues of such development shall administer to the social welfare, as the operation of such developments is administering to the economic welfare, of the communities which they serve."[36] Duke urged the endowment to retain a substantial investment in the Southern Power System, "and I advise the trustees that they do not change such investment except in response to the most urgent and extraordinary necessity."[37]

Duke University was to be the recipient of Duke funds because, Duke wrote, "I recognize that education, when conducted along sane and practical, as opposed to dogmatic and theoretical lines is, next to religion, the greatest civilizing influence." After requesting that students and teachers both possess "character, ability, and vision," he added that

> I advise that the courses at this institution be arranged, first, with special reference to the training of preachers, teachers, lawyers,

and physicians, because these are most in the public eye, and by precept and example can do most to uplift mankind, and, second, to instruction in chemistry, economics, and history, especially the lives of the great of earth, because I believe that such subjects will most help to develop our resources, increase our wisdom, and promote human happiness."[38]

Hospitals were worthy recipients, Duke explained, because they are crucial in "increasing the efficiency of mankind and prolonging human life... So worthy do I deem the cause and so great do I deem the need that I very much hope that the people will see to it that adequate and convenient hospitals are assured in their respective communities, with especial reference to those who are unable to defray such expenses of their own."[39]

The funds for orphans, Duke said, were given "in an effort to help those who are most unable to help themselves." The monies for aiding retired preachers and building and maintaining rural churches were necessary to help men of God who were unable to accumulate retirement funds because of their devotion to religion. Duke said that giving to help build rural churches was part of a larger principle: "it is to these rural districts that we are to look in large measure for the bone and sinew of our country."[40]

In the last paragraph, Duke concluded that

I *have* endeavored to make provisions in some measure for the needs of mankind along physical, mental, and spiritual lines, largely confining the benefactions to those sections served by these water power developments. I might have extended this aid to other charitable objects and to other sections, but my opinion is that so doing probably would be productive of less good by reason of attempting too much. I therefore urge the trustees to seek to administer well the trust hereby committed to them within the limits *set*, and to this end that at least one meeting each year this Indenture be read to the assembled trustees."[41]

This powerful conclusion is noteworthy for two reasons. First, Duke clearly and firmly established his wishes, and left the trustees an extraordinarily specific set of instructions. This was unusual for the time, since prevailing wisdom was that donors should leave vague instructions and trust professionals to do what was best. In an age when the "dead hand" was reviled, Duke created an endowment whose dead hand had sharp claws.

Second, by firmly stating that the endowment would be limited to residents of the two Carolinas and to the causes he favored, Duke ensured that it would be very difficult to break the will. No other philanthropist of his time, and few in ours, would have dared to fix the percentages to be given to causes. By doing this, Duke probably ensured the obscurity of the Duke Endowment, since the foundation has not—and cannot—engage in national crusades. But Duke's foresight ensured that the endowment still supports the causes he favored.

Additional evidence of Duke's intentions comes from an interview be gave to the *New York Times* shortly after the Duke Endowment was announced. In the interview, he explained that "I don't believe that men of wealth should leave their money to their sons unless it is to carry out some specific object. But I have no sons, so that particular problem does not trouble me." (As discussed below, Duke left ample provisions for his daughter, Doris.)[42] He said he wanted to leave funds to a private college rather than a state institution because "the State universities are supported by State funds. I selected private institutions because I believe they are run more efficiently than institutions controlled by the State." *The Times* reporter added, "to make sure that his ideas would be carried out, Mr. Duke explained that he had named as trustees of the endowment mostly men who had grown up in confidence with him, because they understood his ideas."[43]

**Early Criticisms**

Many Carolinians celebrated Duke's beliefs, but the applause was not universal. Some Trinity College alumni were saddened to see their beloved college disappear, and others worried about the source of the university's new wealth. The Trinity College motto was *Education et Religio*, and someone suggested that Duke University should add *et Tobacco*. (Given that the money for the Duke Endowment came from waterpower rather than tobacco, *et Aquia* might have been more appropriate.) Some Trinity College students proposed that the Duke University football team should have this fight song:

"Chesterfield! Bull Durham!
[Lucky] Strikes and Plug!
Duke University!
Slug! Slug! Slug!"[44]

One disgruntled alumnus sent several letters to President Few urging Duke to build his own university in Asheville, over a hundred miles away. "When you go out to get $40,000,000 from a man," Few responded, "you will find that he has some ideas of his own."[45]

Prominent liberals also attacked the Duke Endowment. The *New Republic*, after complaining that Trinity College might well be defaced with billboards for "Duke's Mixture," said that the gift would be controlled by "conservators of established businesses and established educational types" who were "not competent to exercise anything other than a benevolent quietism over the educational institutions intrusted to their care." While not attacking donor intent ("it would be silly to kill the goose that lays the golden eggs because of a special taste for platinum"), the magazine longed for "the equally rare bird, the experimental millionaire," who would fund bold ventures in social change."[46]

The *Raleigh News and Observer*, while supporting Duke's gifts, said that Trinity College's name should not be changed, and attacked Duke as a ruthless monopolist whose fortune was partially built "by heartless destruction of his competitors and fixing a price on tobacco because of the monopoly control that denied proper prices to the grower of the weed."[47] (The circuit court that declared the American Tobacco Company an illegal trust in 1908 noted that during the company's existence, prices paid to farmers for bright-leaf tobacco doubled.")[48]

Duke ignored these criticisms and forged ahead with building Duke University. After acquiring nearly 8,000 acres of land (much of which survives today as a forest preserve), he spent considerable time with landscape architects to determine what sort of stone should be used in constructing the new buildings. One trustee, Watson Rankin, was impressed with Duke's strength. "We walked all over those grounds" of the new campus, Rankin said, "jumping ditches and crossing wagon roads and going through shrubbery and all that kind of thing, with Mr. Duke always in the lead."[49] But it was a vigor that would soon end. In July 1925, Duke contracted a pernicious anemia from which he was to die. On October 10, 1925, Duke died in New York at the age of 68.

# CHAPTER III

The year before his death, Duke gave $16 million to Duke University over and above the funds given to the Duke Endowment. He also pledged that, after all other bequests were made, the residue of his estate, which was worth around $40 million, would go to Duke University. On October 1, 1925, nine days before his death, he gave an additional $7 million to support building construction at the university. Thus, his total gifts to the school, not counting the Duke Endowment, were about $63 million.

## Initial Problems of the Duke Endowment

In order to establish the Duke Endowment, two steps had to be taken. The first was a legal matter. Duke's estate only partially went to charity; part of it also went to support his daughter Doris, while some went to other relatives. The Revenue Act of 1924 declared that such mixed estates were subject to punitive taxes. This would transfer $8 million from the Duke Endowment to the federal government and reduce the endowment's income by $400,000. The Revenue Act of 1926 would remove these restrictions, but as historian James Gifford notes, "Few, Duke's executors, and apparently some congressmen feared that to apply for retroactive relief would seem to the public an appeal for special favors for big business."[50] Working behind the scenes, Few began an extensive lobbying campaign, and persuaded North Carolina Senator Furnifold M. Simmons, an important member of the Senate Finance Committee, to make the relief offered by the 1926 Revenue Act retroactive. This was done, and the Duke Endowment's initial capital was preserved.

A second problem did not affect the Duke Endowment directly, but ensured that Duke's will would spend considerable time in probate. In the early 1920s, Benjamin Duke decided to give distant cousins a portion of his wealth. James Duke decided to follow his older brother's example, and set aside $2 million to be divided among any descendant of his parents or his parents' brothers and sisters. The executors found 167 people qualified to receive funds. In addition, a woman named Elizabeth Duke announced that she was a granddaughter of Thomas Duke, whose father Thomas Duke was allegedly a brother of Washington Duke. She produced a family Bible that allegedly proved Thomas Duke's connection to the Duke family, and demanded that she and her 106 relatives receive their share of the estate.

From January to May 1928, dozens of witnesses debated dusty volumes of Duke genealogy in the Somerset County, New Jersey

Orphans Court. At one point in the trial, one Charles Thomas Duke of Pittsburgh, Texas, when not picking his teeth with a four-inch knife blade, provided what the *New York Times* called "a roistering savor of the Western plains" by declaring that his grandfather Thomas Duke's brothers were David, Russell, and John. When asked about Elizabeth Duke's claim that the family Bible proved her connection to James Duke, he replied, "if there's any names in the book contrary to the names I gave they're false. If they've been written in there they were done forgily [sic]." He then recited what he knew of his family genealogy, and also volunteered that he had an enjoyable fourteen months in prison for a murder charge, because lots of friends brought him good things to eat.[51]

In May 1928, Orphans Court Judge John A. Frech ruled against Elizabeth Duke. Many close relatives of Washington Duke, as well as the family's genealogist, said there was no evidence that Thomas Duke was Washington Duke's brother. Handwriting experts hired by the executors said that the entry in the family Bible stating that Thomas Duke was Washington Duke's brother was probably written after James Duke died. Judge Frech declared that Elizabeth Duke and the other 106 claimants were spurious relatives, and ordered the $2 million distributed to the 167 legitimate relations of James Duke. The Duke will was finally probated, and the Duke Endowment could proceed.[52]

## The Duke Endowment and the Doris Duke Charitable Foundation Contrasted

To assess the fidelity of the Duke Endowment to the wishes of James Duke, the history of the Duke Endowment can be compared to the portion of Duke's estate given to his daughter Doris. According to biographers Tom Valentine and Patrick Mahn, when Duke was on his deathbed, he summoned Doris to his side and told her to "promise to me that you will keep our fortune safe until I return in another life and lay claim to it once again." Valentine and Mahn allege that Duke told his daughter not to trust anyone, to "deny yourself nothing" and to never succumb to anyone else's will. Part of this message, they say, was delivered in Duke's last "glimmer of consciousness before coma cleaved it from his falling body."[53]

Valentine and Mahn provide no evidence for this episode, and the scene is inconsistent with other accounts of Duke's character. But whether it actually happened or was merely gossip from Duke's servants,

## CHAPTER III

it is certainly consistent with Doris Duke's character, as throughout her life she was extremely secretive. This secrecy is understandable; Doris Duke received most of her inheritance when she turned 21. But this was in 1933, when America's revulsion against inherited wealth was at a peak. Given Doris Duke's enormous fortune, she understandably would want to stay out of the public eye.

Doris Duke married James Cromwell, a major backer of the Democratic Party who was rewarded by President Franklin Roosevelt with the ambassadorship to Canada. They divorced in the early 1940s, and Duke had a series of brief marriages thereafter, most notably to Porfirio Rubirosa, the Latin adventurer. She spent most of her career as a philanthropist. Her most notable achievement was funding the restoration of mansions in Newport, Rhode Island.

The Duke Endowment indenture states that Doris Duke was to become a trustee of the endowment on achieving her majority in 1933. She at first dutifully attended board meetings, but her attendance slackened as she began pursuing other interests. Although she remained a life-long trustee of the Duke Endowment, she stopped attending meetings in the late 1960s and refused to accept the fee the endowment paid to all trustees. In a 1988 statement, she explained that her refusal to take part in the Duke Endowment was "because I had disagreed with the policies the endowment was following. I was only one trustee, one voice, wanting to accomplish certain socially progressive objectives. The other trustees, however, disagreed with me."[54]

Duke Endowment trustee Marshall Pickens (who was one of James Duke's pallbearers at his 1925 funeral) told the *Charlotte Observer* in 1988 that Doris Duke had only attended two meetings of the Duke Endowment board since he had become a trustee in 1951. He explained that Doris Duke's estrangement was probably due to politics. She was "a pretty liberal lady in her thinking, socially and otherwise," Pickens said "She probably thought we weren't doing what her father said when actually we were."[55] Similarly, Doris Duke at first regularly attended official functions of Duke University, but after the university's centennial in 1939, she drifted away. While historians debate why this happened, she did occasionally make donations to the university. However, university fundraisers were usually rebuffed in their efforts to acquire a portion of her fortune.

According to biographer Stephanie Mansfield, Doris Duke's last known visit to Duke University was in the early 1970s. The school's president was then Terry Sanford, a former North Carolina governor and future U.S. senator. Sanford told Mansfield that one day a woman walked into his office claiming she was a powerful psychic who had a vision in which James Duke was in the university chapel's crypt "dressed as Jesus". And Mr. Duke said, 'Go see Doris. Tell Doris that I want her to support financial efforts to find the truth about why I can be here.' In other words, psychic research."[56] The psychic said she wanted Sanford to arrange an introduction to Doris Duke. After Sanford declined, the psychic announced that she would use her paranormal powers to make contact with Doris Duke. Several weeks later, Duke and the psychic showed up on campus, and were given a private luncheon with Sanford. Duke then left, and she is not known to have visited the university ever again.

According to Mansfield, Sanford told his fundraisers not to ask Doris Duke for any more money. "I was tired of everyone suggesting, 'Let's get Doris Duke to do this. We only need $6 million.' Her position was quite justifiably: My father's already done all of this, why should I? I think the university played it rather badly in the way they dealt with her. I think she had been mistreated. They hadn't paid attention to her and the students felt compelled to ridicule her."[57]

In the 1980s, Doris Duke began to worry about her estate. She had no children, and the terms of the Doris Duke Trust, created in 1924, stated that barring legitimate heirs, 21 years after her death the trust would dissolve and the assets would revert to the Duke Endowment. In 1986, Doris Duke sued to alter this provision, but lost.

For a time, Doris Duke had an heir. In the early 1980s, she met Charlene "Chandi" Heffner, a fellow student of her belly-dancing instructor. In 1985, Heffner moved into Doris Duke's Somerville, N.J. estate, and changed her name to "Chandi Duke Heffner." In 1988, Duke adopted Heffner. By 1991, however, the relationship had soured, and Duke disavowed the adoption. In her last will, written on March 8, 1993, she stated that "it is my intention that Chandi Heffner not be deemed my child for purposes of disposing of my property under this my Will (or any Codicil thereto). Further, it is not my intention, not do I believe that it was ever my father's intention, that Chandi Heffner be deemed to be a child or lineal descendant of mine for purposes of disposing of the trust estate of May 2, 1917, which my father established for my benefit or the Doris Duke Trust, dated December 11, 1924, which my father established for the benefit of me, certain other members of the Duke family and ultimately for charity."[58]

# CHAPTER III

Heffner then sued for damages, charging that her relationship to Duke was so close that they had traveled to Russia, Romania (for "fountain of youth" treatments), and had shopped for a $35-million Boeing 737. The press quickly called Heffner's suit "galimony."[59] In October 1993, Doris Duke died, leaving an estate worth about $1.2 billion, a considerable improvement on the $40 million she inherited upon her father's death in 1925.

**The Super Bowl of Probate**

But Duke's wishes led to a twisted and convoluted probate case. Part of the problem lay in her choice of executors. She wrote at least six wills between 1987 and 1993, and each had a different executor, including Chandi Heffner, Irwin Bloom (her accountant), Harry Demopoulos (one of her doctors) and Walker P. Inman, Jr., son of Duke's half-brother and her closest living relative. By 1993, Duke had settled on her butler, Bernard Lafferty, to be sole executor. That choice, *Los Angeles Times* reporters Paul Lieberman and John J. Goldman observe, led to "the Super Bowl of probate battles" that consumed as much as $50 million in legal fees.[60]

In August 1994, Lafferty selected trustees for the Doris Duke Charitable Foundation. They included himself, Duke University president Nan Keohane, actress Elizabeth Taylor, New Jersey governor Christine Todd Whitman, former National Gallery of Art director J. Carter Brown, and Marion Oates Charles, a long-time friend of Doris Duke. Chandi Heffner continued her suit against the Doris Duke estate. According to the *Raleigh News and Observer*, Heffner accused Lafferty of turning Doris Duke against her. She also said Duke was not of sound mind when she named Lafferty to execute her will.[61]

The Doris Duke probate case began to make national headlines in January 1995 when Tammy Fayette, a nurse to Doris Duke, charged that Duke did not die of natural causes, but as a result of a "massive sedation regime" imposed by her doctors, including a fatal dose of morphine on the day of her death."[62] Duke's former chef, Colin Shanley, charged that on the day of her death, he had received a large package addressed to Lafferty containing Demerol, a powerful narcotic. Shanley charged that Lafferty leapt across the kitchen, grabbed the parcel out of my hands, and stated that 'Miss Duke is going to die tonight.'"[63]

One month later, Shanley charged that Duke "did not understand what she was doing" when she signed her last will. Duke's housekeeper,

Ann Bostich, charged that Duke was disoriented after a stroke in February 1993. When the day came to sign the will, she testified, Duke's lawyer, William Doyle, obtained Duke's signature by sliding "his own hand under her wrist. He propped her hand up with his hand. Doyle then pushed her hand along the page, guiding her hand" as she signed the final version of her will.[64] Subsequent medical records admitted into the Duke probate case revealed that during the hospital stay in question, Doris Duke was taking as many as 25 drugs a day, including such powerful mood-altering drugs as Valium, Zoloft, Darvocet, and Halcion.[65]

A week later, lawyers for Bernard Lafferty charged that Surrogate Court Judge Eve M. Preminger, a Manhattan judge overseeing the probate case, had appointed an investigator, Richard Kuh, who was trying to determine if Doris Duke's will was valid. Lafferty's lawyers revealed that Kuh was investigating the Duke estate to see if it was properly managed.[66] Nurse Payette, whose allegations ensured that the Duke case was front-page news, was arrested in April 1995 and subsequently charged with stealing $450,000 in jewelry, artwork, and other valuable objects from six of her clients, including Doris Duke and Max Factor, the cosmetics tycoon. Police sources told the *Los Angeles Times* that Payette's original allegations had led private detectives and Los Angeles police officers to pursue her, and that she was caught trying to pawn stolen items. Payette's attorney, Curt Livesay, claimed his client was suffering from "classic self-destructive behavior," but a jury subsequently found her guilty of theft, which included stealing Duke's jade necklaces and pearls valued at $210,000. In February 1996, Payette was sentenced to eight years for the thefts, and ordered to pay $400,000 in restitution.[67]

In May 1995, Richard Kuh issued his report. Based on his recommendations, Surrogate Preminger removed Bernard Lafferty and U.S. Trust as executors. She contended that Bernard Lafferty had used estate credit cards to indulge in a massive spending spree on Giorgio Armani clothes, antiques, and Cartier jewels, and that he had smashed Doris Duke's Cadillac and billed the estate for a replacement, even though the Doris Duke estate was continuing to pay his $100,000-a-year butler's salary, a sum that would rise to $500,000 annually plus a one-time fee of $5 million if Lafferty survived as executor. She also questioned U.S. Trust's allowing Lafferty to use $260,000 of estate funds to renovate Duke's California home.

# CHAPTER III

Surrogate Preminger ousted U.S. Trust as co-executor, charging that the trust company created a conflict of interest by loaning Lafferty $825,000 at a time when he had no assets. It stood to gain substantially if it were subsequently to manage the Doris Duke Charitable Foundation endowment. Preminger ordered Morgan Guaranty Trust to replace U.S. Trust, and Alexander D. Forger, an attorney who was Jacqueline Kennedy Onassis's executor, to replace Lafferty.[68] But U.S. Trust fought back. In an interview with the *New York Times*, its president, Jeffrey A. Maurer, defended its actions as co-executor, noting its order to Lafferty to reimburse the estate for improper use of Doris Duke's money, including repayment of $18,000 for improper use of her jet.[69]

In June 1995, U.S. Trust won a temporary victory in the New York State Appeals Court. Judge Israel Rubin blocked Surrogate Preminger's ruling and reinstated U.S. Trust as joint manager of the Duke estate with Morgan Guaranty. He also restored Bernard Lafferty as executor on the condition that Lafferty leave Duke's Beverly Hills home. His decision was later overturned in October 1995, when the Court, by a 3-2 vote, overruled Rubin (who voted in the minority) and upheld Preminger. The Court ruled that her decision to oust Lafferty and U.S. Trust was "a proper exercise of discretion" and that "the unfitness of the co-executors to take responsibility for the $1.2 billion estate, bequeathed primarily to charity, was manifest." The Court also ruled that U.S. Trust's loans to Lafferty were a conflict of interest that was "actual and not theoretical, since it was apparent that the corporate co-executor improperly acquiesced in Lafferty's assorted misconduct."[70]

The case took several new turns. Three of Doris Duke's employees complained that U.S. Trust and Lafferty had mishandled several of Duke's pets, including her camels, Princess and Baby. Their complaints were not motivated solely by the love of animals: a clause in Doris Duke's will awarded $100,000 to any dog "owned by me and residing at my death at my residence." Housekeeper Ann Bostich told the court that 10 dogs were qualified legatees and that she was entitled to a million-dollar bounty to care for them." When Preminger was asked to appoint a guardian for Duke's dog Rodeo, a Shar-Pei, she stated, "This court has rarely appointed a guardian for any type of puppy." Meanwhile, Chandi Heffner's case against the estate was settled at the end of 1995. In return for a payment of $65.8 million, Heffner agreed never to discuss her relationship with Duke.[71]

In January 1996, the New York State Appeals Court partially reversed itself. It ruled unanimously that Preminger had indeed acted improperly by ousting Lafferty and U.S. Trust without giving them a chance to appeal her decision. Judge Vito J. Titone ruled that Preminger acted largely on "untested hearsay," and he ordered Lafferty and U.S. Trust reinstated until they were able to properly appeal Preminger's ruling.[72]

U.S. Trust then proposed a deal. It would remain as co-executor, but Lafferty would resign in return for an unspecified payment while remaining one of five members on the Doris Duke Charitable Foundation board. When the deal collapsed, Lafferty sued to have Preminger removed from the case, claiming that her action removing him as executor occurred "without ever seeing Mr. Lafferty or hearing him speak."[73] Even more suits followed. Chemical Banking and Bank of New York charged that Doris Duke ended her relationship with them when she "was not of sound mind." Chemical Banking had been named co-executor of Duke's 1987 and 1991 wills. Bank of New York was named a co-executor in a 1992 will.[74]

By the spring of 1996, there were at least 100 motions in the Duke estate case accusing various people of various misdeeds. In March 1996, the New York State Appeals Court ruled in favor of U.S. Trust, and ordered the estate settlement postponed until a way could be found to continue the proceedings without Preminger. To break the logjam, U.S. Trust revised its settlement offer. It continued to suggest that Lafferty be removed as co-executor in return for a payment, but it proposed to keep him off the board of the Doris Duke Charitable Foundation as well. The board would consist of three trustees appointed by Lafferty-Nan Keohane, Marion Oates Charles, and J. Carter Brown—and three additional trustees: lawyer James Gill; Morgan Stanley president John Mack, a Duke University alumnus; and Harry Demopoulos. Elizabeth Taylor and Christine Todd Whitman would not be trustees under this proposal.[75]

This settlement was agreed to in May 1996. U.S. Trust became sole executor of the estate. Surrogate Preminger ruled that the Doris Duke Charitable Foundation board had to appoint one additional member, a nationally recognized medical expert, and she retained the right to approve any new trustees to the board. But she approved the six proposed trustees. (Subsequently Anthony Fauci of the National Institutes of Health, an AIDS expert, was appointed to the board.)

# CHAPTER III

Bernard Lafferty was removed as executor and kept off the board, but he was paid $4.5 million and given an additional $500,000 annually.[76]

Two remaining questions about the Doris Duke estate also were settled in 1996. In July, the Los Angeles County District Attorney issued a report stating that Doris Duke died of natural causes and that there was "no credible evidence of criminal homicide." And in November, Bernard Lafferty died at age 51, leaving his $3.5 million estate to the Doris Duke Charitable Foundation instead of to his relatives.[77]

In 2000, Surrogate Preminger made one final ruling. She charged that Doris Duke's lawyers engaged in work that was "unnecessary, duplicative, or excessive," and ordered the compensation to these firms slashed from $21 million to $7 million. Hardest hit was the firm of Katten Muchin & Zavis, which requested $15.3 million from the court, a bill Surrogate Preminger cut to $3. 2 million.[78]

## The Doris Duke Charitable Foundation

The Doris Duke Charitable Foundation was now legally established. What would it do? Its first step was to re-establish ties between Doris Duke and Duke University. In November 1996, two plaques (paid for by the Mary Duke Biddle Foundation) honoring Doris Duke were placed in the Duke family chapel on the Duke University campus in a service led by Duke's cousins, Anthony Drexel Duke and Mary D.B.T. Semans. Doris Duke was thus honored in the same area that honored Washington, Benjamin, and James B. Duke.[79] The Doris Duke Charitable Foundation then found a president: Undersecretary of State Joan Edelman Spero, who was given compensation of $400,000 a year.[80]

Doris Duke's instructions were not specific. She stated that she wanted to support "dancers, singers, musicians, and other artists of the entertainment world" as well as scientists fighting cancer, AIDS, and sickle-cell anemia "provided no animals are used to conduct such research." She also had "a special interest in the preservation of wildlife, both flora and fauna, in the United States and elsewhere." She gave the trustees the option to spend out the foundation's endowment if they so chose.

Spero and her staff discovered that Doris Duke had given $97.7 million to various charities during her lifetime, including $22 million to restore Newport, Rhode Island homes and $4 million to Duke University. In 1998, *New York Times* writer Judith H. Dobryznski said that Spero had interviewed "dozens of people" close to Doris Duke to try to find out what her patron was like.

Doris Duke, Spero said, "was a hands-on person. And Oatsie Charles has said that she was a very take-charge person. When she led the restoration of Newport, she purchased the properties herself. These things were rundown, but she had a good eye and knew what had to be done with them."[81]

Based on these interviews, Spero decided that the Doris Duke Charitable Foundation's major efforts would be in the arts, medical research, and the environment. She told the *Chronicle of Philanthropy* that Doris Duke's will "doesn't say, 'You should do this, you should do that.' It says, "Okay, Spero, you figure it out."[82]

In December 1997, the Doris Duke Charitable Foundation gave its first grants. It awarded $5 million to the Open Space Institute and the Trust for Public Land to buy Sterling Forest, a tract of land on the New York-New Jersey border. Other major awards went to the American Dance Festival ($1.9 million), the Nicholas School of the Environment ($1.7 million to endow a chair in ecology in Doris Duke's name), Jazz at Lincoln Center ($2 million), and $4.9 million to create the Doris Duke Clinical Scientist Award Program to provide fellowships for up to 10 promising young medical researchers."[83] Because the Doris Duke Charitable Foundation has an endowment of at least $1.5 billion, it must disburse at least $75 million annually. It remains unclear whether the foundation can award its funds for medical research to credible scientists who don't use animals in research."[84]

The Doris Duke Charitable Trust has continued its emphasis on land preservation and arts funding. It has also helped open Doris Duke's homes in Hawaii and Newport as museums. Duke Farms has also been partially opened to visitors.

The Doris Duke case obviously shows the importance of finding the right executor. By choosing a man clearly unqualified to execute her wishes, Doris Duke allowed her estate to be tied up for years in unnecessary and protracted litigation. And by leaving vague instructions, it's probable that the Doris Duke Charitable Foundation will eventually spend money on causes she would have disapproved. It's also clear that Doris Duke's money will not go to causes that James B. Duke favored. Had James Duke willed that the portion of his wealth scheduled to go to Doris Duke be buried in a vault for 68 years, disinterred, and then given to the charities he admired, those non-profits, even after seven decades of inflation, would have benefited more than they will from Doris Duke's estate.

# CHAPTER III

## The Duke Endowment Today

The Duke Endowment more amply fulfilled Duke's wishes. The residents of North and South Carolina quickly became the beneficiaries of Duke Endowment funds. As early as 1931, journalist Louis Graves noted that all Carolinians, rich and poor alike, benefited from the programs that Duke supported. "The number of people who stand to benefit from the Duke benefactions is incalculable," Graves wrote, "for the stream of gold pours through the cities and trickles into the remotest corners of the two Carolinas."[85]

Duke Endowment funds also ensured that Duke University survived the worst years of the Great Depression. From 1927 to 1930, the endowment supplied half the university's budget. Between 1930 and 1932, it doubled its contributions, enabling the university to increase enrollment. Though donations fell after 1934, Duke University clearly would have encountered severe financial trouble—or like many other schools, temporarily closed—had the endowment not existed.[86] Other schools thanked the Duke Endowment for aid during hard economic times. In a special supplement to the April 26, 1937 *Charlotte Observer* commemorating the Duke Endowment, Davidson College president Walter L. Lingle said that "the income from the Duke Endowment has made it possible for the college to come through seven years of the severest depression on record without debt or deficit and without cutting and slashing salaries."[87]

The Duke Endowment has not changed much in the past 50 years. Only one change in the indenture has been made, and that was a major alteration of James B. Duke's intentions.

According to Robert Durden, James B. Duke "envisioned an ongoing, extremely close relationship between the Endowment and the Duke Power Company." The Duke Endowment indenture states that the profits from the power company "shall administer to the social welfare, so the operation of such developments as administering to the economic welfare of the communities which they serve." He added that he hoped that the trustees of the Duke Endowment "see to it that at all times these [Duke Power] companies be managed and operated by the men best qualified for such a service."[88]

This "symmetrical and symbiotic relationship" between the Duke Endowment and Duke Power continued for decades. Every president of Duke Power between 1924 and 1971 was also a Duke Endowment trustee. As late as 1973 Duke Power chairman Thomas L. Perkins was also a Duke Endowment trustee.

But the Tax Reform Act of 1969 states that a foundation can not own more than 25 percent of the shares of a corporation. When the act passed, the Duke Endowment had 56 percent of Duke Power stock. So the trustees convinced the North Carolina Supreme Court in 1972 to alter the indenture to allow the foundation to sell some of its Duke Power holdings.

The endowment's trustees, however, were blocked by another section of the indenture, in which Duke stated that they could only sell Duke Power shares "except in response to the most urgent and extraordinary necessity." Duke further said that the vote to sell the shares had to be unanimous, and Doris Duke insisted on blocking the sale.

Doris Duke was a trustee of the Duke Endowment her entire life, but ceased to play an active role after 1970. In a deposition in a 1979 court case involving the Doris Duke Trust, Doris Duke stated that "I thought there was little that I as a single vote could contribute... It was always a rubber stamp [process] and I was always the one asking all the questions and bringing up difficult points. It seemed like no one really wanted to hear me. So I said, what's the point of my going? So I stopped."[89]

In the same deposition, Doris Duke said she never sold any of her Duke Power shares, though she might have given some away. She said she opposed the Duke Power sale because it was "contrary to what my father wanted." Doris Duke said that her father told her that it was "the most stable stock he could give" for his foundation and "you couldn't have your money in anything safer."[90]

In his history of Duke Power, Durden adds another reason for Doris Duke's estrangement from the Duke Endowment. In the late 1960s, the United Mine Workers (UMW) engaged in a bloody struggle to organize mines in Harlan County, Kentucky, some of which were owned by Duke Power. The UMW, according to Durden, waged "a masterful, if ethically dubious, campaign against Duke Power."[91]

As part of this campaign, UMW leader Arnold Miller wrote a letter to every Duke Endowment trustee informing them of the miners' struggle. "In Harlan County, Kentucky," Miller wrote, "Duke Power Company has shown a callousness to human needs and suffering that flies in the face of everything the Duke Endowment stands for."[92]

While all of the other Duke Endowment trustees ignored Miller's letter, Doris Duke, a political liberal, responded. "I was horrified to learn of the appalling conditions" in Harlan County, Doris Duke wrote. She

# CHAPTER III

said she wrote to her cousin and fellow trustee, Mary D.B.T. Semans. According to Doris Duke, Semans "as extremely distressed to learn of these conditions,"[93] and promised that a representative of the Duke Endowment trustees would be sent to Harlan County.

The trip never took place, and the Duke Endowment made no further involvement in the Harlan County battles. But the episode illustrates Doris Duke's increasing estrangement from the Duke Endowment. For most of the 1970s and 1980s, the Duke Endowment trustees tried to have a meeting with Doris Duke. In 1981, they voted to convene a special meeting at the Mayfair Regent Hotel in the hopes that Doris Duke would show up and change her mind about the Duke Power stock. Doris Duke refused to show up.

While the stock sale was delayed, Duke Power had issued massive numbers of new shares, ensuring that the percentage of stock held by the endowment fell from 56 percent to 11 percent between 1973 and 1994.

In March 1994, six months after Doris Duke's death, the Duke Endowment announced plans to sell 16 million of the 26 million Duke Power shares it still held, reducing the endowment's holdings to five percent of Duke Power's stock. Endowment spokesman Elizabeth Locke told the *Charlotte Observer* that the board tried to sell the shares earlier, but was blocked by Doris Duke. "I have heard that this was something she was opposed to," Locke said. "The board was never able to reach agreement because, perhaps, Miss Duke was against it."[94] Even after the proposed sale, however, Duke Power would remain the largest single holding in the endowment's investment portfolio, and it would still be the largest single shareholder in Duke Power.

While the recipients of Duke Endowment funds have not changed, some of the programs have. The endowment still contributes to orphanages, but they are now mostly called "children's homes." The funds to rural Methodist churches in North Carolina are still given only to churches that qualify under the terms of the 1924 indenture, though they are used for weatherization programs and not just construction. And while James Duke may have been confused by some of the grants made to Duke University, Davidson College, Furman University, and Johnson C. Smith University ($800,000 in 1996 to buy computers at Duke University, $75,000 to Furman University for "a minority faculty recruitment initiative"), he never sought to control the curriculum either at Duke University or any institution mentioned in the Duke Endowment indenture.

Much of the money the Duke Endowment gives to education is used in ways that honor the Duke family. In 1996, the endowment gave $4.5 million to Duke University for the Benjamin N. Duke Leadership Program, which provides scholarships and loans to North and South Carolina students, as well as $100,000 to endow the James B. Duke 100th Anniversary Fellowship Fund and $500,000 to endow the Angier B. Duke Memorial Scholarship Program. (Angier B. Duke was a grandson of Benjamin Duke.) In addition, $500,000 was awarded for the Mary D.B.T. and James Semans Distinguished International Visitor I Ambassador fellowship and $500,000 to create a building honoring Doris Duke in the Sarah P. Duke Gardens. Funds for James B. Duke Scholarships were given to Johnson C. Smith University ($2.2 million), Furman University ($2.2 million), and Davidson College ($2.2 million).

Between December 11, 1924 and December 31, 1996, the Duke Endowment gave $1,287,543,190 to charity. In 78 years, it has given $528,369,992 to Duke University, $447,773,433 to hospitals, $55,823,645 to orphanages, $53,217,751 to Davidson College, $53,101,741 to Furman University, $45,517,709 to Johnson C. Smith University, $30,394,105 for building rural churches, $20,683,091 for maintaining rural churches, and $16,380,046 to assist superannuated preachers. In the Duke Endowment's 1991 annual report, chairman Mary D.B.T. Semans, a granddaughter of Benjamin Duke, says that because the endowment has given to a limited range of causes, it has been a more optimistic endeavor than many other foundations. Most grantmakers, she says, have been pessimistic because their funds could be used for anything, and when not denying grants to scores of worthy recipients, they have been faced with million-dollar grants that could not ease the ravages of AIDS or end hunger. Moreover, the professionals working for nonprofits, "who really know their fields, who are aware of national and global trends, see all the more clearly how complex and difficult the problems are, how costly and precarious the solutions. Then they go to conferences, and it's all reinforced again."[95]

Because the Duke Endowment was limited to causes James Duke favored in North and South Carolina, its has often worked with the same grant recipients year after year; this has enabled it to see their work grow and progress. By giving local, long-term support, the endowment has been able to show, in a small but steady way, progress in solving the social problems of our time. Such a plan, Semans says, might make more sense than broad national studies. It "is helpful to carve out a piece of the problem," she writes,

# CHAPTER III

so that we can manage to have an effect, so that we can recognize success when it occurs, so that we can rejoice with the individuals who achieved it. We cannot, alone, solve the problems of health care, or education, or children; but we can identify the issues in one community, we can find partners and work on those issues. We can *see* some successes."[96]

Semans also stresses the importance of donor intent:

I suggest that we look back to our roots and gain strength and renewal from our founders' dreams... [I]n some cases, this is easy to do. The founders are still part of the foundation. In other cases, it involves going back into history, archives, and memories. But just as we now recognize the importance of children knowing their heritage, so, too, is it important for philanthropy to know from whence it came."[97]

The indenture that created the Duke Endowment provides one way for the trustees to understand James Duke's intentions. Once a year, following Duke's instructions, the Duke Endowment board of trustees reads aloud the entire indenture. "After the reading," Semans explains, "there is always a time of reflection and comment about Mr. Duke, his ideas, and our mission. This closeness to the founder renews us and gives us a sense of new energy."[98]

The Duke Endowment has, however, since made the news because of one clause of the endowment's indenture stating that trustee compensation was divided from three percent of the annual investment income made by the endowment. In 2001, this meant that trustees were paid $132,709.61.

Trustee Juanita Kreps, a former commerce secretary, defended her pay to the *New York Times*. "We do a lot of work," Kreps said. "We meet two full days ten times a year in Charlotte, which isn't the easiest place to get to, and there's a great deal of correspondence to deal with in between."[99]

By 2004, the Duke Endowment had given $2 billion to the causes James B. Duke favored. In that year, the endowment gave $22.5 million to colleges, $20 million to hospitals, $7.1 million for rural Methodist churches and for providing pensions for pastors, and $3.5 million for children's homes.

"When James B. Duke created the Duke Endowment in 1924," said endowment chairman Russell H. Robinson II, "he clearly stated that he wanted to help the people of North and South Carolina. We know that he would be pleased that more than $2 billion of his generosity has gone to the people and organizations in the Carolinas that he instructed us to assist."[100]

## The Conrad N. Hilton Foundation

The story of the Conrad N. Hilton Foundation shows how donor intent can be preserved in our time. It can be contrasted with the story of Henry Ford, who created the Ford Foundation largely as a way of ensuring family control of the business he created.

Conrad Nicholson Hilton (1887-1979) faced the same problem. He wanted to be a philanthropist and also ensure that his son, Barron Hilton (born 1927), would control the Hilton Hotels Corporation. One obstacle was the Tax Reform Act of 1969. This states that a foundation cannot control more than 20 percent of the stock of any business. The resulting battle between Barron Hilton and the Conrad N. Hilton Foundation shows the difficulties this act has created for donor intent.

**Innovator in the Hotel Market**

Conrad Hilton did not invent the modern hotel chain, nor was he the largest hotel proprietor. Throughout his life, he had to compete with hundreds of competitors. Though he was able to build an international corporation, he never dominated the highly decentralized hotel market. His two great innovations were in marketing and financial control.

Hilton ensured that every inch of space in his hotels was used to make money. When renovating the Waldorf-Astoria, for example, he discovered that two of the hotel's central pillars were hollow. He converted them into highly profitable "vitrines," or display cases, for merchandise. While not micromanaging his hotels, Hilton received daily financial reports from each property. This enabled him to quickly detect potential problems, and also ensure that his company would make profits with relatively low occupancy rates.

Hilton also enjoyed the limelight. His hotels were often large, old, and prestigious Chicago's Palmer House, New York's Plaza and Waldorf-Astoria, and Washington's Mayflower. They were also quite valuable. By 1990, the Palmer House, Waldorf-Astoria, and Hawaiian Village in Honolulu were worth an estimated $2 billion.[1] Because his hotels were

CHAPTER III

a major employer of nightclub acts, Hilton knew many Hollywood stars. Zsa Zsa Gabor was his second wife. (His eldest son, Conrad "Nick" Hilton, Jr., was married to Elizabeth Taylor for a time.) Whenever he opened a new hotel, Hilton ensured that plenty of stars were on hand, and the resulting publicity helped make "Hilton" a household word.

**Hilton's Spiritual Concerns**

From about 1950 onwards, Hilton decided to speak his mind on non-partisan public issues. He was not active in politics, except for the period between 1912 and 1913, when he served two terms in the New Mexico state legislature as a Republican. He also gave $250 to Ronald Reagan in his 1976 effort to defeat President Gerald Ford. But Hilton is not known to have made any other political contributions, or to have tried to change public policy in a partisan way.

Hilton was, however, very interested in spiritual matters. He was a devout Catholic and, in his autobiography *Be My Guest* (1957), credits the nuns of New Mexico for providing him with a strong faith in God that helped him endure the near-bankruptcy of his firm during the Great Depression. Prayer also helped him in the business world. Biographer Whitney Bolton notes that during negotiations to buy the Waldorf-Astoria, Hilton and his partners arose every morning at 6:15 to go to St. Patrick's Cathedral for a half-hour of prayer. After the sale of the hotel was complete, Hilton's partners thought they could finally sleep in; but the next day they received a 6:15 wake-up call. "But Connie," one pleaded, "you've got the Waldorf!" Hilton responded, "You can't pray for something you want and then not give thanks when you get it. Let's get started."[2]

Hilton saw prayer, in part, as a weapon to fight communism. In the early 1950s, he worked with noted author Fulton Oursler to compose an ecumenical prayer that would increase America's faith. "America on its knees," the prayer began, "not beaten there by the hammer and sickle. Freely, intelligently, responsibly, confidently, powerfully, America now knows it can destroy Communism and win the battle for peace. We need fear nothing or no one... except God." The Hilton Hotels Corporation donated more than 200,000 copies of the prayer to Americans. According to Bolton, it was a favorite of President Eisenhower.[3] Later in the 1950s, Hilton placed public-service ads in international editions of *Time* and *Newsweek* that described what he called "the power of prayer in opposing imperialistic Communism." These received an enthusiastic response abroad."[4]

Though Hilton sought to increase America's spirituality, he was not an evangelical; nor was he a crusader for Catholicism. He was a founder of the National Prayer Breakfast and was a major sponsor of the National Conference of Christians and Jews, an ecumenical organization devoted to combating anti-Semitism. In 1950, Hilton used an awards dinner held by the conference in his honor to warn of the perils of Communism. The "spreading, deadly perils of communism," he said, "has seeped into the councils of our own nature, and, what is infinitely worse, has found defense and protection from irresolute officials in high office."[5]

In a 1957 address to the organization, he said that the world was divided into thirds-one-third Communist, one-third democratic, and one-third uncommitted. In order to help this uncommitted third toward freedom, he said, helpfulness rather than arrogance should be the order of the day. "The arrogance, bad manners, and tactlessness of our politicians, businessmen, and colonists in these countries have been so thoroughly resented. Exploitation of this resentment is one of the most effective features of Communist propaganda."[6]

Hilton also believed that "the military situation is at stalemate, so we have only the choice of living together as one family or destroying each other." To convince Third World nations that democracy and capitalism were better than communism, Hilton saw trade and God as the primary resources Americans could use in anti-communist efforts. Trade would improve a poor country's standard of living, and show the developing nations that American ideals were greater than armies and warheads. Religion would bind the peoples of the world in a way that was more permanent and important than any political effort. "The great question confronting us today is whether that religion will be strong enough to re-create its unity, and in consequence serve as the basis for a single civilization embracing all the spiritual riches of the world, all the cultures of the world, all the peoples of the world-including the uncommitted third."[7]

Hilton also discussed these themes in a 1961 address. In the frostiest period of the Cold War, he compared America to the Western Roman Empire in the fifth century, shortly before it collapsed and was replaced by barbarian kingdoms. He predicted that in the struggle for world mastery, over half the world's 111 nations "are betting on Soviet Russia to win" because Communism could promise the gospel of revolution while America could "only hug itself in selfishness:

## CHAPTER III

> For years America has been trying-and failing-in its efforts to convince the people of the world, that we are their friend, that we are willing to share with them the knowledge, the technology, the industrial know-how which we have accumulated over the centuries. We have got to recapture that image of America as the hope of all the little people in the world.[8]

Hilton did this in his business career by becoming America's first international hotel operator. In the 1950s and 1960s, he operated scores of hotels overseas. These were not only highly profitable, since Hilton persuaded other investors to put up most of the investment capital needed for construction, but provided a way for Hilton to show the rest of the world American manners and customs which they would otherwise never directly see.

In at least one case, Hilton personally fought communism. It took over ten years for him to persuade the Rome city government, one-third of which was communist, to allow construction of the Rome Hilton. "I guess they didn't want free enterprise in action there," Hilton said in a 1965 interview. "The Commies said the hotel was being built for billionaires. I guess they were talking about lira, not dollars."[9]

### Challenges to Hilton's Estate

Most of Hilton's efforts to advance international understanding were done personally or through Hilton businesses. Though the Conrad N. Hilton Foundation was created in 1944, it remained small throughout most of Hilton's business career. When Hilton in 1972 gave $10 million to the Mayo Foundation for a laboratory at the renowned Mayo Clinic (saying that the gift was made because he liked to see "what makes man tick"), he gave the money personally and not through the foundation."[10]

As the years passed, Hilton became less active in the enterprises he created. But he did not retire until 1978, at the age of 91. Even in his eighties, he still showed up at his office at eight every morning, six days a week, to put in a full day's work."[11] In his last years, he was increasingly preoccupied with the future of the Hilton Foundation. According to James Bates, Hilton's lawyer from the mid-1940s onwards, Hilton drafted 32 wills, and with each, the portion of the estate given to the foundation rose while the amount given to his children Barron, Eric, and Constance Francesca fell. As Bates remarked in a 1985 interview with the *Los Angeles Times*, Hilton intended to "give back to the public all the wealth he had created."[12] In Hilton's last will, Barron Hilton received $750,000, Eric Hilton $300,000, and Constance Francesca Hilton $100,000. (Conrad "Nick" Hilton, Jr. died in 1969.)

When Hilton died in January 1979, his estate faced two major lawsuits. Constance Francesca Hilton, who said that her father was suffering from "insane delusions" by only leaving her $100,000, filed the first. These delusions, she alleged, were due to the fact of her paternity. When Hilton married her mother Zsa Zsa Gabor in 1942, he obtained a civil divorce from the marriage, but the Catholic Church refused to annul it, leaving Hilton allegedly guilt-ridden about having a daughter. This guilt, she charged, led to "the ravages of old age, illnesses, cerebral accidents, and his extreme obsession with his religious beliefs."[13]

Constance Francesca Hilton demanded that her share be increased to $50 million. Her attorney, Robert D. Walker, told the *Los Angeles Times* that this sum was needed so that she was "treated in the way that a daughter should be treated." Los Angeles County Superior Court Judge Jack D. Swink noted that there were doubts about Constance Francesca Hilton's paternity, since Hilton and Gabor were separated in 1945 and Constance Francesca Hilton was not born until 1947. Judge Swink dismissed the suit, but appeals kept the case alive until it was finally dismissed in 1983.[14]

The second effort to change Hilton's will came from Barron Hilton, who succeeded his father as president of Hilton Hotels on his father's death in 1979. When Conrad Hilton died, he owned 6.8 million (27.4 percent) shares in Hilton Hotels, making him the largest single owner. He could not transfer all of this to the Conrad N. Hilton Foundation because of the Tax Reform Act of 1969, which prohibits a foundation from owning more than 20 percent of the stock of any corporation.

Hilton saw this problem, which he tried to address by declaring that all his shares would be willed to the foundation except for those which, according to the Tax Reform Act, were an "excess business holding" that the foundation had to sell. He willed that Barron Hilton had an option to buy these shares at $24.20 each, the market price on the day of Hilton's death. (Barron Hilton already owned 3.6 percent of the Hilton Hotels stock, and Conrad Hilton had transferred 1.3 percent of the stock to the Hilton Foundation before his death.) The debate centered on how many shares qualified as "excess business holdings." The Hilton Foundation believed that only 7.4 percent of the Hilton Hotels

## CHAPTER III

stock qualified, while Barron Hilton argued that he was entitled to buy all the shares.

The dispute remained unsettled for six years. In April 1985, the Golden Nugget Corporation, a Nevada casino operator, announced plans to buy the Hilton Foundation's shares for $72 each, or a total of $488 million. James Bates, executor for the Hilton estate, rejected this offer, declaring it "inadequate" since the value of the firm's assets was between $94 and $110 a share. The Hilton Hotels' management, with the support of the Hilton Foundation, adopted anti-takeover provisions at its annual meeting, including a requirement that any mergers would need a 75 percent approval by shareholders. This caused the Golden Nugget offer to be withdrawn.

The battle between the Conrad N. Hilton Foundation and Barron Hilton continued. James Bates told the *Los Angeles Times* that he believed that Conrad Hilton wanted his foundation to receive most of his fortune as well as to control Hilton Hotels, which it could do even if it held only 20 percent of the stock. Bates said that Hilton tried to ensure that his wishes would be carried out by selecting trustees who were "members of his family, his longtime associates, those he had great confidence in carrying out the charitable purposes that he had eloquently provided for." Barron Hilton's attorney, Ronald Gother, responded that "we don't disagree with the basic thrust of Bates's feeling about Conrad's desire" that the foundation should own 20 percent of the Hilton Hotels stock. "It's just unfortunate that that's wrong. That's what we're struggling with here. The law is otherwise."[15]

Bates asked the Los Angeles County Superior Court to let him transfer 3.6 million Hilton Hotels shares from the Conrad Hilton estate to the Conrad N. Hilton Foundation. This would increase the foundation's holdings to 16 percent of the corporation's stock. The court refused the request. A few months later, Bates allied himself with the California attorney general's office, asking that Conrad Hilton Foundation president Donald Hubbs disqualify himself from the dispute. Hubbs, who was Hilton's accountant and an attorney for over 30 years, admitted in a 1984 deposition that he had persuaded Hilton to insert the "excess business holdings" clause in the will in 1973, and that he had hired an attorney to persuade the Internal Revenue Service to declare the entire 27 percent an "excess business holding." The California attorney general charged that Hubbs was nominated for his position by Barron Hilton—an act, as deputy attorney general James Cordi told the *Wall Street Journal*, that "may make anyone in Hubbs's position reluctant to bite a hand which has fed him over almost his entire career."¹⁶ The state of California also asked Conrad Hilton's son Eric, a member of the foundation's board of trustees, to disqualify himself on the grounds that he was also a Hilton Hotels vice-president, and thus had a conflict of interest. Eric Hilton declined to do this, and remained on the Hilton Foundation board.¹⁷

In February 1986, the Internal Revenue Service, in three private letter rulings, declared that the Conrad N. Hilton Foundation could keep the entire block of Hilton Hotels stock if it created a "public supporting organization." This would have a fixed set of grantees that would receive funds, and would give one-third of its funds to a single organization, most likely a group supporting Catholic Sisters, which Hilton said in his will should receive the largest share of support. The supporting foundation, the IRS declared, could have the same board of directors as the Hilton Foundation and operate out of the same offices, as long as it was a legally distinct organization.

Barron Hilton's attorney, Ronald Gother, responded that a supporting organization would contravene Hilton's will since "the will didn't say leave it to a support organization, it said leave it to 'the Conrad N. Hilton Foundation, a private foundation.'" The Conrad N. Hilton Foundation promptly voted to turn itself into a public supporting organization that could give funds only to 169 charities. (Foundation directors Eric Hilton and Barron Hilton voted in opposition.)¹⁸

**The Trial Over Hilton's Will**

In March 1986, the trial between Barron Hilton and the Conrad N. Hilton Foundation began in Los Angeles County Superior Court. In a last-minute effort to end the dispute, Roger Mahoney, the archbishop of Los Angeles, tried to act as a mediator. His attempt collapsed after an hour of negotiations, and he decided to side with the foundation against Barron Hilton.

The trial swiftly became a dispute over Conrad Hilton's intentions in drafting his will. Barron Hilton testified that his father's main concern was ensuring family control of the business he created. "My father was a philanthropist but also a businessman," Hilton testified. "He didn't want to see his company taken over by an unfriendly group. That's the primary consideration of his will." He added, "My father's first interest was his hotels. His second interest was charity." Further, his father was so interested in financial matters that "he used to follow the stock market prices sometimes on a basis of once every five minutes."¹⁹

# CHAPTER III

Conrad Hilton's executor James Bates testified that he believed Hilton created the foundation because he believed in a "strong work ethic," and that "his desire was to have all of his relatives, his children, get out and go to work and earn their own living." He added that Hilton's desire "was not to leave unearned wealth to relatives and members of his family."[20]

Hilton Foundation president Donald Hubbs said that Conrad Hilton was not worried about family control of Hilton Hotels, and, at one point in the mid-1970s, he nearly sold his share of the company to RCA.

Los Angeles County Superior Court Judge Robert Weil ruled in favor of the Conrad N. Hilton Foundation. He declared that, by transforming itself into a public support organization, the foundation had come close "to mirroring what Conrad Hilton might have wanted and did in fact want for his private foundation." He ruled that when Conrad Hilton, a "very wise man," inserted the clause in his will allowing Barron Hilton to buy the shares that were declared to be excess business holdings, no one, including James Bates, "perceived or realized that by creating this option it was possible that Barron Hilton could receive 100 percent of the shares of the estate."[21] (Judge Weil also said that Donald Hubbs was "a good man" who was placed in "an intolerable position" by being both the president of the Conrad N. Hilton Foundation and Barron Hilton's accountant and lawyer.)

Barron Hilton sued in district court to try to overturn the IRS' private letter rulings. In November 1987, he achieved a partial victory when U.S. District Court Judge Francis C. Whelan ruled that the IRS' decision to allow the Conrad N. Hilton Foundation to become a public support organization was invalid under existing tax law. In March 1988, the California Court of Appeals overturned the Superior Court's decision to award the entire block of Hilton Hotels stock to the Hilton Foundation, and ruled that Barron Hilton could buy the entire block of shares. The appeals court also ruled that the foundation had to become a private foundation, which it did.

In November 1988, an out-of-court compromise was finally reached. This divided the disputed shares into three parts. Barron Hilton received four million shares, worth about $212 million. The Conrad N. Hilton Foundation received 3.5 million shares, valued at about $184 million. The remaining six million shares, worth some $315 million, were placed in a charitable remainder trust. Sixty percent of the income from this trust goes to Barron Hilton, while forty percent goes to the Hilton Foundation. Upon either Barron Hilton's death or in the year 2008, whichever is earlier, the shares in the trust will be transferred to the Hilton Foundation.

The court also ruled that Barron Hilton should be trustee of these shares and be allowed to vote them in Hilton Hotels stockholder meetings. This means that Barron Hilton owns 25 percent of the shares and controls the votes of another nine percent, giving him voting control of 34 percent of the Hilton Hotels stock. He says that this agreement ensures that "my father's two objectives, retaining control of the stock in family hands and benefiting charity through the Conrad N. Hilton Foundation, can both be achieved. I am confident that my father would be pleased with this accord."[22]

With the end of the dispute, the litigants assumed the positions they had before the struggle began. Donald Hubbs remained the foundation's president until his retirement in 2005; Barron Hilton, Eric Hilton, and two other members of the Hilton family continue to serve as directors. In the fiscal year ending February 1993, the Conrad N. Hilton Foundation had assets of $494 million while the charitable remainder trust had $276 million. (A third, much smaller trust had $15.6 million.)

In 1998, the 9.7 percent of the Hilton Hotels stock owned by the charitable remainder trust (officially known as the "Barron Hilton Charitable Remainder Unitrust") was sold, earning Barron Hilton a $700 million profit. The charitable remainder trust still exists, and is, as of August 2006, worth $860 million. By selling the stock, the Hilton Foundation and the Conrad Hilton Fund for Sisters reduced their holdings in Hilton Hotels to below five percent.[23]

**Fulfilling Hilton's Intent**

In a recent Conrad N. Hilton Foundation annual report, president Donald Hubbs explains that the foundation operates primarily to fulfill the wishes of its founder. Arguments against donor intent, such as a fear of "dead hand" control or a donor's lack of professional philanthropic training, Hubbs writes,

> are nothing but excuses for those who would justify an arrogant conduct, avoiding moral and ethical responsibility by substituting their own judgment for that of a donor who had

the wisdom, capability, and industry for creating the wealth in the first place... Individuals during their lifetime can use their wealth—on which taxes have been paid—in any manner that is desired no matter how whimsical, idiosyncratic, or bizarre it may seem. Upon death, the funds suddenly become sacrosanct to the whims, fancies, and social causes of many strangers who may or may not consider themselves to be morally or ethically responsible for honoring the philosophy of the donor.

The lack of training in philanthropy, Hubbs adds, "does not preclude a donor from having certain strongly held beliefs and philosophies [which are] usually soundly grounded in the life experience of the donor and, therefore, should be honored. Regrettably, we have no rule that makes it morally and ethically wrong to do otherwise."[24]

The Hilton Foundation's annual report includes excerpts from Hilton's will, which the foundation uses to show its support for donor intent. The foundation funds a limited number of programs with multi-year grants, enabling it to operate with a very small staff and thus fulfilling Conrad Hilton's wish to "beware of organized, professional charities with high-salaried executives and a heavy ratio of expense."[25]

The largest grants the foundation makes are to the Conrad N. Hilton Fund for Sisters, a legally distinct organization controlled by the archdiocese of Los Angeles. It receives 11.2 percent of the income produced by the foundation and its two allied trusts, which amounted to $990,170 in 1992. This was divided into 113 grants for programs operated by Catholic Sisters in Haiti, the former Yugoslavia, South Africa, Lebanon, the South Bronx, and other areas. Such Catholic charities receive the largest single part of the foundation's grants because of a clause in Hilton's will specifying that the foundation support Catholic Sisters "who devote their love and life's work for the good of mankind, for they appeal especially to me as being deserving of help from the Foundation."[26]

Conrad Hilton also stated in his will that the foundation's trustees should "be ever watchful for the opportunity to shelter little children with the umbrella of your charity; be generous to their schools, their hospitals and their places of worship."[27] The main way this is done is through programs to combat drug use in schools. Over the past decade, the foundation has given over $20 million to anti-drug programs. In the

1980s, it awarded grants to the RAND Corporation to prepare antidrug education materials; in 1992, it gave $3.6 million to the BEST Foundation For a Drug Free Tomorrow to distribute these materials in schools and to train teachers to detect and combat drug use.

The foundation also helps blind children through a five-year, $15-million grant to the Perkins School for the Blind, the institution that Helen Keller attended. In *Be My Guest*, Hilton said that at age 15, he learned of Helen Keller's achievements in overcoming her disability. "I regarded Helen Keller," Hilton wrote, "with an awed understanding which I have never lost."[28] To honor Helen Keller's memory, the Hilton/Perkins National and International Program uses foundation funds to train teachers, support families with blind children, publish scholarly research, and supply equipment to dozens of needy nations around the world, including five Central and Eastern European ones.

Other Hilton Foundation programs include a joint program with World Vision to provide clean water to rural villages in Ghana, a program to provide prenatal care to low-income women in Los Angeles County, a program that helps mentally-ill homeless people in New York City, and several grants to groups addressing domestic violence.

The Conrad Hilton Foundation continued to fund programs about the blind and Catholic charities. It created the Hilton Humanitarian Prize, which awards a $1.5 million annual award to a deserving charity. In 2005, the prize went to Partners in Health, which runs medical clinics in Third World countries.

In 2005, Donald Hubbs retired, and was succeeded as Hilton Foundation president by Steven Hilton, a son of Barron Hilton who had worked at the Conrad Hilton Foundation in various capacities since 1983,

In an interview with the *Chronicle of Philanthropy,* Steven Hilton said that the practices instituted by Donald Hubbs would not change The foundation, Hilton said, would continue to pursue a "major project" approach. "Rather than taking the foundation's monies and spreading them over many organizations in one-year grants," Hilton said, "we thought we'd be more effective if we selected an area where there is a great need that might have been overlooked. Then we'd focus our attention and make one big grant."[29] As an example, Hilton said that the Hilton Foundation would give a multi-million, multi-year grant to provide clean water in Africa—and continue it if the program worked.

# CHAPTER III

In an interview with the *Los Angeles Business Journal,* Hilton said that the foundation would honor his grandfather's intentions in two ways: first, by having a majority of the trustees be Hilton family members, and second, by honoring Conrad Hilton's wish that the foundation be run with low overhead.

"Conrad Hilton's will advises future directors to be wary of charities with high salaried executives and a heavy ratio of expense," Steven Hilton said. "Although he was referring to the non-profit charities to which we give funds, we at the Hilton Foundation take that to heart regarding our own operations. One way we do that is by operating with a staff of only 14."[30]

# CHAPTER IV

# A Legal History of Donor Intent

And besides, what right has the State, or those called upon to administer a charity, to dictate conditions to its founder? Those conditions may seem to us foolish fancies; we may deem ourselves far more competent to establish such as will secure the general object, but it is not ours to say. When we see fit to create such a foundation out of our own fortunes, we shall be at perfect liberty to show our wisdom, but it is out of place in administering the fortunes of others.
— *State v. Adams,* Missouri Supreme Court (1869)[1]

Was John Hiram's will fairly carried out? That was the true question; and if not, was it not his especial duty to see that this was done-his especial duty, whatever damage it might do to his order-however ill such duty might be received by his patron and his friends? — Anthony Trollope, *The Warden* (1854)[2]

The law of donor intent is quite old. The battle between donors and inheritors predates the founding of the United States by several hundred years. Some scholars trace the roots of the conflict to the Charities Act of 1601; others to the mortmain laws of the 13th century; and at least one expert, historian H.F. Jolowicz, to the late Roman Empire.

Given that the history of charitable trust law is at least 400 years old, it would take a book (and possibly a bookshelf) to exhaust the subject. This chapter provides a general overview of the legal history of donor intent, including a discussion of the terms often used in legal cases so that donors better understand what they can and cannot do in creating a foundation or charitable trust. Donors need to know what mortmain was, why the Rule Against Perpetuities is important, and why the Victorians found the subject of "the dead hand" so controversial.

**The Statute of Mortmain**

The problems of donor intent begin in medieval England. The English church by this time had grown quite wealthy, as generations of people had willed it land and other property, which it controlled in

## CHAPTER IV

perpetuity. To limit the church's ability to derive increasing amounts of income from estates, the Statute of Mortmain *(De viris religiosis)* was passed in 1279. This prohibited the church from buying or receiving property that could be perpetually controlled, ordering that "no one at all, whether religious or anyone else, may presume to buy or sell any lands or tenements, or to receive them from anyone under the colour of gift or lease or any other title whatsoever, or to appropriate them to himself in any other way or by any device or subterfuge, so that they pass into mortmain in any way, under pain of their forfeiture."[3]

As Cambridge University historian Sandra Raban notes, however, after 20 years the church managed to devise ways to avoid the statute, often by acquiring short-term leases to land, which were then constantly renewed. Not until the 16th century, when Henry VIII (1491-1547) eliminated most British monasteries and established the Church of England, did mortmain cease to be a problem.

But even after the Church of England was nationalized, thus putting property it acquired under state control, the notion that mortmain was a bad idea persisted. By now, the French term "mortmain" became the English "dead hand," a term that one 19th-century historian said was derived from the "resemblance to holding of a man's hand that is ready to die, for what he then holdeth he letteth not go till he be dead. So that an inheritance is supposed to remain in men of religion as long as the house itself continues."[4]

In the 14th and 15th centuries, "trusts" or "uses" were created, whereby a testator could will land or an estate to a third party and thus avoid punitive death duties. During the same time, the church in England, seeking to avoid mortmain penalties, encouraged donors to will their estates to third parties that would use them to perform good works. By the time of the reign of Elizabeth I (1558-1601), these third parties had evolved into charitable trusts. In the 16th century, private charities were created in England that had little to do with religion.

As historian W.K. Jordan notes, such charitable trusts had been evolving for a long time. As early as the reign of Henry V (1413-1422), the British courts had created a commission to encourage donations to support hospitals, and several laws passed between 1530 and 1597 were intended to discourage gifts to religious organizations while encouraging aid to the poor and the sick. The next step was to determine what sort of gifts were and were not charitable. Passing the Statute of Charitable Uses in 1601, which defined which organizations were charities, did this. It also established a set of commissioners to ensure that charities were properly run.

## Cy Pres

How were the wishes of donors who created charities to be upheld? That was the function of the Court of Chancery. During the 17th century, judges in this court set a series of precedents by establishing *cy pres* doctrine. Historians are uncertain how *cy pres* evolved over the centuries, but as Cambridge University's Gareth Jones notes, by the early 17th century, it had become "a sophisticated and mature doctrine."[5]

The *cy pres* doctrine in 1600 varied little from today's. The Court of Chancery would not alter a will unless a donor's wishes were illegal, impossible, or indefinite. Consider *Emmanuel College, Cambridge v. English,* a 1617 case. A donor asked his executors to spend £1,000 on land. The income from the land would be given to Cambridge University's Emmanuel College at a rate of £50 a year to support two fellows, to be paid £10 a year each, and six scholars, whose annual salary would be £5 a year.

Emmanuel College objected, saying that no one, even in 1617, could live on £5 a year. Sir Francis Bacon, who was Lord Keeper (chief judge) of the court, ruled that the donor's intentions were impossible to carry out, and declared that the scholars should be paid £5, six shillings, and eight pence a year. Bacon, said a court report of the era,

> did not intend to alter anything concerning the disposition of the legacy contrary to the will, except it were in that which was impossible to he performed, which might prove a hindrance and inconvenience to the college; and also that, in that which was necessary to be altered in respect of impossibility and inconvenience as aforesaid, he desired to tie himself to come as near as might he to the will and meaning of the testator in the ordering and disposing thereof.[6]

But Bacon's ruling was unusual. In most cases, English judges applying *cy pres* tests did as little as possible to alter a donor's intentions. In a 1682 case, a donor gave money to a Cambridge University college to endow a professorship in divinity, with stipulations that the professor hold a bachelor's degree or a doctorate in divinity, be at least 50 years old, deliver five lectures a term, and deliver legible copies of these lectures to the university once each term. The university asked the courts to alter the will so that the endowed professor be over 40 years old, give three lectures a term, and deliver his copies once a year. The courts rejected the petition, ruling that the donor's wishes were neither illegal nor impossible, and thus should be followed.

Perhaps the best example of the attitude of 17th-century English courts was in *Man v. Ballet*, another 1682 case. A donor left money to help the poor, repair local roads, and refurbish the parish church. The trustees petitioned the court to alter the will so that the church would receive nothing, claiming that the trustees own "greatness and excess" in other worthy affairs absolved them from fulfilling the donor's intentions. Lord Nottingham, the chief judge, denied the petition, charging that if this exemption were made,

> at this rate we should have all persons' charities given away to preaching ministers and lecturers; but they should not think to rob Peter to pay Paul; however, for as much as this money for a long time had been thus promiscuously applied for the time past, they should not be punished for that mis-employment in anything, saving us to what was paid to the parson, for which they should not be allowed one farthing.[7]

**The Rule Against Perpetuities**

Another innovation of late 17th-century English courts was the Rule Against Perpetuities, intended to prevent estates from using charities as a means to pass wealth through a family. Still the law in England and America, this rule states that only charitable trusts can be continued through successive generations. Other trusts can be passed through only one generation. As an example, consider the fortune of the Rockefellers. The Rockefeller Foundation is immortal, at least until its endowment runs out. But the Rockefeller family fortune must be willed anew by each generation. Further, the Rule Against Perpetuities forbids "mixed trusts," which give money to heirs and to charity. By 1700, the courts repeatedly warned donors that they must divide their estates should they wish to give money to both heirs and charity.

The English Parliament tightened rules regarding donor intent with the Mortmain Act of 1736. Under this act, all gifts of land to charities were illegal unless made at least one year before the donor's death and unless the deed of gift was registered at the Court of Chancery

A Legal History of Donor Intent

within six months after it was made. Further, such transfers were unconditional and could not be revoked by any later wills the donor might make. The only exemptions were for Oxford and Cambridge universities and three public schools—Eton, Winchester, and Westminster. It is unclear why this law was passed. As historian David Owen notes, the act "was not one of Parliament's more inspired decisions in the charity field, nor, for that matter, one of the more readily intelligible."[8]

The English courts chose to interpret the Mortmain Act of 1736 in a very strict manner. In a series of decisions, they ruled that charities could not acquire land or anything whose income derived from land, such as railway or canal shares, or mortgages for toll roads. Moreover, should a donor die less than a year after preparing a will, and should the will include any enterprise that involved land acquisition, the courts would declare it illegal and nullify donor intent. This was what happened to 19th-century philanthropist George Moore, who wished to leave £15,000 for a hospital. Because he died less than a year after making his will, and because land for the hospital had not yet been acquired, the Court of Chancery declared the will illegal.

Interestingly, the English Parliament in the 19th century allowed a series of private exemptions to the Mortmain Act of 1736. Some London hospitals could receive land while others could not. It was legal under the Mortmain Act to will the bonds of the Leicester Corporation to charity, but illegal to will the company's stock. Not surprisingly, long-established organizations petitioned the courts to declare that they were not charities in order to exempt themselves from the Act. In 1826 the British Museum (the English equivalent of both the Smithsonian Institution and the Library of Congress) unsuccessfully tried to persuade the Court of Chancery to declare it a non-charitable institution.

Nonetheless, during the first half of the 19th century, the Court of Chancery was very strict in maintaining donor intent. Provided a donor followed the Mortmain Act, the courts generally upheld his wishes.

**Donor Intent in 19th-Century Great Britain**

The Court of Chancery in the 19th century was headed by a series of strict constructionists. None was more uncompromising than Lord Eldon, who headed the court from 1805 to 1828. Eldon ruled that Leeds Grammar School could not teach French and German since the trust that established the school specified that the school's purpose was to teach "learned languages," specifically Greek and Latin. When asked to divert one bequest to aid the poor, Eldon refused, saying, "I have nothing to do with policy. If the Legislature thinks proper to give the power of leaving property to charitable purposes, recognized by law as such, however prejudiced, the Court must administer it."[9]

A typical example of Lord Eldon's hard-headedness was *Morice v. The Bishop of Durham,* decided by the Court of Chancery in 1804. Ann Cracherode died in 1801, and left her estate to the Bishop of Durham "to dispose of the ultimate residue to such objects of benevolence and liberality as the Bishop of Durham in his own discretion shall most approve of." Cracherode's heirs sued to break the will on the grounds that Cracherode's intentions were indefinite.

Lord Eldon agreed, on the grounds that Cracherode's wishes were "too indefinite to create a trust." Because Cracherode did not precisely define what she wanted done with her wealth, Eldon ruled that the Bishop of Durham should spend Cracherode's wealth immediately on any purpose "not for his own benefit."[10]

The result of such case law was that by 1850, England was filled with charities that were very old, founded by donors with very specific wishes, and functioning in ways that, at least to social reformers, seemed very outmoded. Trustees of the Victorian era were still fulfilling the wishes of a donor named Greene, who wanted to give green clothes to the poor; a donor named Grey, who thought that gray was the ideal color for the poor; and a man named Rose who willed that his town should always have plenty of rosebushes. In Chester, England, a 17th-century donor named Owen Jones willed his inheritance to poor members of 23 trading companies (or guilds) in that city. But as income from the endowment grew, funds were given to all guild members without a means test. By 1869, 369 of 412 members of the Chester trading companies were receiving funds, including some who were soldiers in Australia. Only one of the companies still practiced its trade; the rest were shells that survived solely to receive money.

In enforcing donor intent, Victorian courts did not seek to redistribute income from an endowment if the funds exceeded the amount needed to fulfill a donor's wishes. This led to such cases as that of Christ's Hospital in Durham, England, founded in the 12th century to help lepers. The hospital's endowment, invested in minerals, land, and mines, grew so that by 1850, it had expenses of £1,700 a year and income of £4,700 a year.[11] Author Anthony Trollope used the Christ's

Hospital case and similar examples as the basis for *The Warden,* a novel in which Septimus Harding is paid £80 a year for religious duties and an additional £800 for being warden of Hiram's Hospital. Ultimately, Harding resigns his position as warden, but his real-life counterparts generally preferred to clutch their sinecures.

### Sir Arthur Hobhouse's Legacy

These antiquated charities eventually prompted a major debate between John Stuart Mill and Sir Arthur (later Lord) Hobhouse. Mill believed that charities should be subject to state control and modification 50 to 100 years after a donor's death; Hobhouse preferred to entirely eliminate perpetual charitable trusts.

In *The Dead Hand* (1880), Hobhouse explained that what infuriated him were cases such as *Thornton v. Howe,* an 1862 Court of Chancery case that contested an 1843 will by Ann Essam. Essam wanted to publish the writings of Joanna Southcote, a 17th-century mystic who believed she was to give birth to a second Messiah. Master of the Rolls Lord Romilly declared the will void, since it involved the transfer of land and thus violated the Mortmain Act of 1736. But Romilly noted that had the estate not included land, "this Court would, in my opinion, have enforced the bequest and regulated the application of it as well as it could."[12]

For Hobhouse, *Thornton* was an example of pernicious donor intent, since Southcote had no followers. But Hobhouse's goal was not to revise the wills of antiquated foundations; he wanted to eliminate foundations entirely. "But of the greater Foundations, will anybody confidently assert that they produce more good than evil?" Hobhouse asked.

> Will any contemporary of mine at Eton assert that the then state of the College was useful or edifying? Will any contemporary of mine at Oxford say that the Foundations of Merton or Waynflete or Chichele were then playing their part in the world? There may be times of awakened conscience and active exertion, but the question is whether rich Foundations derived from private origin do not invariably gravitate towards sloth and indolence? It is difficult to point to one instance of a private endowment for learning achieving great results by itself alone.

# CHAPTER IV

> To me, it seems that in this matter of Charitable Foundations we are reaping simply as we have sown. We have committed a vast power to fortuitous and irresponsible hands; and they have used it according to the measure of their goodness and wisdom... If the plans of our noblest spirits—our Mertons and Wykehams and Colets—are found unsuitable as time runs on, what are we to expect from the easy and self-complacent spirit of the ordinary testator?[13]

While Hobhouse did not expect to entirely eliminate the influence of the dead hand, he did want to end all foundations that a state tribunal would declare as "interfer[ing] with the public welfare." This tribunal would be "charged with the duty of adjusting to new objects all Foundations which have become pernicious or useless." After the tribunal had its way for a period of time, "the living principle of using property so as to benefit mankind would, with the assent of the great majority, prevail over the deadly superstition of blind obedience to the commands of the dead."[14]

Hobhouse's views did not prevail. *Cy pres* rules in Britain were loosened somewhat, and the Mortmain Act of 1736 was partly repealed in 1888 (and totally repealed in 1960 after a government commission found it to serve no useful purpose). The British courts, however, still concerned themselves with trifling details. In a notorious 1939 case, the courts decided that the will of Caleb Diplock, which left £250,000 "for such charitable or benevolent object or objects" as his executors could determine, was void because "benevolent" and "charitable" were not synonymous, and that therefore the will did not meet the *cy pres* test for certainty. (Had Diplock's lawyer used the phrase "charitable and benevolent," the will would have been declared valid.)[15]

## The Dead Hand Problem in America

Hobhouse did, however, have a lasting influence in America. Granted, American charities rarely had the dead hand problem; the cases in which a donor's intentions have been completely nullified have been few. But the fear of the dead hand was far more influential than any "dead hand" foundation. This threat was one reason for the rise of community foundations. It was also Julius Rosenwald's main reason for inventing the term limit for charitable trusts. Further, since most major foundations in America were created *after* the idea of the dead hand became common, their vague, amorphous charters ensured that the dead hand was not guiding the foundation and that the donor's living hand was pushed aside at the earliest possible time.

But it took over a century for this to happen. American courts first had to establish what the legal rules were for donor intent. They had to decide whether English precedents would be considered in rulings. Was the Statute of Charitable Uses something to which American courts were bound? What about *cy pres* doctrine? Was it a principle American courts should adopt?

These questions were debated for decades. As Edith L. Fisch, Doris Jonas Free, and Esther R. Schachter note in their authoritative analysis of the laws regulating charities,

> the new nation vehemently condemned anything reminiscent of English sovereign power or of an aristocratic society as being unfit for a democracy. Not only did some states repeal all English statutes including the Statute of Charitable Uses, but some jurisdictions rejected the notion of *cy pres* because it was mistakenly regarded as being exercisable only by the prerogative power of the king and hence contrary to the spirit of our democratic institutions and in conflict with the doctrine of separation of powers."[16]

One of the states that repudiated English law was Virginia, and it was unclear whether charitable trusts could even be established there. This uncertainty was compounded by the U.S. Supreme Court in the *Hart's Executors* case of 1819, in which the court upheld a Virginia decision nullifying a clause of Silas Hart's will that gave much of his estate to the Philadelphia Baptist Association. The association was unincorporated and, in the court's view, did not legally exist.

The *Hart* decision was quite confusing. Some states interpreted the decision to mean that nearly all charitable trusts were illegal. The Virginia courts, in particular, were very strict. In 1833, the Virginia Supreme Court in *Janey's Executors v. Latane* nullified a provision of a will that left $1,000 to educate poor children in a particular school district because the will did not identify what children should be helped. The Maryland Court of Appeals was also very strict. Only four months after *Hart*, it nullified as vague and uncertain a will intended to benefit "the real distressed private poor of *Talbot* county."[17]

# CHAPTER IV

## The Case of Girard College

Only 25 years later, in a case involving the will of Stephen Girard, did the Supreme Court finally declare charitable trusts legal and donor intent constitutional. Girard (1750-1831) was a French immigrant who owned a fleet of ships. He was America's first millionaire and first national philanthropist—the 1820s equivalent of a Rockefeller or Carnegie. Like most of the great philanthropists, he was also very modest. In 1822, a would-be biographer named Stephen Simpson wrote Girard asking for information. Girard declined. "My actions, Mr. Simpson, must be my life," he wrote. "I have no information to give; when I am dead that will speak for itself."[18]

When Girard died in 1831, he left an estate of $6 million—an amount equal to half the federal budget of the time. Some of this was given to the city of Philadelphia (where Girard had spent most of his life) for various good works. But most went to create an orphanage, to be known as Girard College. It was to be endowed by a charitable trust, which would be administered by the city of Philadelphia.

Girard's heirs, who were given small sums, tried to overturn the will on the grounds that the city of Philadelphia could not acquire real estate nor control a private trust. Further, "the objects of the charity were altogether indefinite, vague, and uncertain and therefore the trusts were incapable of execution or of being cognizable in law or in equity."[19]

After several years, the Girard case went to the Supreme Court. Girard's heirs hired Daniel Webster to represent them. Ignoring most of the claims that Girard's intent was uncertain, Webster decided to base his case on the terms by which Girard College was to be created. Clause XXI of Girard's will left very precise instructions, including specifications for the height and length of the college and the placing of windows in buildings.[20] The college was to be open to "as many poor white male orphans, between the ages of six and ten years, as the said income be adequate to maintain."[21] The orphans

> shall be instructed in the various branches of a sound education, comprehending reading, writing, grammar, arithmetic, geography, navigation, surveying, practical mathematics, astronomy, natural, chemical, and experimental philosophy, the French and Spanish languages, (I do not forbid, but I do not recommend the Greek and Latin languages)—and such other learning and science as the capacities of the several scholars may

merit or warrant; I would have them taught facts and things, rather than words or signs.²²

The orphans were not, however, to be instructed by clergymen. "I enjoin and require," Girard wrote, "that no ecclesiastic, missionary, or minister of any sect whatsoever, shall ever hold or exercise any station or duty whatsoever in the said college; *nor shall any such person ever be admitted for any purpose, or as a visitor, within the premises appropriated to the purposes of the college."*

> In making this restriction, I do not mean to cast any reflection upon any sect or person whatsoever; but, as there is such a multitude of sects, and such a diversity of opinion amongst them, I desire to keep the tender minds of the orphans, who are to derive advantage from this bequest, free from the excitement which clashing doctrines and sectarian controversy are apt to produce; my desire is, that all the
>
> instructors and teachers in the college shall take pains to instil [sic] into the minds of the scholars, *the purest principles of morality,* so that, on their entrance into active life, they *may from inclination and habit, evince benevolence towards their fellow creatures, and a love of truth, sobriety, and industry,* adopting at the same time such religious tenets as their matured reason may enable them to prefer.²³

For Webster this clause, if carried out, would mean that America, a Christian nation, would be using its laws to promote atheism. In a nine-hour speech lasting three days, Webster told the Supreme Court that Girard's will was not even charity, since it would deny Christian teaching to the students of Girard College. "If charity denies its birth and parentage," Webster explained, "if it turns infidel to the great doctrines of the Christian religion—if it turns unbeliever—it is no longer charity! There is no longer charity, either in a Christian sense, or in the sense of jurisprudence, for it separates itself from the fountain of its own creation."

Further, Webster argued that Girard's will was illegal since Pennsylvania was not an "infidel state," but founded on Christian principles. Pennsylvania, he said, "has a Christian origin—a Christian code of laws—a system of legislation founded on nothing else, in many of its important bearing upon human society, than the belief of the people of Pennsylvania—their firm and sincere belief, in the divine authority and great importance of the truths of the Christian religion. And she should the more carefully seek to preserve them pure."[24]

The Supreme Court unanimously rejected Webster's argument and upheld Girard's will. In *Vidal v. Girard's Executors,* Justice Joseph Story, writing for the majority, ruled that it was impossible to know what Girard's opinions about Christianity were. He noted that Girard did not say that Christianity was not to be taught at Girard College, only that no ministers would be allowed to enter the college. "In cases of this sort," Story wrote,

> it is extremely difficult to draw any just and satisfactory line of distinction in a free country as to the qualifications or disqualifications which may he insisted upon by the donor of a charity as to those *who* shall administer or partake of his bounty. . . . In America, it has been thought, in the absence of any express legal prohibitions, that the donor might select the studies, as well as the classes of persons, who were to receive his bounty without being compellable to make religious instruction part of these studies.[25]

### Establishing Cy Pres in America

*Vidal* not only determined that charitable trusts were legal in America; it was the first major decision to confirm that donor intent was to be part of American law.

Not until the case of *Jackson v. Phillips,* however, did the *cy pres* doctrine become firmly established. In 1867, the Massachusetts Supreme Court considered the case of Francis Jackson, an abolitionist who died in 1861. Jackson willed $10,000 to a board of trustees "for the preparation and circulation of books, newspapers, and delivery of speeches, lectures, and such other means as, in their judgment, will create a public sentiment that will put an end to negro slavery in this country."[26]

The Massachusetts Supreme Court ruled that the Thirteenth Amendment, which outlawed slavery, had nullified Jackson's original plans. But because blacks still faced considerable problems after slavery, the court ruled that *cy pres* applied, and ordered that a master be appointed to assist the trustees in creating an organization to provide general assistance to African-Americans.

*Jackson* was the first case in which *cy pres* was used to alter donor intent. But the doctrine was not immediately established everywhere. Some states still wrongly believed that *cy pres* was exercised by the English crown rather than English courts, and was therefore a doctrine inapplicable in America. Other courts, even in the late 19th century, questioned a will that left funds for a charitable cause rather than to specific individuals. In *Tilden v. Green (1891)*, Samuel Tilden, a prominent politician and the Democratic presidential candidate of 1876, willed a portion of his estate to create a library in New York City. The New York Court of Appeals nullified the will since it did not specify what persons would receive the benefit. In 1893, however, the New York legislature overturned the decision, allowing bequests to charities to be made.

According to legal historian Ronald Chester, the changing attitude of the courts to *cy pres* law reflects differing attitudes that generations have had toward private property. By Chester's count, before 1860 fifteen states had considered cases where *cy pres* might be invoked, and in ten states the courts had rejected *cy pres* as unconstitutional. Between 1850 and 1900, Chester says, the courts received the notion of charitable trusts more favorably because they "saw that by encouraging private contributions, they were reducing the costs of government…The intent of the donor was paramount. Charitable trusts were construed by detailed inquiries into the state of the testator's mind and his wishes at the time of the making of the gift, instead of being seen in light of changing social conditions."[27]

## Early 20th-Century Challenges to Cy Pres

In the 19th century, courts were reluctant to apply *cy pres* because they wished to do as little as possible to disturb a donor's wishes. Most 19th-century judges believed that an estate was private property, and that property was something that must be preserved.

This attitude, however, began to change in the more socialist-minded 20th century. Some judges eager to modify donor intent cited Andrew Carnegie's belief that his wealth was a public trust for future generations. Other judges followed the views of the Legal Realists, whose leader, Harvard Law School dean Roscoe Pound, firmly opposed donor intent. "No amount of admiration for our traditional system,"

CHAPTER IV

Pound wrote in 1906, "should blind us to the obvious fact that it exhibits too great a respect for the individual, and for the entrenched position in which our legal and political history has put him and too little respect for the needs of society, when they come in conflict with the individual, to be in touch with the present age."[28]

As Ronald Chester notes, only between 1900 and 1950 did courts begin to use *cy pres* doctrine liberally to divert wills from uses thought insufficient. In *Will of Neher,* a 1938 case, the New York Court of Appeals considered the will of a donor who left land for a hospital which a town could not afford to build. The court ruled that the donor's main intention was to build a memorial to her husband, and allowed the town to construct an administration building instead.

But if the dead hand was loosened, it was not loosened much, as exemplified by the Mullanphy Trust. Created in 1849 "to furnish relief to all poor immigrants and travelers coming to St. Louis on their way, *bona fide,* to settle in the West,"[29] the Mullanphy Trust by 1900 had outlived its purpose. It was cited by everyone from Julius Rosenwald to the organizers of community foundations as an example of outdated charity. But it took no less than seven court cases spanning three decades for the trust to be broken. In *Thatcher v. Lewis (1934),* the Missouri Supreme Court modified the trust, allowing it to become a traveler's aid program.

**Modern Donor Intent Case Law: Suggestions for Donors**

*Will of Neher and Thatcher* mark the beginning of modem donor intent case law. Nearly all recent cases involve small foundations and estates. Large foundations have generally avoided donor intent problems because donors' intentions, philosophies, and principles are usually ignored when creating them. *Estate of Buck,* discussed in Chapter Three, is unusual in that it involves a large fortune.

Just as problems relating to wills have generally been seen as a matter of state, not federal, law, most decisions regarding donor intent have been made by municipal and state courts. Justice Hugo Black noted in *Evans v. Abney* (1970), one of the few donor intent cases to reach the Supreme Court, that "the construction of wills is essentially a state-law question."[30]

The rest of this chapter highlights recent court cases involving donor intent. It seeks to provide potential donors with a better understanding of how to establish general charitable intent while avoiding the invocation of *cy pres* law. What does it take to establish charitable intent, and what do the three pillars of *cy pres* doctrine—illegality, impossibility, and impracticality—actually mean?

The first rule in creating a charity is to avoid invoking the Rule Against Perpetuities. As noted, perpetual charitable trusts are allowed while non-charitable ones are not. "Mixed trusts," which seek to combine charitable and non-charitable uses, are likewise forbidden. Care should also be taken to ensure that the proposed foundation is, in fact, a charitable institution. While courts have upheld as valid wills that simply give money "to charity" without qualification, a charity must relieve poverty, advance religion, promote education, further public health, serve governmental or municipal purposes, or provide other services that benefit others.

Donors should also not use the word "benevolent" in creating foundations. While there has never been a case in America equivalent to the British case of Caleb Diplock's will, the precedents suggest that "benevolent" is not equivalent to "charitable," and that using the phrase "charitable or benevolent" at any point in a will or deed of trust will almost certainly be grounds for protracted—and unnecessary—legal action.

### Hardage v. Hardage

In *Hardage v. Hardage* (1954), a man named J.J. Hardage sought to create an endowment whose income would be used "to defray the hospital and medical expenses of any of my blood relatives who may be in need of such care and who because of poverty, hardship, or old age are unable to properly provide such care out of their own resources." His endowment would also have made "educational loans at not greater than 4% interest to any person of reasonable college age, who is a dependent of any of my blood relatives and has shown by his or her character, mental ability, and desire for education to be deserving thereof."[31] The Supreme Court of Georgia ruled that Hardage's plan was not charity, but a private trust meant to benefit his family. Such a trust violated the Rule Against Perpetuities, and the two clauses establishing the trust were struck down.

### Estate of Scholler

It is also doubtful that a valid charitable trust can be created that has clauses benefiting a particular class of persons, even if benefits

## CHAPTER IV

are unrestricted by race or gender. Frederick C. Scholler, the sole shareholder of Scholler Brothers, Inc., created the Scholler Foundation in 1939 to help the poor, promote scientific research, assist people with disabilities, and help hospitals, educational institutions, and churches. But distributions from the foundation were

> not to be limited geographically to the United States of America; (and specifically for the purpose of providing hospitalization, medical care, and educational, literary, and recreational facilities for employees and/or former employees of Scholler Brothers, Inc. and/or Schuller Brothers, Ltd., and/or Trisco Products, Inc. [parts of Scholler Brothers, Inc.] and their families, and/or employees of any other corporation, a majority interest in the voting stock of which is subsequently acquired by The Scholler Foundation, or by Scholler Brothers, Inc., or Scholler Brothers, Ltd., or Trisco Products, Inc.)"[32]

In 1947, the Treasury Department granted the Scholler Foundation charitable status. But Canadian authorities would not consider the foundation a charity under Canadian law unless the clause benefiting Scholler Corp. employees were removed. Scholler did this in 1951, and died six years later. His heirs sued in 1959, saying that the Scholler Corp. employee clause, although it had been removed, was evidence that Scholler sought to create an illegal trust. In 1961, the Pennsylvania Supreme Court rejected the heirs' requests, stating that the Scholler Foundation's revised deed of trust was a valid charity.

After *Estate of Scholler;* the law of trusts became clearer. The general rule that emerged was that a donor could create a charitable trust to study particular ideas, and even to glorify himself. But when a donor tried to restrict distributions of a charity to a narrow class of beneficiaries—heirs, associates, former employees—the courts would almost certainly declare it an illegal mixed trust.

### *Estate of Carlson*

It *is* legal, however, to have a foundation provide scholarships that benefit particular individuals, provided that they are not limited by race or gender (or possibly religion). It is also legal to create a foundation to aid a particular person, as long as that person uses grants to perform services that benefit an entire community. In *Estate of Carlson* (1961), the

Kansas Supreme Court ruled that it was legal to create a charitable trust to send a person to medical school, as long as the person returned to his community after earning his M.D.[33] Similarly, land trusts that preserve a family's home and property are generally legal, provided that the property has "historic worth" and would therefore benefit the community and future generations.[34]

### Register of Wills for Baltimore City v. Cook

It is also charitable to will money to nonprofit organizations that seek to change the law or public policy. This precedent was established in *Register of Wills for Baltimore City v. Cook* (1966), in which a donor willed money to the National Women's Party, a nonprofit whose main goal was to convince states to ratify the Equal Rights Amendment. The Baltimore register of wills imposed a 7 percent tax on the estate. The estate paid, sued, and won a rebate, which did not apply to gifts made to charitable organizations. The Maryland Court of Appeals ruled that the National Women's Party's goals fell within the definition of a charity:

> Whatever may be the views of individuals, laymen, or judges, as to the need or desirability of the passage of the Equal Rights Amendment or similar legislation, our system of government is not opposed to attempts to secure legislative changes by legal means. Indeed, the channeling of efforts to effect social or political changes to the public discussions involved in proposed constitutional amendments or legislation, rather than by possible violence or subversion, is fundamental to our democracy.[35]

### Shenandoah Valley National Bank v. Taylor

In 1951, the Supreme Court of Virginia in *Shenandoah Valley National Bank v. Taylor* provided another clarification of what a donor cannot do. A Winchester, Virginia donor named Charles B. Henry tried to use his $86,000 estate to create the "Charles B. Henry and Fannie Belle Henry Fund." Income would be divided among first-, second-, and third-grade students of an elementary school in Winchester and paid each year on the last school day before Easter and again on the last day before Christmas. The Virginia Supreme Court ruled that while the students would certainly welcome the money (it would "no doubt cause them to remember or think of their benefactor with gratitude and thanksgiving"), the proposed fund did not qualify as a charity, and the will was nullified.[36]

# CHAPTER IV

## *Estate of Robbins*

Until 1965, courts generally declared a charity illegal if the beneficiaries had to perform illegal actions to receive funds. In *Estate of Robbins* (1962), the Supreme Court of California considered the case of a donor who left money "for the care, comfort, support, medical attention, education, sustenance, maintenance or custody of such minor Negro child or children, whose father or mother, or both, may have been incarcerated, imprisoned, detained, or committed in any federal, state, county or local prison or penitentiary, as a result of a conviction of a crime or misdemeanor of a political nature."[37]

The donor's grandnephew, an heir, tried to void the will, claiming that such a provision might encourage people to commit crimes so that their children could claim benefits. The court rejected the argument, stating that this possibility was "far more remote than that which the Legislature itself may have created by provision for the care of children that extends to those of convicted prisoners."[38]

## *Commonwealth of Pennsylvania v. Brown*

Courts have been increasingly willing to modify charitable trusts, however, if they contain restrictions based on race and gender. These used to be very common: an 1886 Connecticut Supreme Court case *(Beardsley v. Selectmen of Bridgeport)* upheld a bequest to benefit "worthy, deserving, poor, white, American, Protestant, Democratic widows and orphans residing in the town of Bridgeport, Conn."[39] Precedents regarding race and gender begin with the will of Stephen Girard. As noted, a clause limited entry to Girard College to "poor white male orphans." According to legal historian David Luria, this ensured that Girard's will would be "the most litigated will in American history."[40]

In 1954, in the wake of the Supreme Court's *Brown v. Board of Education* decision, two black orphans sued to be admitted to Girard College, claiming discrimination based on race. The Orphans Court of Philadelphia rejected the request twice, and the Pennsylvania Supreme Court upheld the ruling. In 1957, the U.S. Supreme Court overturned the Pennsylvania decision, ruling that because Girard College's board of trustees was appointed by the city, the city was violating the Fourteenth Amendment clauses against discrimination. In turn, the city of Philadelphia replaced these trustees with private trustees and continued to refuse admission to blacks. The Pennsylvania Supreme Court upheld the action, and the U.S. Supreme Court refused to consider the case. (Meanwhile, Girard College had modified Girard's will to allow admission of needy boys whose mothers were still alive.)

By 1957, the legal questions regarding Stephen Girard's will seemed to be resolved. But in 1965, another group of blacks began to sue in federal courts. This time, they won. After five more decisions in district and circuit courts over a three-year period, concluding in *Commonwealth of Pennsylvania v. Brown* (1968), Girard College was required to modify Stephen Girard's will to admit blacks. (As Luria notes, a second modification of the will in 1984 to admit girls "seems to have been accomplished with relatively little litigation or controversy."[41])

### *Evans v. Newton and Evans v. Abney*

Other well-established educational institutions had the wills of their founders modified in the 1960s to remove racial restrictions. *Guillory v. Administrators of Tulane University* (1962) eliminated the clause of merchant Paul Tulane's will that required the university to benefit "young white persons." *Coffee v. William Marsh Rice University* (1966) voided the clause of the founder's will saying that the university educate "white inhabitants of the City of Houston, and State of Texas."

The U.S. Supreme Court considered donor intent racial discrimination in *Evans v. Newton* (1966) and *Evans v. Abney* (1970). In 1911, Senator Augustus O. Bacon of Georgia willed a piece of land known as Baconsfield to the city of Macon, Georgia for "a park and pleasure ground" for whites. He believed that "in their social relations the two races (white and negro) should be forever separate."[42]

In the 1960s, the Macon city government said it could no longer enforce discrimination on property it administered. Bacon's heirs sued, charging that Bacon's wishes had been violated and that Bacon's estate was entitled to the land. While the Supreme Court of Georgia ruled in favor of the heirs, the U.S. Supreme Court reversed the decision. Justice William O. Douglas, writing the majority decision, stated that because the state was involved in administering the bequest, and because the park was not like a social club or an academy but was open to everyone, it should continue to operate and be open to all races.

The heirs of Senator Bacon sued again, and convinced the Supreme Court of Georgia that because Bacon's wishes for a park for whites only could not be fulfilled, the court should use *cy pres* doctrine to have the land revert to the estate. In *Evans v. Abney* (1970), the U.S. Supreme Court upheld the lower court ruling. "The loss of charitable trusts such as Baconsfield is part of the price we pay for permitting deceased persons to exercise a continuing control over assets owned by them at death," Justice Hugo Black wrote in his majority decision. "This aspect of freedom of testation, like most things, has its advantages and disadvantages. The responsibility of this Court, however, is to construe and enforce the Constitution and laws of the land as they are and not to legislate social policy on the basis of our own personal inclinations."[43]

### *Trammell v. Elliott*

Clem Boyd left her estate to Agnes Scott College, Emory University, and the Georgia Institute of Technology for scholarships "for the benefit of deserving and qualified poor white boys and girls." The state of Georgia sued, stating that Georgia Tech, as a state-controlled school, could not award scholarships with an illegal racial restriction. In 1973 the Supreme Court of Georgia agreed, stating that the donor, in another section of her will, said, "adults do not need my life's earnings, and the children who need a college education are the ones who interest me most." The court, using the two *Evans* cases as precedents, upheld a lower court ruling that "the doctrine of *cy pres* was correctly applied in excluding the illegal racial classification from the charitable grant." The court declared that the scholarships be awarded without racial restrictions.[44]

### *Howard Savings Institution v. Peep*

In the 1960s, courts also began striking down bequests that imposed religious tests. In *Howard Savings Institution v. Peep* (1961), the New Jersey Supreme Court considered the bequest of C. Edward McKinney, Jr., an alumnus of Amherst College, who left $50,000 to his alma mater on condition that it be "held in trust to be used as a scholarship loan fund for deserving American-born, Protestant, Gentile boys of good moral repute, not given to gambling, smoking, drinking or similar acts. (It being my thought that if a young man has enough funds to allow the waste of smoking, he certainly does not need help.")[45] McKinney also left most of his estate to Amherst, provided that it agree to accept his scholarship plan.

Amherst College sued, saying that its charter barred it from discrimination based on religion, and asked the courts to strike down the religious clause in McKinney's will. (Amherst had no difficulty accepting McKinney's restrictions on smokers.) The New Jersey

Supreme Court agreed, ruling that because the college's charter prohibited discrimination based on religion, the college could not accept the McKinney bequest as it stood.

But in making the decision, the court warned that recipients could not arbitrarily restrict donor intent, citing *Connecticut College v. United States* (1960), in which the U.S. Military Academy sued to block a donor bequest for a new building, saying that it did not fit the academy's expansion plans. While the Academy wanted to use the funds for an addition to an existing building, a circuit ruled that *cy pres* could not be invoked "merely because the variation will meet the desire and suit the convenience of the trustee."[46] Because the McKinney bequest violated the Amherst charter, it had to be modified in order for the bequest to be accepted; but modifications made simply to ease burdens on the recipient would not be allowed.

### Lockwood v. Killian

*Howard Savings Institution v. Peep* is important because it established a precedent courts could follow, particularly when stricter federal anti-discrimination laws were enacted in the 1960s and 1970s. Sometimes the courts upheld restrictions based on religion. In *Lockwood v. Killian* (1979), the Connecticut Supreme Court considered the will of Frank Russell Fuller, who willed his estate to create a "Fuller Scholarship Fund" to benefit boys in Hartford, Connecticut and its suburbs who were "members of the Caucasian race and who have severally, specifically professed themselves to be of the Protestant Congregational faith." The court ruled that the fund had to be open to women and minorities from other parts of the state. But the court upheld Fuller's limits on aid to Protestants, stating that the restriction should not be considered under the anti-discrimination clauses of the Fourteenth Amendment, but was an exercise of the donor's religious freedom, and thus was constitutionally protected under the First Amendment."[47]

### Kamehameha Schools v. Equal Employment Opportunity Commission

The U.S. Supreme Court's recent ruling in *Kamehameha Schools v. Equal Employment Opportunity Commission* (1993) may signify a more restrictive attitude toward religious restrictions in wills. The Court upheld a ruling that charged that private schools in Hawaii could not discriminate against non-Protestants when hiring teachers, despite a clause in an 1884 will by Bernice Bishop (which established the schools) specifying that only Protestants should be teachers. The Supreme Court ruled that because the schools were not church-affiliated, the religious restriction in Bishop's will violated the Civil Rights Act of 1964. While it is too early to predict how state courts might interpret the decision, it may be that donors can only limit their bequests on religious grounds if they give to a church or a church-affiliated institution.[48]

### *In Re Estate of Wilson*

Courts have generally been more restrictive in upholding bequests that limit funds based on race and gender. In *In Re Estate of Wilson* (1983), the New York Supreme Court considered two scholarship funds created to help boys in a particular school district. In one case (known as the "Wilson Trust"), the school superintendent was to certify who the best students were. In the other (the "Johnson Trust"), the local board of education, acting as trustee, was to pay scholarships to the best students. The school district refused to cooperate, saying that it would be enforcing and approving discrimination.

Lower courts removed the superintendent's certification function in the Wilson Trust and allowed women to apply for the Johnson Trust scholarships. The New York Supreme Court upheld the decision in the matter of the Wilson Trust, but reversed the ruling in the Johnson Trust. Following the precedent of *Shelley v. Kraemer* (1948), which states that the Fourteenth Amendment "erects no shield against merely private conduct, however discriminatory or wrongful," the court ruled that the two trusts were private institutions. Unlike the park considered in *Evans v. Newton*, they had no "indelible public character."[49] The court concluded that it had no jurisdiction in modifying the bequest, except in the case of the Wilson Trust, because the school superintendent refused to honor his obligation under the terms of the trust.

### *In Re Certain Scholarship Funds*

In a similar case, however, the Supreme Court of New Hampshire came to a strikingly different conclusion. In *In Re Certain Scholarship Funds* (1990), the court considered two trusts left to the city of Keene, New Hampshire. One was for "some poor... boy," and the second for "some worthy protestant boy." The city of Keene, acting as trustee, refused to administer the trusts unless they were open to all students, citing a clause in the New Hampshire state constitution that prohibited discrimination by creed or gender.

The New Hampshire Supreme Court noted two precedents to follow: *Matter of Wilson* and *Commonwealth of Pennsylvania v. Brown*. The court ultimately sided with Brown, ruling that the trusts had to be modified to remove gender and religious restrictions. "Our society permits discrimination in the private sector in recognizing that the desire of human beings is to associate with, and confer benefits upon, other human beings and institutions of their own choosing," Justice William F. Batchelder wrote in his majority decision. "Such private decision-making is a part of daily life in any society. However, when the decision-making mechanism, as here, is so entwined with public institutions and government, discrimination becomes the policy statement and product of society itself and cannot stand against the strong and enlightened language of our constitution."[50]

Chief Justice David A. Brock, however, wrote a vigorous dissent:

> Freedom of testation is a cherished right which permits a testator to breathe his last, secure in the expectation that the law will venerate, and not frustrate, his last wishes. A court may, accordingly, replace an unfit or unsuitable trustee as part of its general duties in supervising the administration of a charitable testamentary trust, but the court is not free to rewrite a decedent's will or to attribute to him, posthumously, a desire to spend his bounty for the collective good when the designated and preferred class of beneficiaries has not been exhausted."[51]

### In Re Los Angeles County Pioneer Society

Generally, courts have ruled that charitable trusts are impossible or impracticable for two reasons. In some cases, donors unintentionally leave money to organizations that do not exist. In other cases, bequests are vague, and courts use *cy pres* formulas to assign beneficiaries. In *Estate of Tomlinson* (1976), a donor left funds to a nonexistent "Cancer Research Fund." *Cy pres* doctrine was used to award the gift to the American Cancer Society. *Estate of Bernstrauch* (1981) left money to a nonexistent "Masonic Lodge for Crippled Children." A court awarded the funds to the Shriners Lodge for Crippled Children after discovering that the donor was handicapped but not a Mason.

Courts, however, are more skeptical about efforts to overturn wills because donors made minor mistakes or omissions in naming beneficiaries. In *Vadrnan v. American Cancer Society* (1980), the American

# CHAPTER IV

Cancer Society tried unsuccessfully to use *cy pres* to acquire a bequest made to the "National Cancer Foundation" instead of the National Cancer Foundation, Inc.[52] In other cases, donors leave fortunes to organizations that do not exist after their deaths. In *Re Los Angeles County Pioneer Society,* decided by the Supreme Court of California in 1953, centered on the Los Angeles County Pioneer Society, an organization that honored the founders of that city. In 1946, Emma Stoltenberg left $53,000 to the organization, which it used to buy a building for meetings. But membership in the society was falling, and in 1948 it voted to disincorporate, distribute its assets (which totaled $95,243.54) among its members, and continue as an unincorporated association.

The courts ruled that in doing so, the Pioneer Society ceased to be a charitable association and had become a profit-making enterprise. They appointed the Historical Society of Southern California as trustee of all Pioneer Society assets. The Pioneer Society responded that it still existed, that it still conducted activities, and that Emma Stoltenberg had willed her funds as a personal gift to her friends, not as charity.

The California Supreme Court ruled that Emma Stoltenberg was acting charitably when she made the gift, since she had said before her death that the money was to be used for a new building. The court likewise ruled that the Pioneer Society was no longer a charity, since it reorganized after the Stoltenberg bequest (and two years before it disincorporated) by closing its membership and saying that each member had a proprietary interest in its assets. While Stoltenberg's general charitable intent had been established, the Pioneer Society was no longer a charity, and its assets were held in trust until a suitable recipient was found.[53]

## *Freme v. Maher*

*Los Angeles County Pioneer Society* is very unusual in that a court overturned a bequest because its intended recipient was no longer a charity. Usually, courts will honor gifts to specific charities even if they are failing or bankrupt. In *Freme v. Maher* (1984), a Maine court considered a bequest made in 1976 to Ricker College, a school that went bankrupt several months after the donor's death in 1978. Though Ricker College had sold its buildings and other assets, it still existed as a corporation, and the college trustees asked the court to use the bequest for scholarships for students in Aroostook County, Maine. A court-appointed referee, having established the donor's general charitable intent, sought to use *cy pres* powers to divert the estate and divide it between Bates College, Bowdoin College, and Colby College, three nearby private schools.

The court rejected the referee's request and awarded the estate to Ricker College for scholarships. The court declared that since part of the college bylaws stated that the school existed to "provide an opportunity for a college education at modest cost to great numbers of deserving youths of Aroostook County," providing scholarships was consistent with the donor's intentions, even though the college only had a corporate and not a physical existence. "A resort to *cy pres* would tend to defeat, rather than further, the general charitable intent expressed in the Knox will," the court ruled, "and application of the doctrine under the circumstances of this case was therefore error as a matter of law."[54]

### In Re Estate of Crawshaw

Chester Crawshaw, a donor in Salina, Kansas, died on May 4, 1989. In his will, he left 15 percent of his estate to the Salvation Army and 85 percent to Marymount College, to form the "Mary Anne and Chester D. Crawshaw Trust Fund" to benefit students studying nursing. Marymount College went out of business on June 30, 1989, and was succeeded by the Marymount Memorial Education Trust Fund, which awarded scholarships to students planning to be nurses.

The Salvation Army sued to get control of the entire $140,000 estate, claiming that Crawshaw's will could not be fulfilled on grounds of impractability, because Marymount College no longer existed. The Supreme Court of Kansas ruled against the Salvation Army, declaring that Crawshaw's intent was to help potential nurses. Since the Marymount Memorial Education Trust Fund awarded scholarships in many fields, the court ruled that the fund could receive the Crawshaw funds, provided they were restricted to scholarships for nurses.[55]

### Summary

The record of American courts in matters of donor intent, then, is as follows: courts tend to uphold donor intent so long as the bequest is fairly small and does not involve restrictions based on race, gender, or religion. However, once donors have severed their interests in the philanthropies they have created, either through vague charters or through the actions of trustees, courts have never restored their control.

# CONCLUSION
# What Donors Can Do

The previous chapters have examined how donor intent became a problem, how the law has addressed the issue, and how foundations, both large and small, have either followed or abandoned the wishes of their founders. This chapter seeks to draw general conclusions about the problems of donor intent and to outline a set of principles for those who wish to create a foundation of their own.

As should be evident by now, there is no iron-clad guarantee that families, friends, and associates will honor one's wishes after one's death. Far too often, the stories of great fortunes begin with heirs who agreed with a donor's intentions when alive, but end with betrayal after the donor's death. Trusted family lawyers have also helped create foundations that betray donors' wishes. John D. MacArthur's lawyer, William Kirby, helped ensure that the John D. and Catherine T. MacArthur Foundation would not fund any cause that John MacArthur supported. John D. Rockefeller's lawyer, Starr Murphy, not only ensured that Rockefeller would have little say in the Rockefeller Foundation's affairs, but that Rockefeller would be kicked out of the foundation by 1920-even though Rockefeller lived until 1937.

Consider the case of Harry John, an heir who at one time owned 47 percent of the Miller Brewing Company. In the 1950s, he transferred these shares to De Rancé, Inc., an organization that supported Catholic charities.[1] John declared that when he died De Rancé's assets would be transferred to the Southern Cross Foundation, which would fund similar charities.

Over the years, Harry John grew more eccentric. He reportedly ordered the walls of the De Rancé offices shielded against nuclear attack, and insisted that nuns applying for grants wear traditional habits. According to the *Chronicle of Philanthropy*, in 1986 two other De Rancé trustees—John's former wife, Erica John, and former philosophy professor Donald A. Gallagher—met with Archbishop Pio Laghi, the Vatican's ambassador to the United States, and J. Peter Grace, president of the Knights of Malta, a well-known lay Catholic organization. Laghi and Grace urged Erica John and Gallagher to oust Harry John.

In 1986, Wisconsin Circuit Court Judge Michael J. Barron ordered Harry John ousted from De Rancé, charging that he had engaged in such illegal activities as selling stocks to De Rancé for a profit (a transaction known as "self-dealing") as well as buying stocks personally and then having the foundation buy large amounts of the same stocks, ensuring that he illegally profited from De Rancé's investments. Not only was John ousted from De Rancé, but his credit cards were cancelled and the foundation's locks were changed.

For the rest of his life, John sued to regain control of De Rancé, charging that the punishment imposed on him was too harsh and that with most of his assets seized, he could do little to contest his far richer foes. "I had to borrow heavily to pay my legal fees, and now I am literally broke and plagued with debts," he wrote in a letter to foundations, from which he sought aid. "I am a donor turned beggar."[2]

On December 15, 1992, as John lay dying in a coma, Erica John called a meeting of the De Rancé board of directors. They voted to spend the foundation's $100 million in assets before a clause in John's will, which would transfer the assets to the Southern Cross Foundation, took effect. The De Rancé board gave $30 million to Catholic charities in Milwaukee and transferred $70 million to the Archdiocese of Milwaukee Supporting Foundation, a newly created organization whose three trustees were Archbishop of Milwaukee Rembert Weakland, Erica John, and Paula John, a daughter of Harry John. *The Chronicle of Philanthropy* reports that Harry John refused to give to the Milwaukee Archdiocese after Weakland became archbishop because he thought Weakland was too liberal. (Erica John was divorced from Harry John in 1985.)

"For anyone who takes seriously the matter of respecting donors' intent, and that donors are a central and essential element in the whole philanthropic process," foundation historian Waldemar Nielsen told the *Chronicle of Philanthropy*, "the De Rancés story has extremely damaging and dangerous implications."[3] The affair provides one rule for potential donors: *trust no one*. The histories of foundations many countless cases of children, spouses, and close family friends betraying donors' intentions. Certainly donors should ask for advice, but they should take it with a healthy dose of skepticism.

A second rule for donors is that *the donor is the best judge of his or her intentions*. People intelligent enough to acquire fortunes are smart enough to know what charities or causes they wish to support. Donors should be wary of any advisor who suggests leaving money to vague causes, or who suggests leaving no instructions on how an endowment should be used.

# CONCLUSION

But in selecting charities to receive aid, the donor should ensure that these actually want aid. This advice may seem obvious, but consider donor Robert T. Alexander, a Falls Church, Virginia investor. Alexander was graduated from the Coast Guard Academy in 1931 and later taught chemistry and physics at that school. He parlayed his investments into an estate of $1.1 million which he left to the academy as an endowment to be awarded as an annual prize of between $65,000 and $130,000 to "the graduating cadet who has attained the highest grade average in chemistry and physics."

The Coast Guard Academy objected, charging that such a large award would encourage cheating and corruption. A U.S. District Court judge agreed, and ordered the funds diverted to provide a scholarship for a graduate student planning to teach science at the academy, for guest science lecturers, and for grants supporting student science research projects. Five years after Alexander's death, the funds were still tied up in court and unused.[4] It is unclear whether the Coast Guard Academy was ever consulted about Alexander's plans, but if Alexander had talked with the institution he loved, he might have devised a plan that would have been more acceptable.

Alexander's case is not unusual. Donors often encounter unforeseen problems in preparing their wills. Consider George Bernard Shaw, who originally wanted to leave the funds from his estate to promote a simplified spelling scheme, which would replace complex English words with their phonetic equivalents (e.g., "enuf" rather than "enough"). The courts ruled that this was unacceptable, and ordered the funds diverted to a set of residual legatees Shaw had selected, including the British Museum, which at the time controlled Britain's national library. In 1973, the British Library seceded from the British Museum, a move that, in America, would be equivalent to the Library of Congress seceding from the Smithsonian Institution. Although Shaw declared that he left the British Museum money "in acknowledgement of the incalculable value to me of my daily resort to the Reading Room of that institution at the beginning of my career," when the library and museum split, the museum kept the Shaw funds, and spent both capital and interest.[5]

In a letter to the *Times Literary Supplement,* British Museum director R.G.W. Anderson noted that Shaw imposed no restrictions on how the funds from his estate should be used; therefore, "there is no legal obligation to spend the Shaw money in any particular way." In Anderson's view, the only obligation the British Museum had was "to spend the money in the way which most effectively promotes its own purposes."[6]

Anderson is legally correct. Whenever donors choose to relinquish their intentions by leaving wills with no restrictions, the law states that the recipients are under no moral or legal obligation to follow the donors' wishes or philosophy. Should the presidents of the Ford or Rockefeller foundations decide that the best use of their endowments is to convert the funds into cash, open the office windows, and shower the passing crowd with money, there is nothing that the Ford or Rockefeller families—or anyone—can do to stop them.

Moreover, any attempt to alter the law to allow third parties to contest foundation indentures would be unwise. The law of donor intent, refined over seven centuries, works reasonably well. To weaken or alter cy pres any further would open the door to those wishing to use estates only for "socially responsible" (i.e., establishment liberal) philanthropy. Attempts to give third parties legal standing in donor intent cases would likely do more harm than good.

Third parties do have a role to play in donor intent cases by advising heirs and executors. They should be entitled to file *amicus curiae* briefs and to reassure donors and their heirs that donor intent will be properly fulfilled. Above all, third parties can act as watchdogs to urge that donor intent is observed. Morally, foundation officers should have a decent respect for the dead and give grants that are consistent with their founders' views. While it is natural for heirs to rebel against their parents, and for foundations to act in ways their founders would have abhorred, such tendencies are not immutable. The story of The JM Foundation shows how Milbank family traditions ensured that Jeremiah Milbank's wishes endured beyond one generation.

What can donors do to ensure that their intentions are preserved? The best answer combines the timeless wisdom of Andrew Carnegie, Julius Rosenwald, and James Buchanan Duke. Likewise, the advice Andrew Carnegie gave in "The Gospel of Wealth" is still sound. Donors can ensure that their wishes are fulfilled by spending funds on projects they prefer within their lifetimes. Living donors are better able to ensure that their fortunes are appropriately spent than dead ones.

To preserve donor intent, donors should make their wills as specific as possible. The fundamental problem of philanthropy today is not "dead hand" control. It is donors who meekly follow prevailing wisdom and leave their fortunes to professionals who spend the money

# CONCLUSION

on causes *they* like—which are usually not the causes preferred by the donors. Philanthropy needs bolder donors who are unafraid to assert their wills. The more strongly worded and precise the will, the less likely that a donor's wishes will be subverted by future generations. The case of the Duke Endowment shows how one donor left very precise instructions that ensured that his wishes are still being followed 70 years after his death.

Yet donors should realize that the longer a foundation exists, the less likely it is to heed donor intent. This is due in part to fading memories, as friends and associates of donors die and are succeeded by people who did not personally know the founder. But the fading of donor intent is also a consequence of the professionalization of philanthropy, as far too many program directors and grants officers wrongly believe that their views are more important than donors'.

The longer-lived the endowment, the more likely that donor intent will be undermined. Therefore, donors should follow Julius Rosenwald's advice and create foundations that have a term limit, probably no more than 25 years from the donor's death. Support for term-limited foundations is not confined to any ideology. Both Julius Rosenwald, who invented the idea of limiting the life of foundations, and Rosenwald's grandson, Philip Stern, who used his grandfather's ideas in setting a date for terminating his own foundation, were both liberals. Another prominent liberal who created a term-limited foundation was Max Fleischmann, the yeast heir (and *New Yorker* backer) whose Max Fleischmann Foundation expired in 1980, 20 years after the death of Fleischmann's widow.

The best known term-limited foundation, however, is the conservative John M. Olin Foundation. In 1991, Olin grant recipients were informed that the foundation would spend itself out of existence by the end of the decade. after the death of Olin's widow, Evelyn Olin. In an interview with the *Chronicle of Philanthropy,* Olin Foundation executive director James Pierson said that John M. Olin, before his death in 1982, "said many times that he did not want this foundation to exist in perpetuity. He feared that, over the long haul, a new generation unknown to him would come on the scene and bend the foundation to a different direction." Olin's fears, Pierson added. were in part caused by Henry Ford II's departure as a Ford Foundation trustee in 1977.[7]

Donors should realize that creating a perpetual endowment will not ensure that they will be revered forever. John Harvard's *name* may be known because he founded Harvard University, but only antiquarians know anything about Harvard's life or achievements. Henry Ford's presence in the Ford Foundation is little more than a photograph on a wall. And it's unlikely that anyone at the Russell Sage Foundation knows, or even cares, about Russell Sage.

If more foundations had fixed spans of existence, the nonprofit world might become more entrepreneurial. Corporations are not assured immortality; they rise or fall as demand for their products changes. As late as the 1950s, such meatpackers as Swift and Armour were among America's largest businesses. Today, these names survive only as subsidiaries of more successful firms. Likewise, if big foundations were required to terminate, they might be superseded by foundations better able to meet the challenges of our time.

In conclusion, donors should give as much money as possible during their lifetimes. If they wish to leave their wealth to foundations, they should limit their lives. They should leave explicit instructions for using bequests, and act on the premise that their wills will be challenged in court by heirs or other parties who will want the money for themselves. Lastly, they should be very skeptical of those who argue that the ideas, principles, and passions of donors are unimportant.

# Notes

## Introduction
1. Cited in Frederick T. Gates, *Chapters in My Life* (New York: Free Press, 1977), p. 212.
2. *Ibid.*, p. 265.
3. Barry D. Karl and Stanley N. Katz, "The American Private Philanthropic Foundation and the Public Sphere 1890-1930," *Minerva*, Summer 1981.
4. Kathleen D. McCarthy, "The Gospel of Wealth: American Giving in Theory and Practice," in Richard Magat, ed., *Philanthropic Giving: Studies in Varieties and Goals* (New York: Oxford University Press, 1989), p. 58.
5. Marvin Olasky, *The Tragedy of American Compassion* (Washington, D.C.: Regnery Gateway, 1992), p. 127.
6. Cited in John M. Glenn, Lilian Brandt, and F. Emerson Andrews, *Russell Sage Foundation, 1907-1946* (New York: Russell Sage Foundation, 1947), p. 6.
7. Joseph J. Thorndike, Jr., *The Very Rich: A History of Wealth* (New York: American Heritage, 1976), p. 337.
8. *The Russell Sage Foundation, 1907-1946, op. cit.*, p. 7.
9. *Ibid.*, p. 13.
10. *Ibid.*, p. 26.
11. Scott M. Cutlip, *Fund Raising in the United States: Its Role in American Philanthropy* (New Brunswick, N.J.: Transaction, 1990), pp. 206-207.
12. By 1907, Ward and Pierce's whirlwind techniques had been successfully used in Duluth, Dallas, Denver, and St. Paul. Ward and Pierce even went to Australia and New Zealand, but found little enthusiasm for their high-pressure salesmanship. "The smart Yankee 'organizing' secretary of the Victorian Y.M.C.A. is growing monotonous with his glorious schemes for collecting cash," the Sydney, Australia *Bulletin* editorialized in August 1907, adding that however worthy the Y.M.C.A. might be, "it isn't good enough to justify the eternal importunities of a begging secretary, who presumably draws commission on his 'order' in addition to a fat salary." *Ibid.*, p. 249.
13. *Ibid.*, p. 116.
14. Such appeals, however, were not new. When America's first great philanthropist, Stephen Girard, began making major donations in the 1820s, he was besieged with charitable requests. After giving to Philadelphia's St. Mary's Catholic Church, other churches in Boston, Cincinnati, Annapolis, Maryland, and Perryville, Missouri begged for loans. Yale University sought a new building; Dickinson College wanted an endowed chair in chemistry; and a man with the pseudonym "Amicus Patriae" insisted that with $800,000 he could start a "University of the United States." Someone from Ohio also wrote Girard, claiming that "the Supreme Being having revealed himself to me for the execution of His purposes on the earth directs me to call on you in His name for $25,000. He will demonstrate His concern in the matter by showing you what must be considered a miracle. For that purpose, when you have perused this letter you must lay it on a table and the Supreme Being will restrain you or deprive you of the power of touching it for one minute by the exercise of His omnipotency." Girard gave the alleged ambassador from God no money. Harry Emerson Wildes, *Lonely Midas: The Story of Stephen Girard* (New York: Farrar and Rinehart, 1943), pp. 267-271.
15. The study was conducted by the New York Bureau of Municipal Research. Most grantseekers assured Mrs. Harriman that she would never miss the money. "Please

do sit down and write a check for one million dollars," one woman wrote. "It will look so small that you will see you'll never miss the sum and make me famous and fortunate." William H. Allen, *Modern Philanthropy: A Study of Efficient Appealing and Giving* (New York: Dodd, Mead, 1912), p. 4. While most recipients wanted unconditional loans or grants, 216 people wanted to sell Mrs. Harriman a total of $8,000,000 in goods, including a farm, magazine subscriptions, old coins, a fire escape, a "crazy patch silk quilt," and a "horn that was taken from the head of a steer that was eat [sic] for breakfast by a company of Virginia soldiers." *Ibid.*, p. 29.

16. *Ibid.*, pp. 189-190.
17. *Ibid.*, p. 203.
18. *Ibid.*, p. 204.
19. *Ibid.*, p. 204.
20. *Ibid.*, p. 290.
21. Frederick Goff, a banker who created the Cleveland Foundation, was so preoccupied with the problem of the dead hand, his wife recalled, that his youngest child once "asked in a frightened tone to be told where it was and what it did." Diana Tittle, "Cleveland's Best Idea," *Foundation News,* September/October 1989.
22. Walter Greenough, "The Dead Hand Harnessed: The Significance of Community Trusts," *Scribner's Magazine,* December 1923.

## Chapter I-The Rockefeller Legacy

1. Herbert N. Casson, "The Rockefeller Foundation," *Munsey's Magazine,* June 1910.
2. John Ensor Harr and Peter J. Johnson, *The Rockefeller Century* (New York: Scribner's, 1988), pp. 24-25.
3. Frederick T. Gates, *Chapters in My Life* (New York: Free Press, 1977), p. 161.
4. Rockefeller was such a prominent donor to the school that when he visited in 1896, he was serenaded by undergraduates, who shouted, "John D. Rockefeller, wonderful man is he/Gives all his spare change to the U. of C." Cited in Gerald Jonas, *The Circuit Riders: Rockefeller Money and the Rise of Modern Science* (New York: Norton, 1989), p. 32.
5. *Ibid.*, p. 27.
6. Ron Chernow, *Titan: The Life of John D. Rockefeller, Sr.* (New York: Random House, 1998), p. 468.
7. *Ibid.*, p. 469.
8. Peter Collier and David Horowitz, *The Rockefellers: An American Dynasty* (New York: Holt, Rinehart, and Winston, 1976), p. 3.
9. *Ibid.*, p. 3. Capitalization original. The cartoon was reprinted in the April 13, 1905 *Independent.*
10. James L. Barton, "The Correspondence on the Rockefeller Gift," *Independent,* April 13, 1905.
11. According to historian Ray Eldon Hiebert, in 1884 the president of the University of Rochester wrote to Rockefeller saying that he was writing a paper that would show how Rockefeller's consolidation of the oil industry was resulting in better quality goods at lower prices. Rockefeller refused to cooperate, fearing that the president's reputation would be harmed.

That same year, a woman sought an interview with Rockefeller for articles she was writing on prominent Americans of the day. She believed "it is a good thing for the world to know that the President of the great Standard Oil Company is a Christian, a gentleman, an earnest temperate man, and generous in all good works." (Emphasis original.) Rockefeller's response was that "in accordance with a decision reached some time hence, I have declined to allow anything to be written in the manner as suggested, but I appreciate the kindness of my friends desiring to say something favorable to me and that might be helpful to others." Cited in Ray Eldon Hiebert, *Courtier to the Crowd: The Story of Ivy Lee and the Development of Public Relations* (Ames, Iowa: Iowa State University Press, 1966), pp. 110-111.

After Ida Tarbell published the *History of the Standard Oil Company* in 1904, Standard Oil hired a public-relations specialist. But Rockefeller, who had retired from the company in 1897, did nothing. As a result, notes Hiebert, "few people thought of Rockefeller as a human being, but only as a billion-dollar machine that crushed everything in its path. He was pictured as a stingy old man who would step on anyone to make another dollar. He was commonly described as morose and mean, fearful of being attacked by people he had ruined, and ringed by bodyguards. When he gave sizable sums to church or charity, it became 'tainted money' with which he was seeking to salve his guilty conscience." *Ibid.*, p. 110.

12. Cited in Raymond B. Fosdick, *John D. Rockefeller, Jr: A Portrait* (New York: Harper, 1956), p. 110. In his memoirs, Gates says that by 1905, "I came to disbelieve altogether in the peculiar tenets of the Baptist Church, or in the doctrines generally held by orthodox Protestants, and to reject the inspiration and inerrancy of the Scriptures. . . . My religion became, and still is, simply the service of humanity in the Spirit of Jesus. It is the religion of Jesus, of science, and of evolution alike. Creeds, churches, sects, religious organizations, and all the agencies of civilization are to be valued and used only as they are agents to the service of humanity on earth." Gates, *op. cit.*, pp. 206-207.

Rockefeller's fortune dramatically increased in the late 1890s, after gasoline became a common fuel for cars instead of a useless byproduct of refining. An 1897 editorial in the *New Era* calculated that Rockefeller's wealth was increasing at the rate of $55 million a month, equivalent to $972 million today. Ron Chernow estimates that Rockefeller's wealth increased tenfold after 1897. Chernow, *op. cit.*, p. 397.

13. Gates, *op. cit.*, p. 208.
14. *Ibid.*, p. 209.
15. Harr and Johnson, *op. cit.*, p. 83.
16. Allan Nevins, *Study in Power.: John D. Rockefeller, Industrialist and Philanthropist* (Westport, Connecticut: Easton Press, 1989), p. 308.
17. Raymond B. Fosdick, *The Story of the Rockefeller Foundation* (New Brunswick, New Jersey: Transaction, 1989), p. 15.
18. Gates, *op. cit.*, p. 234.
19. Fosdick, *Rockefeller Foundation*, p. 16.
20. *Ibid.*, p. 17.
21. Henry F. Pringle, *The Life and Times of William Howard Taft* (New York: Farrar and Rinehart, 1939), pp. 662-663. Other prominent Americans also joined in opposing the Rockefeller charter, including former president Theodore Roosevelt, who said that "of course no amount of charities in spending such fortunes can compensate in any way for the misconduct in acquiring them." American Federation of Labor president Samuel Gompers charged that the most noble act John D. Rockefeller could do was to create a foundation to "help other people see in time how they can keep from being like him." Collier and Horowitz, op. cit., p. 64.

22. Chernow, *op. cit.,* p. 565.
23. Barry Karl and Stanley Katz, "Foundations and Ruling Class Elites," *Daedalus,* Winter 1987.
24. *Ibid.*
25. Robert E. Kohler, P*artners in Science: Foundations and Natural Scientists 1900-1945* (Chicago: University of Chicago Press, 1991), p. 47.
26. Priscilla Long, "Ludlow Massacre," in Mari Jo Buhle, Paul Buhle, and Dan Georgakas, *Encyclopedia of the American Left* (New York: Garland, 1990), p. 441.
27. According to Mackenzie King, "Mother" Jones thought that John D. Rockefeller, Jr. was "a man with a thin, hard jaw, who kept his teeth and mouth firmly compressed and his hands clutching out for money all the time." F.A. McGregor, *The Fall and Rise of Mackenzie King, 1911-1919* (Toronto: Macmillan of Canada, 1962), p. 137.
28. "In accepting I had to consider that I was prejudicing my political future for all time to come," King wrote to John D. Rockefeller, Jr. "My battles henceforth would not be with the political issues but against the Rockefeller prejudice.... I would not be harangued against as a Liberal politician but as a `Standard Oil man.' Still I felt I was not going to be governed by prejudice, and had decided on this basis." Harr and Johnson, *op. cit.,* p. 135.
29. H. M. Gitleman, *Legacy of the Ludlow Massacre: A Chapter in American Industrial Relations* (Philadelphia: University of Pennsylvania Press, 1988), p. 222.
30. Graham Adams, Jr., *Age of Industrial Violence, 1910-15: The Activities and Findings of the United States Commission on Industrial Relations* (New York: Columbia University Press, 1966), p. 162.
31. *Ibid.,* p. 163.
32. Karl and Katz, "American Private Philanthropic Foundations."
33. McGregor, *op. cit.,* p. 139.
34. Kohler, *op. cit.,* p. 47.
35. *Ibid.,* p. 47.
36. Albert F. Schenkel, *The Rich Man and the Kingdom: John D. Rockefeller, Jr., and the Protestant Establishment* (Minneapolis: Fortress Press, 1995), pp. 59-60.
37. After Mackenzie King returned to Canadian politics in 1917, Harr and Johnson note that John D. Rockefeller, Jr. would never again "ask the Foundation to become involved in an activity that had anything to do with a personal or family problem, or for that matter with any highly personal preference of his own as to where money should go." Harr and Johnson, *op. cit.,* p. 145.
38. *Ibid.,* p. 146.
39. *Ibid.,* p. 146.
40. Karl and Katz, "Foundations and Ruling Class Elites."
41. Harr and Johnson, *op. cit.,* p. 147.
42. Edwin R. Embree and Julia Waxman, *Investment in People: The Story of the Julius Rosenwald Fund* (New York: Harper, 1949), p. 31.
43. Julius Rosenwald, "Principles of Public Giving" *Atlantic Monthly,* May 1929.
44. Rosenwald, "The Trend Away From Perpetuities," *Atlantic Monthly,* December 1930.
45. Rosenwald's views did, however, influence his family, including his grandson, Philip Stern (1926-1992), whose Stern Family Fund has been a leading source of grants

*Notes*

for liberal nonprofits. Stern's will declares that the Stern Family Fund, which as of January 1994 had assets of $2 million, must spend its endowment by 2017. In an interview, Stern's son David explained that his father imposed this restriction because Philip Stern did "not want the dead hand to rule." Juliet Eilperin, "Phil Stern: Muckraking With Dollars," *Washington City Paper,* January 28, 1994.

For more information about Julius Rosenwald's views about perpetuity, see Martin Morse Wooster, *Should Foundations Live Forever? The Question of Perpetuity* (Capital Research Center, 1998).

## Chapter II–Undermining Donor Intent

**The Ford Foundation**

1. Cited in Harry S. Ashmore, *Unseasonable Truths: The Life of Robert Maynard Hutchins* (Boston: Little, Brown, 1989), p. 317.
2. Waldemar A. Nielsen, "The Donor's Role in Donor Intent," in *Donor Intent* (Indianapolis: Philanthropy Roundtable, 1993), p. 19.
3. William Greenleaf, *From These Beginnings: The Early Philanthropy of Henry and Edsel Ford, 1911-1936* (Detroit: Wayne State University Press, 1964), p. 7.
4. George Bernard Shaw, "Socialism for Millionaires," *Contemporary Review*, February 1896.
5. Ibid.
6. Ibid.
7. Ford N. Bryan, *Clara: Mrs. Henry Ford* (Dearborn, Michigan: Ford Books, 2001), p. 113-114.
8. Greenleaf notes that Ford even received requests from peasants and factory workers in the Soviet Union, who "asked whether it was true that Ford was wealthier than any of the Czars." Greenleaf, *op. cit.*, p. 9.
9. Henry Ford with Samuel Crowther, *Today and Tomorrow* (Cambridge, Massachusetts: Productivity Press, 1978), pp. 179-180.
10. Greenleaf, *op. cit.*, p. 15.
11. By 1942, Ford Motor had 11,163 disabled employees, including 1,208 blind or partially blind employees, 322 with "organic heart ailments," 260 with one crippled arm, 157 with one leg amputated, and 111 deaf mutes. Edsel Ford, "Why We Employ Aged and Handicapped Workers," *Saturday Evening Post,* July 6, 1943.
12. David L. Lewis, *The Public Image of Henry Ford: An American Folk Hero and His Company* (Detroit: Wayne State University Press, 1976), p. 120.
13. Henry Ford with Samuel Crowther, *Moving Forward* (Garden City, New York: Doubleday, Doran, 1930), pp. 97-98.
14. Greenleaf, *op. cit.,* p. 126.
15. "Ford Calls Charity a Barbarous Thing," *New York Times,* May 30, 1932.
16. Ibid.
17. Judson C. Welliver, "Mr. Ford Is Interviewed," *American Review of Reviews,* September 1925.
18. Garet Garrett, *The Wild Wheel: The World of Henry Ford* (London: Cresset Press, 1952), pp. 153-154.

19. Allan Nevins and Frank Ernest Hill, *Ford: Decline and Renewal*, 1933-1962 (New York: Scribner's, 1963), p. 411.
20. Greenleaf, *op. cit.*, p. 185.
21. Nevins and Hill, *op. cit.*, p. 410.
22. Greenleaf, *op. cit.*, p. 188.
23. Lally Weymouth, "Foundation Woes: The Saga of Henry Ford II, Part II," *New York Times Magazine,* March 12, 1978.
24. *Tax-Exempt Foundations: Hearings Before the Select Committee to Investigate Tax-Exempt Foundations and Comparable Organizations* (Washington, D.C.: Government Printing Office, 1952), pp. 221-222.
25. See Kate O'Neill, "Model Ts and Do-Si-Dos: Henry Ford and Traditional Dancing," *Michigan History,* January/February 2001. According to O'Neill, lovers of old dances have revived them in recent years using facilities built by Henry Ford.
26. Thomas C. Reeves, *Freedom and the Foundation: The Fund for the Republic in the Era of McCarthyism* (New York: Knopf, 1969), p. 284. In a 1978 interview with Lally Weymouth, Forest Marden, a long-time friend and associate of Henry Ford II, said that in its early years, the Ford Foundation's chief asset was some land in Dearborn, Michigan which had some apartment buildings. "To everyone in Dearborn then," Marden said, "that land was the Ford Foundation." Weymouth, *op. cit.*
27. Francis X. Sutton, "The Ford Foundation: The Early Years," *Daedalus.* Winter 1987.
28. *Ibid.*
29. Cited in Sidney Hyman, *The Lives of William Benton* (Chicago: University of Chicago Press, 1969), p. 426.
30. Ashmore, *op. cit.*, p. 323.
31. *Ibid.*, p. 330.
32. *Ibid.*, pp. 330-331.
33. Weymouth, *op. cit.*
34. *The Fulton Lewis Jr. Report on the Fund for the Republic* (Washington: Special Reports, 1955), p. 9.
35. Weymouth, *op. cit.*
36. Leonard Silk and Mark Silk, *The American Establishment* (New York: Basic Books, 1980, p. 129.
37. Reeves, *op. cit.*, p. 332.
38. *Ibid.*, p. 337.
39. William F. Buckley, Jr., "A Letter to Mr. Henry Ford," *National Review,* December 14, 1955.
40. "Ford's Letter on Fund," *New York Herald Tribune,* December 8, 1955.
41. "Robert Hutchins's Platonic Grove," *The Nation,* January 30, 1988. Ferry later became a philanthropist. The *Washington Post* reported in October 1993 that he was a "major benefactor" of the radical Institute for Policy Studies, and was honored by IPS during that organization's 30th anniversary. Hutchins, observed *American Scholar* editor Joseph Epstein, "was never able to attract truly serious people permanently to the Center; despite everything the place offered in the way of luxury and the little it asked for in the way of work, it must have resembled nothing so much as an endless talk show to which no one was tuned in." Joseph Epstein, "The Sad Story of the Boy Wonder," *Commentary,* March 1990.

42. This confusion between the Ford Motor Company and Ford Foundation continued even after the foundation began selling Ford Foundation stock. When the foundation gave a grant in the early 1960s to the Center for Community Change, a nonprofit headed by United Farm Workers organizer Cesar Chavez, California farm owners announced a boycott of Ford trucks. An early 1960s grant to the Mozambique Institute, a nonprofit branch of the Mozambiquean Marxist-Leninist revolutionary group FRELIMO, prompted a Portuguese boycott of Ford Motor and some friction in U.S. negotiations over military bases in the Azores Islands. Peter D. Bell, "The Ford Foundation as a Transnational Actor," *international Organization*, Summer 1971.
43. Joe McCarthy, "The Ford Family," *Holiday*, September 1957.
44. Silk and Silk, *op. cit.*, p. 131.
45. *Ibid.*, p. 131.
46. William L. Cary and Craig B. Bright, *The Law and the Lore of Endowment Funds* (New York: Ford Foundation, 1969), p. 17.
47. Peter Collier and David Horowitz, *The Fords: An American Epic* (New York: Summit, 1987), pp. 363-364.
48. These "Kennedy grants" were quite controversial at the time; Senator John J. Williams (R-Delaware) even introduced a bill that would have banned any foundation grants for two years to government officials who left their posts. Senator Albert Gore, Sr. (D-Tennessee) argued that supporters of defeated Democratic presidential contender Eugene McCarthy were also entitled to aid, since "they were not only broken-hearted but broken-nosed. They were disappointed and beaten up." See Joseph Goulden, *The Money Givers* (New York: Random House, 1971), pp. 278-279.

    In a 1989 interview, Peter Edelman was still defensive about receiving a Kennedy grant. Edelman told *Foundation News'* Roger M. Williams that the grants were "very constructive and important, something the Ford people should be proud of. Instead, they put their tails between their legs and said, 'I'm very sorry.'" Roger M. Williams, "To Each His Own," *Foundation News*, May/June 1989.
49. Weymouth, *op. cit.*
50. Collier and Horowitz, *op. cit.*, p. 397.
51. In 1966, the value of the Ford Foundation's investments was $3,051,000,000; by 1977, it had fallen to $2,091,100,000.
52. Waldemar A. Nielsen, *The Golden Donors: A New Anatomy of the Great Foundations* (New York: Dutton, 1985), p. 70. Despite this massive spending spree, the Ford Foundation managed to remain the nation's largest until 1998, when it was superseded by the Lilly Endowment, which in 1998 had $12.7 billion in assets compared to the Ford Foundation's $9.4 billion. Judith Havemann, "Lilly Endowment Is Nation's Top Giver," *Washington Post*, February 15, 1998.
53. Walter Hayes, *Henry: A Life of Henry Ford II* (New York: Grove Weidenfeld, 1990), p. 56.
54. "Excerpts from Henry Ford Letter," *New York Times*, January 12, 1977.
55. Weymouth, *op. cit.*
56. *Ibid.*
57. Jon Pepper, "The Henry Ford II Tapes: Ford Was Main Catalyst for Building Renaissance Center," *Detroit News*, September 21, 1994.

*Notes*

58. Hayes, *op. cit.*, p. 56.
59. Ian Wilhelm, "Michigan Asks Ford Foundation to Show It Is Following Donor's Intentions," *Chronicle of Philanthropy,* April 27, 2006.
60. Daniel Howes, "Bill Challenges Ford Foundation," *Detroit News,* June 7, 2006. See also Ian Wilhelm, "Bill Triggered by Ford Foundation Would Require Funds Set Up in Michigan to Direct Half of Giving Within State," *Chronicle of Philanthropy,* June 14, 2006.
61. Thomas Bray, "Raiding the Ford Foundation," *New York Sun,* June 14, 2006.
62. John J. Miller, "Charity Begins at Home, But Must it Stay There?" *New York Times,* May 15, 2006.

## The Carnegie Corporation of New York

1. Andrew Carnegie, *Triumphant Democracy, or, Fifty Years' March of the Republic* (New York: Scribner's, 1886), p. 479.
2. *Ibid.,* p. 169.
3. Aileen McLaughlin, "Prenuptial Reveals Carnegie's True Plan," *Glasgow Sunday Herald,* May 1, 2005.
4. Andrew Carnegie, "The Gospel of Wealth," in Joseph Frazier Wall, ed., *The Andrew Carnegie Reader* (Pittsburgh: University of Pittsburgh, 1992), p. 133.
5. *Ibid.,* p. 135.
6. *Ibid.,* p. 135.
7. *Ibid.,* p. 139.
8. Andrew Carnegie, "The Best Use of Wealth," in Burton J. Hendrick, ed., *Miscellaneous Writing of Andrew Carnegie* (Garden City, New York: Doubleday, 1933), p. 206.
9. *Ibid.,* p. 207.
10. Frederick Lynch, *Personal Recollections of Andrew Carnegie* (New York: Fleming H. Revell, 1920), p. 135.
11. *Ibid.,* p. 135.
12. William C. Greenough, *It's My Retirement Money, Take Good Care of It: The TIAA-CREF Story* (Homewood, Illinois: Irwin, 1990), p. 15.
13. Information provided in emails from Gay Clyburn and Ann Whitfield of the Carnegie Foundation for the Advancement of Teaching, July 24, 2006.
14. Joseph Frazier Wall, *Andrew Carnegie* (Pittsburgh: University of Pittsburgh Press, 1989), p. 881. Historian Larry Fabian describes how one university president courted Carnegie during this period. "I'll tell you how I felt," the president said. "I felt like backing him up in the corner and saying, 'Give it!' And then I kept saying to myself, 'It's his money, it's his money. Larry L. Fabian, *Andrew Carnegie's Peace Endowment: The Tycoon, the President, and their Bargain of 1910* (Washington: Carnegie Endowment for International Peace, 1985), p. 22.
15. Michael Rosenthal, *Nicholas Miraculous: The Amazing Career of the Redoubtable Dr. Nicholas Murray Butler* (New York: Farrar, Straus, and Giroux, 2006), p. 161-62.
16. *Ibid.,* p. 162.
17. For Edwin Ginn's role in the creation of the World Peace Foundation, see Richard

*Notes*

Marchand, *The American Peace Movement and Social Reform, 1898-1918* (Ann Arbor, Michigan: University of Michigan Press, 1972), p. 99-103. The World Peace Foundation is now controlled by Harvard University.

18. Rosenthal, *op. cit.,* p. 167.
19. Fabian, *op. cit.,* p. 41. Carnegie asked Secretary of State Philander Knox to serve on the new endowment's board, and at one point inserted a clause (later removed) saying that the Carnegie Endowment for International Peace could contribute to political parties if "one party ever stand for measures leading to international peace and the other against this, contributions be made to the former."
20. Philip C. Jessup, *Elihu Root: Volume 2, 1905-1937* (New York: Dodd, Mead, 1938), p. 491.
21. Robert M. Lester, *Forty Years of Carnegie Giving* (New York: Scribner's, 1941), p. 166.
22. Wall, *op. cit.,* p. 883.
23. Burton J. Hendrick, *The Life of Andrew Carnegie* (New York: Harper, 1932), Vol. II, p. 351. Philip C. Jessup observes that Carnegie, while he obeyed Root's decision, dislike it intensely. Root, Jessup wrote, observed many years later that "Carnegie had a distrust of lawyers, regarding them as people who tried to prevent him from doing what he wanted to do." Jessup, *op. cit.,* p. 491.
24. Robert E. Kohler, *Partners in Science: Foundations and Natural Scientists, 1900-1945* (Chicago: University of Chicago Press, 1991), p. 56.
25. Theodore Jones, *Carnegie Libraries Across America: A Public Legacy* (New York: Preservation Press / Wiley, 1997, p. 101.
26. Alvin Johnson, *Pioneer's Progress: An Autobiography* (New York: Viking, 1952), p. 236.
27. *Ibid.,* pp. 236-237.
28. *Ibid.,* p. 238.
29. *Ibid.,* p. 239.
30. Jones, *op. cit.,* p. 102.
31. *Ibid.,* p. 66.
32. *Ibid.,* p. 68.
33. According to a 1965 profile in *Fortune,* Gardner became president of the Carnegie Corporation as a result of connections he made serving in the Office of Strategic Services during World War II. Robert P. Elson, "An 'In' Man for the Cabinet," *Fortune,* November 1965.
34. Waldemar Nielsen, *The Golden Donors: A New Anatomy of the Great Foundations* (New York: Dutton, 1985), p. 134.
35. I discuss the role the Carnegie Corporation played in creating public television in Martin Morse Wooster, *Great Philanthropic Mistakes* (Washington, D.C.: Hudson Institute, 2006).
36. Ellen Condliffe Lagemann, *The Politics of Knowledge* (Middletown, Connecticut: Wesleyan University Press, 1989), p. 242.
37. Paul Desruisseaux, "What Would Andrew Carnegie Think About How His Money Is Used Today?" *Chronicle of Higher Education,* August 7, 1985. See also Paul Desruisseaux, "Celebrating the Legacy of Andrew Carnegie's Philanthropy," *Chronicle of Higher Education,* September 11, 1985.
38. *New York Times,* January 22, 1993.
39. Claudia Dreifus, "It Is Better to Give than to Receive," *New York Trees Magazine,* December 14, 1997.

40. Patrick Reilly, "Replacing Welfare with Child Care: Foundations Lay Groundwork for Clinton's Costly Proposals," *Foundation Watch,* June 1998.
41. Debra Viadero, "Carnegie Corp. Repeats History With New Library Grants," *Education Week,* June 16, 1999.
42. Tamar Lewin, "Leading Philanthropists Get Carnegie Medals," *New York Times,* December 11, 2001. I discuss Gregorian's role as philanthropic adviser to Walter Annenberg in *Great Philanthropic Mistakes.* For an extended interview with Gregorian, see "A Conversation with Vartan Gregorian," *Humanities,* September 2003.

## John D. and Catherine T. MacArthur Foundation

1. T.A. Wise, "The Incorrigible John MacArthur," *Fortune,* July 1958.
2. William Hoffman, *The Stockholder* (New York: Lyle Stuart, 1969), p. 19.
3. "John D. MacArthur of Bankers Life and Casualty," *Nation's Business,* July 1974.
4. Lewis Beman, "The Last Billionaires," *Fortune,* November 1976.
5. Joshua Muravchik, "MacArthur's Millions," *American Spectator,* January 1992.
6. Anne Matthews, "The MacArthur Truffle Hunt," *New York Times Magazine,* June 7, 1992.
7. Richard T. Griffin, "The Feuding MacArthurs," *New York Times,* January 23, 1977.
8. Phyllis Berman with R. Lee Sullivan, "Limousine Liberal," *Forbes,* October 26, 1992. In January 1994, the J. Roderick MacArthur Foundation announced that it was shrinking. Its long-time president, Lance Lindblom, was not replaced when he departed for a professorship at DePaul University, and the foundation's staff was cut from four to one. In addition, the foundation announced that it would no longer consider unsolicited grants, and with the exception of three organizations fighting the death penalty and censorship, would be devoted to the personal philanthropic interests of Rod MacArthur's children, Solange, Gregoire, and John R. "Rick" MacArthur. Charles Storch, "Foundation Shrinks Its Circle of Recipients," *Chicago Tribune,* January 21, 1994.
9. Jon Nordheimer, "Florida's Accessible Billionaire," *New York Times,* June 3, 1973.
10. Ruth Dean, "The MacArthur Foundation," *Foundation News,* March/April 1982.
11. According to T.A. Wise, MacArthur was "thrifty to the point that would embarrass a professional Scot." MacArthur's frugal habits included saving half-smoked cigarettes and refusing collect calls-and then returning them collect. According to Wise, someone once burnt the baked beans at a Bankers Life picnic. The frugal MacArthur showed up next day in the staff cafeteria with a syrup that he claimed would make burnt baked beans tasty. Wise, *op. cit.*

    By 1976, MacArthur looked so poor that Lewis Beman declared that he "looks less like a billionaire than a retired postal clerk whose Social Security check was being stretched too thin." At the time of the interview, the windows in MacArthur's five-year-old Cadillac were broken, and MacArthur's apartment "is furnished with odds and ends that might have been picked up decades ago." Beman, *op. cit.*
12. Brenda Shapiro, "Shaking the Foundation," *Chicago,* June 1992.
13. Muravchik, *op. cit.*
14. Shapiro, *op. cit.*
15. Muravchik, *op. cit.*
16. Shapiro, *op. cit.*

17. See Martin Morse Wooster, "The MacArthur Fellowships: The Oscars of the Multicultural Elite," *Philanthropy Culture, & Society*, January 1996.
18. Matthews, *op. cit.*
19. Denise Shekerjian, *Uncommon Genius: How Great Ideas Are Born* (New York:Viking, 1990), pp. 97-98.
20. Liz McMillen, "MacArthur Foundation Expected to Review, and Perhaps Revise, Its Grants Program," *Chronicle of Higher Education*, March 8, 1989. However, Daniel Socolow, who became director of the MacArthur Fellows Program in 1997, said that he would like to give MacArthur Fellowships to entrepreneurs. "I'd like to see more entrepreneurs (winning)," Socolow said. "We wouldn't fund Steve Jobs when he had Apple Computer, but maybe when he was in his garage playing with a strange box." Dyan Machan, "Venture Capital for Geniuses," *Forbes*, February 23, 1998.
21. John Leo, "MacArthur Awards More About Gender Than Genius," *New Orleans Times-Picayune*, June 28, 1995. I discuss the MacArthur Fellows program at greater length in *Great Philanthropic Mistakes*.
22. Mark Scheffler, "Genius Grants Don't Pay Off in Literature," *Crain's Chicago Business*, January 24, 2005.
23. Paul Deruisseaux, "MacArthur Fundation Seeks a Narrower, Deeper Focus," *Chronicle of Higher Education*, July 14, 2000.
24. For details of recent MacArthur Foundation grants, see Martin Morse Wooster, "The MacArthur Foundation," *Foundation Watch*, September 2005. See also Neil Hrab, "The MacArthur Foundation on Foreign Policy and Defense," *Foundation Watch*, September 2003.
25. Cheryl L. Reed, "MacArthur Brass Lives Large–Frugal Founder Didn't," *Chicago Sun-Times*, May 23, 2004.

**The Pew Charitable Trusts**

1. Scott Allen, "The Greening of a Movement," *Boston Globe*, October 19, 1997.
2. J. Howard Pew, *Governmental Planning and Control as Applied to Business and Industry: A Common Sense Plea by an American Citizen* (Princeton, New Jersey: Guild of Brackett Lecturers, 1938), pp. 9-10.
3. August W. Giebelhaus, *Business and Government in the Oil Industry A Case Study of Sun Oil, 1876-1945* (Greenwich, Connecticut: JAI Press, 1980), p. 207.
4. "The Republican Party: Up From the Grave" *Fortune*, August 1939.
5. Dan Rottenberg, "The Sun Gods," *Philadelphia Magazine*, November 1975. Rottenberg estimates that the Pew family gave about $2.7 million to Republicans during the Roosevelt administration and $600,000 between 1945 and 1972.
6. Nielsen, *op. cit.*, pp. 170-171.
7. Potomacus (pseudonym), "Pew of Pennsylvania," *The New Republic*, May 8, 1944.
8. "J. N. Pew Jr.'s Help to Dewey Scorned," *New York Times*, March 20, 1960.
9. Mary Sennholtz, ed., *Faith and Freedom:The Journal of a Great American, J. Howard Pew* (Grove City, Pennsylvania: Grove City College, 1975), pp. 86-87.
10. Lucinda Fleeson, "How a Foundation Reinvented Itself," *Philadelphia Inquirer*, April 27, 1992.
11. Jack Willoughby, "Putting on Heirs," *Institutional Investor*, March 1997.
12. "Sun Oil," *Fortune*, February 1941.

13. *The Chairman's Final Report to the Members of the National Lay Committee* (New York: National Council of Churches, 1956), p. 169.
14. John Wicklein, "Layman Charges Church Meddling," *New York Times,* March 20, 1960.
15. Arnold Forster and Benjamin R. Epstein, *Danger on the Right* (New York: Random House, 1964), p.191. Forster and Epstein say the Christian Freedom Foundation's positions included calling Social Security "the older generation stealing from the younger," the income tax as "Communist doctrine," and labor unions as "stemming from Socialism."
16. Nielsen, *op. cit.,* p. 163.
17. *J. Howard Pew Freedom Trust Annual Report 1985* (Philadelphia: Glenmede Trust, 1985), pp. 16-17.
18. Eileen Shanahan, "House Tax Panel Eases Rule on Foundation Spending," *New York Times,* October 14, 1971.
19. Rottenberg, *op. cit.*
20. David Diamond, "The Pews of Philadelphia: The Subtle Control of a Vast Fortune," *New York Times,* October 25, 1981.
21. Fleeson, *op. cit.*
22. Kathleen Teltsch, "Pew Memorial Trust Issues Report, First in 22 Years of Discreet Charity," *New York Times,* June 23, 1980.
23. Kristin A. Goss, "New Head of Pew Trusts Stirs Strong Passions in Quest for Radical Philanthropy," *Chronicle of Philanthropy,* November 8, 1988.
24. "Reorganization at Glenmede Trust: Philanthropy in the 1980s," *Chronicle of Philanthropy,* January 1988.
25. *Pew Charitable Trusts 1988 Annual Report* (Philadelphia: Pew Charitable Trusts, 1989), p. 13. For an obituary of Langfitt, see Adam Bernstein, "Pew Trusts Leader Thomas Langfitt Dies at 78," *Washington Post,* August 9, 2005.
26. Roger M. Williams, "From Inside Right to Out Front," *Foundation News,* May/June 1991.
27. Dan Rottenberg, "The Pew Charitable Trusts: Foundation for the Future," *Town and Country,* December 1991.
28. Lucinda Fleeson, "Trusts' New Direction Leaves Region Behind," *Philadelphia Inquirer,* April 26, 1992.
29. Fleeson, "How a Foundation Reinvented Itself," *op. cit.*
30. Kathleen Teltsch, "2d-Largest Philanthropy Widens Role," *New York Times,* August 27, 1990.
31. Williams, *op. cit.*
32. Jennifer Moore, "Council on Foundations Hobbled by "Political Correctness," Report Charges," *Chronicle of Philanthropy,* May 4, 1993.
33. Letter to the author, dated December 16, 1997.
34. Paul Starobin, "Raging Moderates," *National Journal,* May 10, 1997.
35. Judith Havemann, "Bankrolling an Activist Agenda," *Washington Post,* March 29, 1998.
36. Robert Lerner and Althea K. Nagai, "The Pew Charitable Trusts: Revitalizing 'the Spirit of the '60s,'" Capital Research Center, *Alternatives in Philanthropy,* November 1995.
37. *The Pew Charitable Trusts Public Policy Program-1996 Grants.*

## Notes

38. *The Pew Charitable Trust Environment Program-1996 Grants.*
39. Nathan Gorenstein, "Pew Charitable Trusts Sells Last of Sun Oil Stock," *Philadelphia Inquirer,* August 5, 1997.
40. Richard O'Mara, "Buzzword for Pew: 'Pro-Active,'" *Baltimore Sun,* March 17, 1997.
41. Reichert has worked with J. Howard "Howdy" Pew H, a grandnephew of J. Howard Pew and an ardent conservationist.
42. Starobin, *op. cit.* For an interview with Reichert, see "Forging, Founding, and Funding," *Foundation News and Conmentary*; July I August 1994. Pew activities have been denounced by liberals, who perceive its program directors as arrogant. "They're a bully," Beth Daley of the National Committee for Responsive Philanthropy told Paul Starobin. "Some of us were joking around that we should have a Pew liberation front–committed to getting environmental organizations off the Pew dole." Starobin, *op. cit.*
43. Alicia Shepard, "Buying Press Coverage: How Pew's Civic Journalism Movement Put Newspapers, Radio, and Television Stations on the Payroll," *Foundation Watch,* August 1996, G. Bruce Knecht, "Why a Big Foundation Gives Newspapers Cash to Change Their Ways," *Wall Street Journal,* October 17, 1996, and Howard Kurtz, "The New Reform School," *Washington Post,* May 12, 1997. For an analysis of the ideas behind the civic journalism movement, see Scott Sherman, "The Public Defender," *Lingua Franca,* April 1998.
44. David S. Broder, "Panel Urges Americans to Turn Off TV, Get Involved," *Washington Post,* June 25, 1998.
45. Ben Wildavsky, "Talking the Talk on Social Security," *National Journal,* November 1, 1997.
46. Howard Kurtz, "Adversaries Join Campaign to Improve Coverage of State, Local Politics," *Washington Post,* May 28, 1998, Daniel LeDuc and Charles Babington, "A Call for More TV Time for Campaigns," *Washington Post,* June 18, 1998, and Jodie Morse, "Making Dirty Tricksters Behave Themselves," *National Journal,* July 5, 1997.
47. Howard Kurtz, "A Reporter with Lust in Her Hearts," *Washington Post,* July 6, 1998.
48. Rob Gurwitt, "With Strings Attached," *Governing,* April 1998.
49. Annie Groer and Ann Gerhart, "Rap's Social Conscience," *Washington Post,* May 13, 1998.
50. "A Matter of Trust," *Philanthropy,* May/June 2000.
51. Rebecca W. Rimel, "Charity and Strategy: Philanthropy's Evolving Role," accessed at pewtrusts.com, April 13, 2006.
52. "Pew Charitable Trusts Plans to Split From Money-Management Firm," *Philadelphia Inquirer,* July 27, 2003.
53. David Bank, "Pew Casts Itself in Fresh Role as Public Lobby," *Wall Street Journal,* November 6, 2003. See also Marianne D. Hurst, "Pew Seeks Flexibility Through New 'Public Charity' Status," *Education Week,* November 19, 2003, and Stephanie Strom, "Pew Charitable Trusts Will become Public Charity," *New York Times,* November 7, 2003.
54. For Alice Goldfarb Marquis article, see *New York Times,* August 9, 1999. For Pew proposals, see David N. Dobryzynski, "Heavyweight Foundation Throws Itself Behind Idea of a Cultural Policy," *New York Times,* August 2, 1999.
55. Douglas Jehl, "Charity is New Force in Environmental Fight," *New York Times,* June 28, 2001. For an analysis of Pew efforts to stop global warming, see Ron Arnold,

"The Pew Charitable Trusts: Global Warming Power Nexus," *Foundation Watch,* May 2004.
56. Wendy Tanaka, "Groups Mobilize to Get Nation's Young Adults to Vote," *Philadelphia Inquirer,* September 15, 2004.
57. Ryan Sager, "Buyer 'Reform,'" *New York Post,* March 17, 2005. See also Martin Morse Wooster, "Too Good to be True," *Wall Street Journal,* April 1, 2005, and David Hogberg, "Something Stinks at Pew," *Foundation Watch,* June 2005.
58. *New York Post,* March 25, 2005.

**The Barnes Foundation**
1. Benjamin Forgey, "For Art's Sake," *Washington Post Magazine,* April 11, 1993.
2. *Ibid.*
3. Carl W. McCardle, "The Terrible Tempered Dr. Barnes, *Saturday Evening Post,* March 21, 1942.
4. A.H. Shaw, "De Medici in Person," *New Yorker,* September 22, 1928.
5. Howard Greenfeld, *The Devil and Dr. Barnes: Portrait of An American Art Collector* (New York: Viking, 1987), p. 3.
6. Albert C. Barnes, "Sabotage of Public Education in Philadelphia," in *Art and Education: A Collection of Essays,* 3rd ed., (Merion, Pennsylvania: Barnes Foundation, 1954), p. 276.
7. Greenfeld, *op. cit.,* p. 5.
8. Richard Blow, "The Barnes Collection: Wow!" *Washington Post,* April 29, 1993.
9. Greenfeld, *op. cit.,* p. 27.
10. Henry Hart, *Dr. Barnes of Merion: An Appreciation* (New York: Farrar, Straus, 1963), p. 70.
11. Greenfeld, *op. cit.,* p.31.
12. Albert C. Barnes, "The Barnes Foundation," *New Republic,* March 14, 1923.
13. Gilbert M. Cantor, *The Barnes Foundation: Reality vs. Myth* (Philadelphia: Chilton, 1963), p. 200.
14. Cynthia Flannery Stine, "My Private War with Dr. Barnes," *Harper's Magazine,* August 1956.
15. Milton Esterow, "Barnes Bars Barr," *Art News,* December 1991.
16. Stine, *op. cit.*
17. McCradle, *op. cit.*
18. Cited in Lois G. Forer, "No Place for the Rabble," *Horizon,* Spring 1964.
19. Quotation from "Dr. Barnes Plans to Desert Merion," *New York Times,* April 16, 1927. See also "Negro Center Plan Incenses Merion," *New York Times,* April 14, 1927, and "Barnes Trust in Merion," *New York Times,* April 20, 1927.
20. Greenfield, *op. cit.,* p. 277.
21. *Ibid.,* p. 281.
22. *Ibid.,* p. 281.
23. Cantor, *op. cit.,* p. 187.
24. *Ibid.,* p. 182-184.

## Notes

25. *Ibid.*, p. 194.
26. Hart, *op. cit.*, pp. 117-18. Hart notes that when Barnes sold the A.C. Barnes Company to American Zonite Corp. for $6 Million in 1929, he promptly invested money in tax-exampts, "a fact people should bear in mind when they think, or say, the Barnes Foundation was created to avoid the payment of taxes."
27. Cantor, *op. cit.*, p. 198, 200.
28. *Ibid.*, p. 209.
29. Dorothy McCardle, "Mrs. Barnes Tells Why Doors Bang Again on Art Treasures," *Washington Post,* August 17, 1952.
30. *Ibid.*, p. 145.
31. Forer, *op. cit.* According to Forer, during this era Leningrad University art historian Igor N. Diakonoff applied for admission to the Barnes galleries and was rejected. Diakonoff "declared on the basis of his experience at the Barnes Foundation that America was a police state."
32. Greenfeld, *op. cit.*, p. 290.
33. John Anderson, *Art Held Hostage: The Battle Over The Barnes Collection* (New York: Norton, 2003), p. 93.
34. Carol Vogel, "A Controversial Man in an Eccentric Place," *New York Times,* April 4, 1993. Some evidence of the exaggeration about the expenses needed to restore the Barnes Foundation is provided in A.F. Brown, *The Barnes Case X Grand Scam: How The Trustees Faked It* (Broomall, Pennsylvania: A.F. Brown, 1993) Brown's study should be treated with caution, as he engages in relentless hyperbole, such as comparing the Barnes battles to the Dreyfus case.
35. *Washington Post,* May 2, 1993.
36. David D'Arcy, "Barnes Storm," *Vanity Fair;* August 1991.
37. Dale Russakoff, "A Bitter, Beautiful Legacy: The Bizarre Life-And Afterlife-of Albert Barnes," *Washington Post,* May 2, 1993.
38. "Once is Enough," *Art News,* September 1992.
39. Jennifer Moore, "Barnes Foundation, De Mazia Trust Drop Lawsuits Against Each Other," *Chronicle of Philanthropy,* January 26, 1995.
40. Edward J. Sozanski "The Bottom Line at the Barnes Foundation: It's Now a Museum," *Philadelphia Inquirer,* November 19, 1995.
41. Lee Rosenbaum, "Masterpieces Back Home, Hung in Same Weird Way," *Wall Street Journal,* November 28, 1995.
42. Leonard W. Rosenberg, "Court Allows Barnes' Guests at Dinner a Feast for Eyes, Too," *Philadelphia Inquirer,* November 9, 1995.
43. Robert W. Fowler, "A Cha-Cha Near a Cezanne? Court Opens Barnes Door," *Philadelphia Inquirer,* September 14, 1996.
44. Kyle York Spencer, "Barnes Foundation Ordered to Cut Its Hours," *Philadelphia Inquirer,* December 14, 1995.
45. Anne Barnard, "Barnes to Open for Summer," *Philadelphia Inquirer;* July 3, 1996.
46. Anne Barnard, "Bold Style Was Help and Hindrance to Barnes Chief," *Philadelphia Inquirer,* February 11, 1998, and Anne Barnard, "Barnes, L. Merion Go Back to Court over Zoning Dispute," *Philadelphia Inquirer,* January 28, 1997.
47. Anderson, *op. cit.*, p. 129.
48. Anne Barnard, "Court Curtails Barnes' Hours and Admissions," *Philadelphia Inquirer,*

August 8, 1997, and Ralph Vigoda, "At the Barnes, Court Order Keeps Visitors Out," *Philadelphia Inquirer,* September 4, 1997.

49. Anne Barnard, "Judge Throws Out Barnes Lawsuit Against Lower Merion Township," *Philadelphia Inquirer,* September 27, 1997.
50. Anne Barnard, "2 Montco Judges Affirm Zone Board, Barnes a Museum," *Philadelphia Inquirer,* November 3, 1997.
51. Anne Barnard, "Bold Style Was Help and Hindrance to Barnes Chief."
52. Bernard, *Ibid.* The best analysis of the Rome suit is Shannon P. Duffy, "Rome Sues Glanton, Barnes," *Philadelphia Legal Intelligences,* July 30, 1996. See also Michael Janofsky, "Italians Sue the Barnes Because Show Didn't Go to Rome," *New York Times,* July 31, 1996.
53. See 1998 stories in the *Philadelphia Inquirer:* Larry King, "A Quiet Man Taking the Reins at Barnes," February 11, Rich Henson, Stephanie A. Stanley, and Julia M. Klein, "Barnes Hires Interim Manager," February 11, and Anne Barnard and Peter Dobrin, "Barnes Switches Course," February 15.
54. Edward J. Sozanski, "Glanton's Tenure: A Mission to Alter Albert Barnes' Dream," *Philadelphia Inquirer,* February 18, 1998.
55. Russakoff, *op. cit.*
56. Eric Gibson, "Barnes Storming," *Washington Times,* April 30, 1992.
57. Cited in Lawrence Osborne, "Are a Donor's Wishes Sacred?" *National Law Journal,* July 3, 1995.
58. "The Barnes Foundation Receives Permission to Remain Open During the Summer Months," *PR Newswire,* August 5, 1998.
59. "Troubled Pa. Fund Suffers setback in Civil Rights Case," *Chronicle of Philanthropy,* March 22, 2001. The court declared that evidence of racism against a sixth neighbor was "thin."
60. Joann Loviglio, "Former Lincoln University President Suing Former Barnes Chief," Associated Press, July 30, 2001. "Former Lincoln President's Suit Against Former Counsel Dismissed," Associated Press, August 1, 2001.
61. Jeffrey Toobin, "Battle for the Barnes," *New Yorker,* January 29, 2002.
62. Ralph Blumenthal, "Art Museum Outside Philadelphia Plans Move," *New York Times,* September 28, 2002.

    For a profile of H.G. "Gerry" Lenfest, see Patricia Horn, "Cable Television Magnate Plans to Give Away Entire Fortune," *Philadelphia Inquirer,* February 23, 2004. Lenfest said that he had given away $325 million and planned to give away his remaining $800 million, leaving no money for his children or grandchildren. "I care about what happens when I die, but I can't control that," Lenfest said. "Giving during your lifetime, you can direct how your wealth is spent for the most good. But after your death it is problematic, you don't have the control." Lenfest said that after a donor dies, foundations "are often perpetuated by those who work for them, for the organization. The donor no longer has any control over what the foundations are used for."
63. Patricia Horn, "Philadelphia-Area Museum Fights Student Petition, Hopes to Move Collection," *Philadelphia Inquirer,* October 31, 2002. John L. Pulley, "Barnes Foundation Seeks to Cut Lincoln U.'s Role," *Chronicle of Higher Education,* November 1, 2002.
64. Jennifer Batchelor, "Foes of Barnes Foundation Move Answered by Art

*Notes*

Foundation's Lawyers," *Legal Intelligencer,* November 19, 2002. David R. Caruso, "Barnes Foundation Claims Its Creator Planned to Sever Ties With Lincoln U.," Associated Press, November 19, 2002.

65. Don Sternberg, "Lawyers Argue on Barnes Foundation's Planned Move to Philadelphia," *Philadelphia Inquirer,* November 19, 2002.
66. Don Sternberg, "Bill Would Let University Vero Art Collection's Move to Philadelphia," *Philadelphia Inquirer,* November 30, 2002.
67. Patricia Horn, "Pennsylvania Governor-Elect Offers Help in Battle Over Art Collection's Move," *Philadelphia Inquirer,* January 17, 2003.
68. Patricia Horn, "Lincoln University in Pennsylvania Can Participate in Art Collection Trial," *Philadelphia Inquirer,* February 13, 2003.
69. Patricia Horn, "Pennsylvania Judge Wants Art Foundation to Explain Refusal to Disclose Audit," *Philadelphia Inquirer,* March 12, 2003. During this period, Barnes Watch placed billboards in African-American neighborhoods with Barnes' portrait captioned, "A MAN'S WILL SHOULD NOT BE BROKEN." Kendra Hamilton, "A Battle of Wills," *Black Issues in Higher Education,* July 17, 2003.
70. Don Sternberg, "Philadelphia-Area Foundations Says Financial Audit Contains Embarrassing Data," *Philadelphia Inquirer,* April 12, 2003
71. Ralph Blumenthal, "Release of Audit Roils Trust Fight at the Barnes," *New York Times,* May 5, 2003.
72. Patricia Horn, "Pennsylvania Attorney General Requests Changes to Art Museum's Petition," *Philadelphia Inquirer,* May 29, 2003.
73. Patricia Horn, "Pennsylvania Art Museum Board Members Raise Concerns Over Proposed Expansion," *Philadelphia Inquirer,* June 4, 2003.
74. Don Sterberg, "Philadelphia's Barnes Foundation Was in Chaos, Audit Shows," *Philadelphia Inquirer,* July 2, 2003. Ralph Blumenthal, "Audit Sharply Criticizes Art Institution's Dealings," *New York Times,* July 2, 2003.
75. "Chester County, Pa. University Disagrees With Foundation over Audit Findings," *Philadelphia Inquirer,* July 13, 2003.
76. Don Sternberg, "Chairman of Pennsylvania Art Collection Says Bankruptcy May Be in Future," *Philadelphia Inquirer,* September 4, 2003.
77. Patricia Horn and Don Sternberg, "Petition to Move Art Collection to Philadelphia May be Abandoned," *Philadelphia Inquirer,* September 3, 2003.
78. Patricia Horn, "Philadelphia-Area Foundation Clears Way for Proposed Move of Art Collection," *Philadelphia Inquirer,* September 13, 2003. Patricia Horn, "Chester County Pa. University Board Accepts Smaller Role in Foundation," *Philadelphia Inquirer,* September 21, 2003.
79. Patricia Horn, "J. Paul Getty Trust Backs Moving Art Collection to Philadelphia," *Philadelphia Inquirer,* October 10, 2003.
80. Patricia Horn, "Judge Agrees to Let Students Take Part in Art Collection Case in Philadelphia," *Philadelphia Inquirer,* October 30, 2003.
81. John Anderson, "Will the Pew's Fine Print Determine the Fate of the Barnes Collection?" *Wall Street Journal,* December 9, 2003. Patricia Horn, "Pew Chairtable Trusts, Not Barnes Foundation, Could Control $150 Million," *Philadelphia Inquirer,* November 20, 2003. Don Sternberg, "Philadelphia-Area Foundation Begins Process of Trying to Move its Art," *Philadelphia Inquirer,* December 7, 2003.
82. Patricia Horn and Don Sternberg, "Foundation Head Testifies in Case Concerning

Philadelphia-Area Art Collection," *Philadelphia Inquirer,* December 9, 2003. Patricia Horn, "Philadelphia-Area Foundation Had No Money for Feasibility Study, Director Says," *Philadelphia Inquirer,* December 10, 2003. Patricia Horn, "Judge Expresses Doubt About Art Foundation's Proposal to Move to Philadelphia," *Philadelphia Inquirer,* December 11, 2003.

83. Patricia Horn, "Trial Concerning Art Collection's Proposed Move to Philadelphia Ends Early," *Philadelphia Inquirer,* December 12, 2003.
84. Patricia Horn and Don Sternberg, "Foundation Allowed to Expand Board Over Philadelphia-Area Art Collection," *Philadelphia Inquirer,* January 30, 2004. Asher Hawkins, "Barnes Move Delayed Pending Look At Fund-Raising Options," *Legal Intelligencer,* January 30, 2004.
85. Matthew P. Blanchard and Patricia Horn, "Lower Merion Township, Pa. Neighbors Want Art Collection to Stay," *Philadelphia Inquirer,* March 13, 2004. Matthew P. Blanchard, "Merion, Pa. Resists Push to Move Barnes Art Museum to Philadelphia," *Philadelphia Inquirer,* September 26, 2004.
86. Patricia Horn and Matthew P. Blanchard, "Foundation Attorneys Say Art Collection Can't Stay in Lower Merion, Pa.," *Philadelphia Inquirer,* September 22, 2004.
87. Patricia Horn, "Consultant Says Philadelphia Arts Foundation's Fund-Raising Goal is Workable," *Philadelphia Inquirer,* September 24, 2004.
88. Patricia Horn, "Selling Philadelphia School's Artwork is OK, Expert Says," *Philadelphia Inquirer,* September 25, 2004.
89. Blanchard, "Merion Pa. Resists Push to Move Barnes Art Museum."
90. Patricia Horn, "Philadelphia-Area Foundation Offers $100,000 to Keep Art Gallery in Township," *Philadelphia Inquirer,* September 30, 2004.
91. Melissa Nann Burke, "Barnes Foundation Wins OK to Move to Phila.," *Legal Intelligencer,* December 14, 2004.
92. Patricia Horn, "Judge Amends Ruling Concerning Pennsylvania Art Museum," *Philadelphia Inquirer,* December 22, 2004.
93. Patricia Horn, "Barnes Foundation's Planned Move to Philadelphia Will Face Court Appeal," *Philadelphia Inquirer,* March 10, 2005. For a profile of Jay Raymond, see Amy Donohue Korman, "The Handyman vs. the Billionaires," *Philadelphia Magazine,* September 2005.
94. Asher Hawkins, "State High Court Ends Barnes Appeal," *Legal Intelligencer,* April 28, 2005.
95. Christopher Knight, "What the Court Didn't Know," *Los Angeles Times,* October 16, 2006.
96. "Philadelphia's Foundations, Corporations, Citizens Contribute $150 Million to Relocate Barnes Foundation Gallery," *U.S. Newswire,* May 15, 2006.
97. Stephen Salisbury, "Barnes Search for Leader Ends Here," *Philadelphia Inquirer,* August 8, 2006.
98. Debra Blum, "Court Ruling Could Influence Restrictions," *Chronicle of Philanthropy,* January 6, 2005.
99. Leslie Lenkowsky, "A Risky End to the Barnes Case," *Wall Street Journal,* December 16, 2004.
100. Tom L. Freudenheim, "Intentions Be Damned!–Donors of Art Often Find Themselves Betrayed," *Wall Street Journal,* December 31, 2005.
101. Robert Zaller, "A Manufactured Offer: Is the Barnes Foundation Really in Trouble?", posted on broadstreetreview.com, February 24, 2006.

## Notes

### The Buck Trust

1. Vanessa Laird, "Phantom Selves: The Search for a General Charitable Intent in the Application of the *Cy Pres* Doctrine." *Stanford Law Review,* April 1988. The case has achieved a certain notoriety. It was used as the basis of an episode of *L.A. Law,* in which crusading lawyers at Mackenzie, Brackman pondered whether or not a trust willed "for the poor of Beverly Hills" could be used to benefit the Los Angeles area.
2. Aaron Wildavsky, "Exchange Versus Grants: The Buck Case as a Struggle Between Equal Opportunity and Equal Results," *University of San Francisco Law Review,* Summer 1988.
3. Superior Court of the State of California, County of Marin, *In the Matter of the Estate of Beryl H. Buck, Deceased: Statement of Decision,* filed August 15, 1986, p. 5. (Referred to hereafter as "Decision.")
4. Douglas Bartholomew, "The Battle for the Buck," *Los Angeles Times Magazine,* December 21-28, 1986.
5. Ted Holdrich, "Widow's Request spawns Marin County Headache," *Los Angeles Times,* February 1, 1986.
6. Decision, *op. cit.,* p. 10
7. *Ibid.,* p. 15.
8. *Ibid.,* p. 12.
9. Peg Brickley and Fred Powledge, "Marin County Legacy, or the Curse of the Buck Bucks," *The Nation,* May 14, 1983.
10. Memorandum from Wayne Lamprey to Robert C. Harris, dated July 24, 1979.
11. *Ibid.,* p. 12.
12. Decision, *op. cit.,* p. 21.
13. *Ibid.,* pp. 25-26.
14. Michael Cieply, "The Lotus-Eaters," *Forbes,* July 19, 1982. According to an article in the *Los Angeles Times Magazine,* Public Advocates employees claimed they had thought up the notion of breaking the trust. In a 1982 interview in *Forbes,* Public Advocates partner Robert Gnaizda said that breaking the Buck Trust would be an important precedent. "If the court allows his group to intervene on Buck, he says, the precedent could lead to greater public scrutiny of such private foundations as 'Kresge, Rockefeller, Ford, you name it.'"
15. "California Case Challenges Donors' Rights," *Organization Trends* (Washington, D.C.: Capital Research Center, January 1986).
16. *Ibid.*
17. Robert B. Buck, "Attack on Bay Area Foundation Could Hit Charitable Groups," *Sacramento Union,* December 26, 1985.
18. Roger M. Williams, "When the Buck Stopped," *Foundation News,* November/December 1988.
19. Paul Desruisseaux, "A Foundation Grapples With the Meaning of a 'Magnificent Gift,'" *Chronicle of Higher Education,* March 27, 1985.
20. California Attorney General's petition to the court, p. 5.
21. Katy Butler, "Trial Starts Today over Buck Trust," *San Francisco Chronicle,* February 3, 1986.
22. *Marin Independent Journal,* February 12, 14, and 20, 1986.
23. *Marin Independent Journal,* March 15, 1986.

24. *San Francisco Chronicle,* May 6, 1986.
25. Williams, *op. cit.*
26. *San Francisco Chronicle,* May 6, 1986.
27. From Martin Paley speech in *The Commonwealth,* June 1986.
28. Decision, *op. cit.*, pp. 110-111.
29. "Text of Agreement," *Marin Independent Journal,* July 26, 1986.
30. John G. Simon, "American Philanthropy and the Buck Trust," *University of San Francisco Law Review,* Summer 1987.
31. From article in *San Jose Mercury News,* February 11, 1990.
32. *Marin Community Foundation Newsletter,* Spring 1989.
33. *Marin Connmmity Foundation,* 1997 annual report.
34. Peter Fimrite, "S.F. Supervisors Lack Faith in Trust," *San Francisco Chronicle,* March 5, 2002.

**The Robertson Foundation**
1. "Mrs. Marie H. Reed Engaged to Marry," *New York Times,* October 7, 1936.
2. *Composite Certificate of Incorporation of the Robertson Foundation,* p. 1.
3. *Ibid.* p. 3-4.
4. "Notes by Charles Robertson RE: Woodrow Wilson Graduate Program," document WSR001904. Underlining in original. "B.F." is probably "Banbury Fund," the Robertson family foundation.
5. Letter from Charles Robertson to Robert F. Goheen, dated June 10, 1960 (Exhibit D-83). Woodrow Wilson School Dean Gardner Patterson wrote a report to Goheen on Harvard's international affairs programs, which Robertson also received.
6. Summary of The Results of Our Talks in Washington," dated December 15, 1960, CSR Files 000509.
7. Letter from Eugene Goodwillie to Charles S. Robertson, dated December 22, 1960 (Exhibit P-600).
8. Letter from Brian P. Leeb to Robert F. Goheen, dated January 6, 1961 (Princeton exhibit 000275).
9. *Memorandum of Points and Authorities in Support of Plaintiffs' Motion for Partial Summary Judgment Re Fiduciary Duties and Business Judgment Rule,* submitted by Saul Ewing LLP to Superior Court of New Jersey, Chancery Division, Mercer County January 2006, p. 32. Gen, Goodpaster said he became involved with the Robertson donation in 1960, when he served as President Eisenhower's staff secretary. President Goheen, Gen. Goodpaster recalled, asked him to talk to Charles Robertson about "what Princeton could do to...support the kind of foreign policy and security policy that Eisenhower was carrying out as president." *Ibid*, p. 32.
10. Letter from Charles S. Robertson to William Robertson dated February 2, 1979 (Exhibit P-608).
11. Cited in "Interpreting the Mission of the Robertson Foundation," Princeton University press release, issued June 2, 2003.
12. "$35 Million Given to Princeton for Government Services School," *New York Times,* August 6, 1961.
13. "Wilson School Endowers Identified as a L.I. Couple," *New York Times,* June 14, 1973.

## Notes

14. Letter from Charles Robertson to William Robertson, July 3, 1962 (exhibit P-607).
15. *Memorandum of Points and Authorities*, p. 17.
16. *Ibid.* p. 17.
17. Robertson Foundation IRS Form 4023, submitted to the IRS August 20, 1970 (Document D-1333).
18. Letter from Charles S. Robertson to Gardner Patterson, June 24, 1963 (Exhibit D-114).
19. *Memorandum of Points and Authorities*, p. 19.
20. Letter from Charles S. Robertson to William Bowen dated November 18, 1972 (exhibit P-4). Underlining in original.
21. *Memorandum of Points and Authorities*, p. 27.
22. *Ibid.* p. 31.
23. Susan Warner, "Thriving in a World in Crisis," *New York Times*, December 23, 2001.
24. The number of plaintiffs fell to four when John Robertson died in an accident in February 2003. Daniel Lipsky-Karasz, "Robertson Suit May Be Delayed by Injury to Judge," *Daily Princetonian*, February 3, 2003.
25. Letter from Charles S. Robertson to William Robertson, February 7, 1979 (Exhibit P-608.
26. Maria Newman, "Princeton University is Sued Over Control of Foundation," *New York Times*, July 18, 2002. See also Kelly Heyboer, "Heirs Sue Princeton Over Endowment—College Is Accused of Misusing A&P Gift," Newark *Star-Ledger*, July 19, 2002, "Follow the Money," *Wall Street Journal*, July 19, 2002, Silla Brush, "Donors Allege Misuse of Woodrow Wilson School's $550 M Endowment," *Daily Princetonian*, September 11, 2002, and Jeffrey O. Nelson, "Donor Beware," *National Review Online*, October 3, 2002.
27. "Princeton-Appointed Trustees and the University File for Dismissal of Robertson Lawsuit," Princeton University press release, issued November 4, 2002.
28. Silla Brush, "Princeton Files to Dismiss Robertson Suit," *Daily Princetonian*, November 5, 2002.
29. "New Evidence Displays Princeton's Arrogance in Treating $500 Million Foundation as University 'Piggy Bank,'" Robertson family press release, issued February 4, 2003. See also Daniel Lipsky-Karasz, "Robertsons File Response to Notion to Dismiss Lawsuit," *Daily Princetonian*, February 5, 2003.
30. Daniel Lipsky-Karasz, "Wilson School Defends Use of Endowment," *Daily Princetonian*, March 25, 2003.
31. Jeff Linkous, "Judge Asked to Dismiss Suit Alleging Princeton Misused Endowment," Associated Press, June 5, 2003.
32. John J. Miller, "Giving, and Taking Away: A Controversy at Princeton Offers Broad Lessons," *National Review*, September 29, 2003.
33. Michael Powell, "At Princeton, Feeling Failed: Family Seeks Return of $525 Million, Saying University Has 'Abused' Gift," *Washington Post*, October 8, 2003.
34. Zachary A. Goldfarb, "PRINCO to Advise WWS Endowment," *Daily Princetonian*, November 6, 2003.
35. William Robertson, "It's National Philanthropy Day—Do You Know Where Your Money Is?" *Christian Science Monitor*, November 14, 2003.
36. Joyce Howard Price, "Princeton Sued for Funds Misuse: A&P Heirs Say Money 'Diverted,'" *Washington Times*, June 20, 2004. Erin Strout, "New Complaint in

Lawsuit Alleges That Princeton U. Misused Donors' Money," *Chronicle of Higher Education*, July 2, 2004.

37. Raj Hathiramani, "How A Memo Became a Symbol of Contention," *Daily Princetonian*, October 11, 2004.

38. Raj Hathiramani, "Robertson Family Seeks to Amend Complaint," *Daily Princetonian*, September 13, 2004.

39. John Covaleski, "Fraud Count Added to Donors' Suit That Princeton Misused Endowment," *New Jersey Law Journal*, November 8, 2004.

40. Kelly Heyboer, "Big Stakes as Donor's Heirs Fight Princeton—Suit to Regain Gift Could Spark Others," Newark *Star-Ledger*, November 28, 2004. The largest lawsuit in Princeton's history prior to the Robertson affair was a 1990 case in which an undergraduate won an out-of-court settlement after nearly electrocuting himself after a drinking binge. Raj Hathirimani, "Robertson Lawsuit Most Expensive in U. History," *Daily Princetonian*, November 19, 2004.

41. Chanakya Sethi, "University Files New Claims in Suit," *Daily Princetonian*, February 3, 2005. See also "University Seeks Resolution of Key Issues in Robertson Lawsuit," Princeton University press release, issued February 2, 2005.

42. "Princeton 'Donor Intent' Lawsuit Gathers Steam," Philanthropy News Network Online, June 18, 2005.

43. Chanakya Sethi, "Resignation Sparks Fracas," *Daily Princetonian*, September 21, 2005.

44. Zogby America Poll conducted November 20-22, 2005.

45. "University Seeks Summary Judgment on Three Key Robertson Litigation Issues," Princeton University press release, issued January 9, 2006.

46. Viola Huang, "University Seeks Ruling on Robertson Case," *Daily Princetonian*, January 13, 2006.

47. John Hechinger and Daniel Golden, "Poisoned Ivy: Fight at Princeton Escalates Over Use of a Family Gift, *Wall Street Journal*, February 7, 2006. For more about the McGuire report, see Joyce Howard Price, "Princeton Faulted on Foundation Funds Use," *Washington Times*, February 16, 2006.

48. "Princeton Responds to Feb. 7 WSJ Article," Princeton University press release, issued February 7, 2006.

49. Robert K. Durkee, "Robertson Funds Not Diverted," *Trenton Times*, February 17, 2006.

50. "Scholars in the Nation's Service," *Princeton Weekly Bulletin*, March 7, 2006.

51. Charles Forelle, "Princeton, Amid Donor Flap, Sets Government Scholarship," *Wall Street Journal,* February 27, 2006.

52. Katherine Hamilton, "University Claims it Underbilled Foundation," *Daily Princetonian*, March 16, 2006. See also John Hechinger, "Princeton Claims it Undercharged Donor Foundation," *Wall Street Journal*, March 16, 2006.

53. Stephanie Mansfield, "Lawsuit Turns Against Princeton," *Washington Times*, July 7, 2006.

*Notes*

# Chapter III Preserving Donor Intent

### The JM Foundation

1. Clarence R. Wharton, *Gail Borden, Pioneer* (San Antonio: Naylor, 1941), p. 193.
2. "The Quiet Milbank Millions," *Fortune,* May 1959. When the railroad reached South Dakota, a town first used as a maintenance stop was renamed Milbank.
3. *Ibid.* Elizabeth Milbank Anderson ensured, however, that the "palace" did not serve hard liquor, which she fiercely opposed.
4. For Jeremiah Milbank's obituary, see "Jeremiah Milbank, A Financier Who Aided the Crippled, Dead," *New York Times,* March 23, 1972.
5. John Briggs, *The Face of a Family* (Greenwich, Connecticut: The JM Foundation, 1992), p. 27.
6. "Red Cross to Open School for Cripples," *New York Times,* January 20, 1918.
7. "600 Cripples Guests of Jeremiah Millbank," *New York Times,* July 20, 1929.
8. Cited in "The Quiet Milbank Millions," *op. cit.*
9. Jeremiah Milbank with Grace Fox Perry, *Turkey Hill Plantation* (Ridgeland, South Carolina: Cypress Woods Corporation, 1966), p. 102.
10. Briggs, *op. cit.,* p. 43.
11. *Ibid.,* p. 75.
12. *Ibid.,* p. 1.
13. *Ibid.,* p. 2.
14. *Ibid.,* p.2.
15. "The Quiet Milbank Millions," *op. cit.*
16. *Turkey Hill Plantation, op. cit.,* preface. The preface is by Perry alone.
17. Jeremiah Milbank, "Will Giver Get Hand Bitten after Giving?" *Leaders,* Fourth Quarter 1984.

    Jeremiah Millbank, Jr. was also active in Republican politics. In 1962 he and J. William Middendorf II agreed to donate enough money to keep the "Draft Goldwater" offices operating until after the 1962 mid-term elections, at which time other donors pledged their support. Milbank and Middendorf were such efficient fund-raisers that they were nicknamed "The Brinks Brothers," Lee Edwards, "The Unforgettable Candidate," *National Review,* July 6, 1998.

### Lynde and Harry Bradley Foundation

1. John Gurda, *The Bradley Legacy: Lynde and Harry Bradley, their Company, and their Foundation* (Milwaukee: Lynde and Harry Bradley Foundation, 1992), p. 41.
2. *Ibid.,* p.98.
3. *Ibid.,* p. 120.
4. *Ibid.,* p. 115.
5. *Ibid.,* p. 112.
6. *Ibid.,* p. 116.
7. *Ibid.,* p. 117.
8. *Ibid.,* pp. 115-116.

9. "Harry Bradley, R.I.P.," *National Review*, August 24, 1965.
10. Gurda, *op. cit.*, p. 124.
11. *Ibid.*, p. 121.
12. *Ibid.*, p. 125.
13. Harvey W. Peters, *America's Coming Bankruptcy: How the Government Is Wrecking Your Dollar* (New Rochelle, New York: Arlington House, 1973), p. 118.
14. *Ibid.*, p.121.
15. "Bradley Foundation Gets New Chairman," *Milwaukee Journal Sentinel*, June 9, 2000. For Rader's obituary, see Jason Gertzen, "Industrialist Was Catalyst for a Company: I. Andrew 'Tiny' Rader, 1914-2003," *Milwaukee Journal Sentinel*, February 15, 2003.
16. Gurda, *op. cit.*, p. 157.
17. *Report of the Lynde and Harry Bradley Foundation, Inc., August 1988-July 1990* (Milwaukee: Lynde and Harry Bradley Foundation, 1991), p. 8.
18. Charles Storch, "Money Talks," *Chicago Tribune*, March 4, 1993.
19. James A. Barnes, "Banker with a Cause," *National Journal*, March 6, 1993.
20. Cited in Brian D. Willats, "Restoring Donor Intent: The Philanthropy Roundtable," *Philanthropy, Culture & Society* (Washington, D.C.: Capital Research Center, February 1993).
21. Y. Krysta Tabuchi, "Parade Aid: $50,000 More Will Honor Barkin," *Milwaukee Journal Sentinel*, June 15, 1996.
22. Curtis Lawrence, "School Choice Book Aims to Focus on Real People Involved," *Milwaukee Journal Sentinel*, May 15, 1996. I edited a chapter from this book as an excerpt in *The American Enterprise*.
23. Joe Williams, "Foundation Again Supports School Choice," *Milwaukee Journal Sentinel*, August 29, 1997.
24. Eric Alterman, "The 'Right' Books and Big Ideas," *The Nation*, November 27, 1999.
25. Shawn Zeller, "Conservative Crusaders," *National Journal*, April 26, 2003.
26. Alan Borsuk, "Bush Stresses Faith-Based Efforts," *Milwaukee Journal Sentinel*, July 3, 2002.
27. For a report of a 2005 Bradley Center conference, see Thomas B. Edsall, "Now in Power, Conservatives Free to Differ," *Washington Post*, February 20, 2005. I have edited transcripts of Bradley Center conferences.
28. For an account of the 2005 Bradley Prizes, see Jennifer Frey, "For Bradley Prize Winners, a Conservative Celebration," *Washington Post*, February 17, 2005. Andrew Ferguson, "The Right Stuff," *Weekly Standard*, March 7, 2005, provides a skeptical account of the Bradley Prizes.

    One of the 2006 Bradley Prize winners, Fouad Ajami, had previously been a MacArthur Fellow.
29. Among the more important tributes to Michael Joyce were James Piereson, "Michael Joyce, 1942-2005: The Godfather of Conservative Philanthropy," *Weekly Standard*, March 20, 2006, and William A. Schambra, "Michael Joyce's Mission: Using Philanthropy to Wage a War of Ideas," *Chronicle of Philanthropy*, March 9, 2006.
30. "Staying the Course," *Philanthropy*, July 2003.

*Notes*

**The Duke Endowment**

1. Cited in Joe Maynor, *Duke Power: The First Seventy-Five Years* (Albany, New York: Delmar, 1980), p. 44.
2. Patrick G. Porter, "Origins of the American Tobacco Company," *Business History Review*, Spring 1969.
3. Cited in Watson S. Rankin, *James Buchanan Duke (1856-1925): A Great Pattern of Hard Work, Wisdom, and Benevolence* (New York: Newcomen Society, 1952), p. 9.
4. In April 1994, British-American Tobacco (now known as B.A.T. Industries) announced plans to acquire American Tobacco.
5. While Southern Power System president, Duke continued his thrifty ways. In her memoirs, Cordelia Drexel Biddle, who married Benjamin Duke's son, Tony Duke, recalled that sometime around 1920, James Duke decided to teach his nephew the family trade and took him on a tour of Southern Power System facilities. At one hotel, James Duke found that Tony had booked two rooms. "You'll get nowhere in business wasting money like that," James Duke said. "Give us that room with the double bed that Ben and I always slept in."

    According to Biddle, Tony Duke "never recovered from the fact that one of America's richest men was worrying about saving a dollar a night in a primitive country hotel. However, his admiration for Mr. Duke has never wavered. `After a day on the trail with that wonderful old man,' says Tony, `I was so tired that I could just as easily have slept with a cobra.'" Cordelia Drexel Biddle, as told to Kyle Crichton, *My Philadelphia Father* (Garden City, New York: Doubleday, 1955), p. 195.
6. Cited in Robert F. Durden, *The Dukes of Durham, 1865-1929* (Durham, North Carolina: Duke University Press, 1975), pp. 97-98. Duke University Press published a sequel by Durden, *Lasting Legacy to the Carolinas, The Duke Endowment, 1924-1994*, in 1998.
7. *Ibid.*, p.97.
8. James B. Duke, "Politics and Prosperity," *North American Review*, April 9, 1915.
9. Arthur Pound and Samuel Taylor Moore, eds., *They Told Barron: Conversations and Revelations of an American Pepys in Wall Street* (New York: Harper, 1930), p. 54.
10. *Ibid.*, p. 55.
11. "Duke Calls Power Good in Wealth," *New York Times*, December 16, 1924.
12. "Politics and Prosperity," *op. cit.*
13. Durden, *op. cit.*, p. 113.
14. Robert H. Woody, ed., *The Papers and Addresses of William Preston Few, Late President of Duke University* (Durham, North Carolina: Duke University Press, 1941), pp. 90-91. Benjamin Duke gave Trinity College $120,000 between 1898 and 1901. He also ensured that his children attended the school. His son Angier was graduated with the 1905 class and his daughter Mary was a 1907 alumnus.
15. Durden, *op. cit.*, p. 163.
16. Woody, *op. cit.*, p. 93.
17. *Ibid.*, p. 104.
18. *Ibid.*, p. 93.
19. *Ibid.*, p. 93.
20. *Ibid.*, p. 94.

21. *Ibid.*, pp. 94-95.
22. Durden, *op. cit.*, p. 214.
23. Woody, *op. cit.*, p. 135.
24. *Ibid.*, p. 105.
25. Cited in Robert F. Durden, *The Launching of Duke University, 1924-1949* (Durham, North Carolina: Duke University Press, 1993), p. 22.
26. *Ibid.*, p. 22.
27. James F. Gifford, Jr., *The Evolution of a Medical Center: A History of Medicine at Duke University to 1941* (Durham, North Carolina: Duke University Press, 1972), p. 36.
28. Gifford, *op. cit.*, p. 39.
29. Durden, *Dukes of Durham*, p. 227.
30. *Ibid.*, p. 229.
31. Woody, *op. cit.*, p. 106.
32. *The Duke Endowment Indenture of Trust* (Charlotte, North Carolina: Duke Endowment, n.d.), pp. 10-11.
33. *Ibid.*, p. 12.
34. *Ibid.*, p. 14.
35. *Ibid.*, p. 14.
36. *Ibid.*, p. 17.
37. *Ibid.*, p. 17.
38. *Ibid.*, pp. 17-18.
39. *Ibid.*, p. 18.
40. *Ibid.*, pp. 18-19.
41. *Ibid.*, p. 19.
42. "Duke Calls Power Good in Wealth," *op. cit.*
43. *Ibid.*
44. Ned Glascock, "Slug! Slug! Slug!" *Raleigh News and Observer*, August 11, 1996.
45. Durden, *Dukes of Durham*, p. 235.
46. "The Goose Step and the Golden Eggs," *The New Republic*, December 24, 1924.
47. Cited in "Given Away-The Duke and Eastman Millions," *Literary Digest*, December 27, 1924.
48. Rankin, p. 9.
49. Durden, *Dukes of Durham*, p. 239.
50. Gifford, *op. cit.*, pp. 43-44.
51. "Texan Enlivens Duke Will Trial," *New York Times*, March 17, 1928.
52. "Right to Texas Fund Denied Duke Girl," *New York Times*, May 22, 1928.
53. Tom Valentine and Patrick Mahn, *Daddy's Duchess: The Unauthorized Biography of Doris Duke* (Secaucus, New Jersey: Lyle Stuart, 1989), pp. 13-14.
54. Karen Garloch and Jack Horan, "Their Mission: Give Away $41 Million," *Charlotte Observer*, November 13, 1988.
55. *Ibid.*
56. Stephanie Mansfield, *The Richest Girl in the World: The Extravagant Life and Fast Times*

## Notes

      *of Doris Duke* (New York: Putnam, 1992), p. 260.
57. *Ibid.*, p. 260.
58. Cited in Ted Schwarz with Tom Rybak, *Trust No One: The Glamorous Life and Bizarre Death of Doris Duke* (New York: St. Martin's Press, 1997), pp. 262-263. While this book is a useful guide to legal documents, the authors make many claims unsupported by evidence, including allegations that James Duke was murdered by his wife Nannaline and that James Duke in 1917 (when he was no longer in the tobacco business) suppressed research that showed that cigarette smoking causes cancer.
59. Stephanie Mansfield, "Billionaire's Heir Out of Place," *Washington Post*, March 7, 1993. Duke biographer Schwarz notes that it is unclear whether Duke could legally annul her adoption of Heffner, even though it is clear that Heffner could be disinherited. Schwarz, *op. cit.*, p. 263.
60. Paul Lieberman and John J. Goldman, "Doris Duke's Will Evolves into Ultimate Probate Fight," *Los Angeles Times*, January 1, 1996.
61. Catherine Clabby, "Duke University President, Liz Taylor Get Chance to Dole Out Heiress' Charity," *Raleigh News and Observer*, August 30, 1994.
62. John J. Goldman and Robert J. Lopez, "Police to Investigate Death of Heiress," *Los Angeles Times*, January 25, 1995.
63. James C. McKinley, Jr., "Los Angeles Police Begin Inquiry into Heiress's Death," *New York Times*, January 27, 1995.
64. John J. Goldman and Paul Lieberman, "Former Employees of Heiress Contest Legality of Will," *Los Angeles Times*, February 25, 1995.
65. Schwarz, *op. cit.*, p. 255.
66. John J. Goldman and Paul Lieberman, "New Legal Twist Entangles Heiress's Will," *Los Angeles Times*, March 3, 1995. Surrogate Preminger's uncle was Otto Preminger, the film director.
67. See Paul Lieberman's *Los Angeles Times* stories: "Nurse Who Said Heiress Was Slain Held in Theft," April 2, 1995 (with Stephanie Simon), "Heiress Duke's Nurse Charged in Thefts," May 25, 1995 (with John J. Goldman), "Nurse Admits Thefts from Rich Patients," October 14, 1995 (with John J. Goldman), and "Doris Duke Nurse Gets Eight Years in Theft," February 29, 1996.
68. See James C. McKinley, "Judge Removes the Executors of Duke Estate," *New York Times*, May 23, 1995, Margaret A. Jacobs, "U.S. Trust and Butler Dismissed as Co-Executors," *Wall Street Journal*, May 23, 1995, Cristina Merrill, "Unseemly Case of the Bank, the Butler, and the Billionaire," *American Banker*, June 12, 1995, and David Stout, "Bernard Lafferty, the Butler for Doris Duke, Dies at 51," *New York Times*, November 5, 1996.
69. James C. McKinley, Jr., "Stakes in the Duke Case: A Long Reputation and a Lot of Dollars," *New York Times*, May 31, 1995.
70. James C. McKinley, Jr., "Judge Blocks Replacement of Executors in Duke Case," *New York Times*, June 2, 1995, and McKinley, "Ousting of Doris Duke Executors Is Upheld," *New York Times*, October 11, 1995.
71. George James, "More Than $65 Million for Adopted Duke Daughter," *New York Times*, December 30, 1995.
72. Joseph P. Fried, "Court Reverses the Removal of Duke Estate's Executors," *New York Times*, January 12, 1996, and Goldman and Lieberman, "N.Y. Court Rejects Ouster of Duke Estate's Executor," *Los Angeles Times*, January 12, 1996.
73. Don Van Natta, Jr., "Settlement May Be Reached in Battle Over Duke Estate," *New

*Notes*

York Times, January 25, 1996, and Van Natta, "Lawyers in Duke Estate Case Ask the Judge to Step Aside," *New York Times*, January 30, 1996.

74. Katharine Fraser, "Chemical and Bank of N.Y. Challenge U.S. Trust for Control of Duke Estate," *American Banker*, January 29, 1996.
75. See April 11, 1996 stories in the *New York Times, Raleigh News and Observer, American Banker*, and *Los Angeles Times*.
76. Susan Kaufman, "Judge Gives Blessing to Settlement in Doris Duke Estate Battle," *Raleigh News and Observer*, May 16, 1996, and Don Van Natta, Jr., "Accord Clears the Last Will of Doris Duke for Probate," *New York Times*, May 16, 1996.
77. See stories in *Los Angeles Times*, July 25, 1996, and *Raleigh News and Observer*, November 5, 1996.
78. Salvatore Arena, "Judge Slashes Fees 14M in Heiress Estate Case," *New York Daily News*, May 2, 2000.
79. Susan Kaufman, "Duke University Honors an Heiress," *Raleigh News and Observer*, October 1, 1996.
80. John J. Goldman and Paul Lieberman, "Hoping to End Wrangles, Duke Charity Picks President," *Los Angeles Times*, January 29, 1997, and Susan Kaufman, "As Troubles Recede, Doris Duke's Largesse Poised to Flow," *Raleigh News and Observer*, January 29, 1997.
81. Judith M. Dobrzynski, "Confronting a $1.4 Billion Blank Page," *New York Times*, November 10, 1998.
82. Marina Dundjerski, "At Long Last, a Legacy," *Chronicle of Philanthropy*, December 11, 1997.
83. Susan Kaufman, "Doris Duke's Charity Flows," *Raleigh News and Observer*, December 10, 1997.
84. Joyce Mercer, "Colleges Watch for Signals on Priorities of Doris Duke's Charitable Foundation," *Chronicle of Higher Education*, March 13, 1998.
85. Louis Graves, "Benevolent Water Power," *World's Work*, December 1931.
86. Durden, *Launching of Duke University*, pp. 58-59.
87. Walter L. Lingle, "Endowment Aids Davidson," *Charlotte Observer*, April 26, 1937.
88. Robert F. Durden, "James B. Duke Wins and Loses: The Partial Collapse of His Grand Design for Perpetual Philanthropy in the Carolinas," *North Carolina Historical Review*, January 1997.
89. *Ibid.*
90. *Ibid.*
91. Robert F. Durden, *Electrifying the Piedmont Carolinas: The Duke Power Company, 1904-1997* (Durham, North Carolina: Carolina Academic Press, 2001), p. 111.
92. *Ibid*, p. 111.
93. *Ibid.*, p. 111-12.
94. Dan Chapman, "Endowment Selling 60% of Duke Shares," *Charlotte Observer*, March 3, 1994.
95. *The Duke Endowment 1991 Annual Report* (Charlotte, North Carolina: Duke Endowment, 1992), p. 3.
96. *Ibid.*, pp. 4-5.
97. *Ibid.*, p. 5.
98. *Ibid.*, p. 4.

*Notes*

99. Stephanie Strom, "Fees and Trustees, Paying the Keepers of the Cash," *New York Times*, July 10, 2003.
100. "Duke Endowment Awards $2 Billion," Duke Endowment press release, issued December 15, 2004.

**The Conrad N. Hilton Foundation**

1. Tom Furlong, "Barron Hilton on Hot Seat," *Los Angeles Times*, April 2, 1990.
2. Whitney Bolton, *The Silver Spade: The Conrad Hilton Story* (New York: Farrar, Straus, 1954), pp. xii-xiii.
3. *Ibid.*, pp. xiii-xiv.
4. Conrad N. Hilton, "'The Face of America,'" *Vital Speeches of the Day*, January 15, 1962.
5. "Hilton Gets Prize for Brotherhood," *New York Times*, November 22, 1950.
6. Conrad N. Hilton, "The Uncommitted Third," *Vital Speeches of the Day*, May 15, 1957.
7. *Ibid.*
8. Conrad N. Hilton, "'The Face of America,'" *op. cit.*
9. Joel F. Olesky, "Conrad Hilton's International Shoestring," *Dun's Review and Modern Industry*, April 1965.
10. "Notes on People," *New York Times*, April 20, 1972.
11. Joan Cook, "Conrad Hilton, Founder of Hotel Chain, Dies at 91," *New York Times*, January 5, 1979.
12. Al Delugach, "Bates Vows to Protect Hilton Estate," *Los Angeles Times*, May 9, 1985.
13. "Daughter Contests Conrad Hilton's Will," *Los Angeles Times*, March 13, 1979.
14. Myrna Oliver, "Effort to Break Conrad Hilton Will Fails," *Los Angeles Times*, March 29, 1980.
15. Al Delugach, "Bates Vows to Protect Hilton Estate," *op. cit.*
16. Eileen White, "Claims to Big Hilton Estate Are Heating Up," *Wall Street Journal*, February 20, 1986.
17. *Ibid.* See also Al Delugach, "Head of Hilton Trust Refuses to Step Aside," *Los Angeles Times*, January 31, 1986.
18. David Johnston and Al Delugach, "IRS Says Hilton Estate Can Keep Controlling Block of Stock," *Los Angeles Times*, February 10, 1986, and Johnston and Delugach, "Fight Over Conrad Hilton Estate Gets Increasingly Bitter," *Los Angeles Times*, March 4, 1986.
19. Marcia Chambers, "The Hilton Will in Court: Heir Fights Foundation," *New York Times*, June 16, 1986.
20. *Ibid.*
21. *Ibid.*
22. Al Delugach, "Barron Hilton Wins Battle for Chain," *Los Angeles Times*, November 26, 1988. See also Anne Lowrey Bailey, "Hilton Fund Gets Over $500 Million in Accord, But Charities Disappointed," *Chronicle of Philanthropy*, December 6, 1988.
23. Ricki Fuhman, "Hilton Foundation, Heir Share Interests," *Pensions and Investments*, April 20, 1998. Information on the current status of the Barron Hilton Charitable Remainder Unitrust from an email from Patrick Modugno of the Conrad N. Hilton Foundation, dated August 16, 2006.

*Notes*

24. *Conrad N. Hilton Foundation Annual Report 1992-1993* (Reno, Nevada: Conrad N. Hilton Foundation, 1993), pp. 4-5.
25. *Ibid.*, p. 1.
26. *Ibid.*, preface.
27. *Ibid.*, preface.
28. *Ibid.*, p. 8. For more information about the Hilton/Perkins Program, see Donald H. Hubbs, "Helping the Multi-Handicapped Blind," *Philanthropy*, June 1995.
29. Peter Panepanto, "Once a Wanderer, Hotel Heir is at Home in the Family Foundation," *Chronicle of Philanthropy*, November 24, 2005.
30. Anne Riley-Katz, "Steven Hilton Started in the Hotel Business, Then Switched to Philanthropy Through the Foundation Established by his Father Conrad," *Los Angeles Business Journal*, January, 2006.

## Chapter IV - A Legal History of Donor Intent

1. Cited in Vanessa Laird, "Phantom Selves: The Search for a General Charitable Intent in the Application of the Cy Pres Doctrine," *Stanford Law Review*, April 1988.
2. Anthony Trollope, *The Warden* (New York: Oxford University Press, n.d.), p. 36.
3. Cited in Sandra Raban, *Mortmain Legislation and the English Church, 1279-1500* (Cambridge: Cambridge University Press, 1982), p. ] .
4. Cited in Edith L. Fisch, Doris Jonas Freed, and Esther R. Schachter, *Charities and Charitable Foundations* (Pomona, New York: Lond, 1974), p. 19.
5. Gareth Jones, *History of the Law of Charity, 1532-1827* (Cambridge: Cambridge University Press, 1969), p. 74.
6. *Ibid.*, p. 74.
7. *Ibid.*, p. 73.
8. David Owen, *English Philanthropy, 1660-1960* (Cambridge, Massachusetts: Harvard University Press, 1964), p. 87.
9. Ian Williams, *The Alms Trade: Charities, Past, Present, and Future* (London: Unwin Hyman, 1989), p. 23. Eldon was also opposed to expanding the notion of charity to include political activism. In *De Themmines v. De Bonneval* (1828), he ruled that political organizations were not included in the Charities Act of 1601, and thus could not be considered charities. As late as 1978, this decision was used in Britain to declare that Amnesty International was not a charity.
10. Elias Clark et al., *Cases and Material on Gratuitous Transfers Wills, Intestate Succession, Trusts, Gifts, Future Interests and Estate and Gift Taxation*, fourth edition (St. Paul, Minnesota: West, 1999), p. 563-570.
11. Owen, *op. cit.*, p. 206.
12. Southcote, Lord Romilly continued, "was in my opinion, a foolish, ignorant woman, of an enthusiastic turn of mind, who had long wished to become an instrument in the hand of God to promote some great good on earth. . . . In the history of her life, her personal disputations and conversations with the devil, her prophecies and her inter-communings with the spiritual world, I have found much that, in my opinion, is very foolish, but nothing which is likely to make persons who read them either immoral or irreligious. I cannot, therefore, say that this devise of the testatrix is invalid by reason of the tendency of the writings of Joanna Southcote." Cited in George Gleason Bogert, Dallin H. Oaks, H. Reese Hansen,

## Notes

and Claralyn Martin Hill, *Cases and Text on the Law of Trusts*, 6th ed. (Westbury, New York: Foundation Press, 1991), p. 226.

13. Sir Arthur Hobhouse, *The Dead Hand: Addresses on the Subject of Endowments and Settlements of Property* (London: Chatto and Windus, 1880), pp. 42-44.
14. *Ibid.*, pp. 121-122.
15. Owen, *op. cit.*, p. 546.
16. Fisch, *op. cit.*, p. 21.
17. Howard S. Miller, *The Legal Foundations of American Philanthropy, 1776-1844* (Madison, Wisconsin: State Historical Society of Wisconsin, 1961), pp. 25-26.
18. Harry Emerson Wildes, *Lonely Midas: The Story of Stephen Girard* (New York: Farrar and Rinehart, 1943), p. 277.
19. *Ibid.*, p. 306.
20. *The Will of the Late Stephen Girard, Esq., Procured from the Office for the Probate of Wills, with a Short Biography of His Life* (Philadelphia: Thomas Desilver, 1848), p. 17. In the building's cellar, Girard called for windows to be placed "one half below, the other half above the surface of the ground."
21. *Ibid.*, p.21.
22. *Ibid.*, p. 22.
23. *Ibid.*, pp. 22-23.
24. Hon. Daniel Webster, *A Defence of the Christian Religion and of the Religious Instruction of the Young. Delivered in the Supreme Court of the United States, February 10, 1844, in the Case of Stephen Girard's Will* (New York: Mark H. Newman, 1844), pp. 20-21.
25. Cited in Edith Abbott, *Some Pioneers in Social Welfare: Select Documents with Editorial Notes* (New York: Russell and Russell, 1963), pp. 85, 87.
26. Cited in Eugene F. Scoles and Edward C. Halbach, Jr., *Problems and Materials on Decedents' Estates and Trusts,* 4th ed., (Boston: Little, Brown, 1987), p. 546.
27. C. Ronald Chester, "*Cy Pres*: A Promise Unfulfilled," *Indiana Law Journal*, Spring 1979.
28. Fisch, *op. cit.*, p. 27.
29. Cited in "Trusts-Cy Pres-Construction of Purpose to Permit Aid of Others than Designated Beneficiaries," *Columbia Law Review, March 1935.*
30. Cited in John Ritchie, Neill H. Alford, Jr., and Richard W. Effland, *Cases and Materials on Decedents' Estates and Trusts* (Mineola, New York: Foundation Press, 1982), p. 710.
31. Bogert, *op. cit.*, pp. 210-211.
32. Cited in John T. Gaubatz, Ira Mark Bloom, and Lewis D. Solomon, *Estates and Trusts: Cases, Problems, and Materials* (New York: Matthew Bender, 1989), p. 768.
33. Cited in Jesse Dukeminier and Stanley M. Johanson, *Wills, Trusts, and Estates*, 4th ed. (Boston: Little, Brown, 1990), p. 588.
34. However, the courts have ruled that political parties are not charities. The National Woman's Party, despite its name, did not actively contest elections or nominate candidates. Ritchie, *op. cit.*, p. 710.
35. Bogert, *op. cit.* p. 220.
36. Ritchie, *op. cit.*, p. 673.

*Notes*

37. *Ibid.*, pp. 689-690.
38. *Ibid.*, p. 691.
39. David Luria, "Prying Loose the Dead Hand of the Past: How Courts Apply *Cy Pres* to Race, Gender, and Religiously Restricted Trusts," *University of San Francisco Law Review*, Fall 1986.
40. *Ibid.*
41. *Ibid.*
42. Scoles, *op. cit.*, p. 534.
43. Ritchie, *op. cit.*, p. 712.
44. Clark *et al.*, *op cit.*, p. 594-97.
45. Bogert, *op. cit.*, p. 549.
46. *Ibid.*, p. 550.
47. See Paige Lescure, "Lockwood v. Killian: Connecticut *Cy Pres* and the Restrictive Charitable Trust," *Connecticut Law Review*, Winter 1980.
48. Joan Biskupic, "Court Won't Let 2 Hawaii Schools Hire Only Protestant Teachers," *Washington Post*, November 9, 1993.
49. Gaubatz, *op. cit.*, p. 789.
50. Bogert, *op. cit.*, p. 304.
51. *Ibid.*, p. 307.
52. Bogert, *op. cit.*, pp. 572-573.
53. Ritchie, *op. cit.*, pp. 718-725.
54. Scoles, *op. cit..* p. 551.
55. Valerie J. Wollmar, Amy Morris Hess, and Robert Whitman, *An Introduction to Wills and Estates* (St. Paul, Minnesota: Thomson/West, 2003), 1030-1039.

**Conclusion - What Donors Can Do**

1. As a consequence of the Tax Reform Act of 1969, De Rance sold the shares to Philip Morris in 1969 for $97 Million.
2. Anne Lowrey Bailey, "The Strange Case of Harry John," *Chronicle of Philanthropy*, May 4, 1993.
3. *Ibid.*
4. Bill Miller, "Captain's Orders Entangle Bequest to Coast Guard," *Washington Post*, September 18, 1983.
5. This may have amounted to £3 Million on acquisitions for the museum, although some funds were given to the library for purchases of manuscripts.
6. R.G.W. Anderson, "Shaw's Bequest to the British Museum," *Times Literary Supplement*, May 14, 1993. See also Noel Annan, "Time to Divide the Shavian Spoils," *Times Literary Supplement*, May 7, 1993.
7. Stephen G. Greene, "Why Some Foundations Opt to Go Out of Business," *Chronicle of Philanthropy*, June 30, 1992.

# Index

## A

Abramson, Howland, 97
Abramson, Rudy, 74
Ahmad, Eqbal, 63
Aldrich, Nelson, 14
Alexander, Robert T., 228
Allen, William H., 5
Allen-Bradley Company, 150-153, 155
Alliance for Political Campaigns, 74
Alliance for School Choice, 156
Alterman, Eric, 157
American Academy in Rome, 14
American Cancer Society, 1, 4, 223, 224
American Civil Liberties Union, 57
American Dance Festival, 183
American Enterprise Institute, 69, 72, 156
American Federation of the Blind, 4
American Historical Association., 14
American Legion, 39
American Red Cross, 1, 5
American Tobacco Company, 160, 161, 173
Americans for Constitutional Action, 67
Americans for Democratic Action, 38
Anderson, John, 94, 102
Anderson, R.G.W., 228
Angell, James, 53
Annenberg Foundation, 97, 108
Annenberg, Leonore, 56
Anti-Defamation League of B'Nai Brith, 67
Archdiocese of Milwaukee Supporting Foundation, 227
Arkin, William, 63
Astor, Brooke, 56

## B

Bacon, Augustus, 219
Baker, Houston, 61
Banbury Fund, 128, 136
Bankers Life, 57, 59, 60
Barder, Sarah Doll, 155
Barnes Foundation, 65, 78, 80-85, 87-95
*Barnes Foundation v. Keely,* 88
Barnes, Albert, 78, 80, 88, 90, 93-96, 108

Barnes, Laura, 88, 89
Barron, Clarence, 162
Barton, Clara, 1
Batchelder, William F., 223
Bates College, 225
Bates, James, 192, 194, 196
Beardsley v. Selectmen of Bridgeport, 218
Bendana, Alejandro, 63
Bennett, Harry, 33, 34
Bennett, William, 74
Benton, William, 36
Bertram, James, 53
Beryl Buck Institute for Education, 119, 120
BEST Foundation For a Drug Free Tomorrow, 199
Beucar, Barbara, 105
Big Shoulders Fund, 156
Billington, James, 61
Bishop, Bernice, 221
Black Alliance for Educational Options, 156
Black, George, 66
Black, Hugo, 214, 220
Block, Herbert, 38
Bloom, Allan, 61
Bond, Horace Mann, 84, 98
Bond, Julian, 98, 108
Borden, Gail, 143
Bostich, Ann, 179, 180
Boudin, Leonard, 63
Bowdoin College, 225
Bowen, William, 130
Boy Scouts of America, 4
Boyer, Ernest, 61
Boys Clubs, 4, 149
Bradford, Jr., Earle L., 95, 97
Bradley Center for Philanthropy and Civic Renewal, 158
Bradley Foundation, Lynde and Harry, 149-159
Bradley, Caroline, 151, 155
Bradley, Harry, 150, 151-154, 157
Bradley, Lynde, 149-151, 155
Brady, W.H., 155
Bray, Thomas, 46
British Museum, 27, 205, 228
Brock, David A., 223
Brody, Anita, 94

*Index*

Brookings Institution, 72
Browder, Earl, 38
Brown University, 55
*Brown v. Board of Education,* 218
Brown, Harold, 119
Brown, J. Carter, 178, 181
Buck
  Beryl, 109-115, 117, 119, 120
  Frank, 109
  Leonard, 109
Buck Center for Research on Aging, 119, 120
Buck Trust, 109-120
Buckley, Jr., William F., 39
Building Excellent Schools, 156
Bundy, McGeorge, 42, 43
Bush, George H.W., 89
Bush, George W., 157
Butler, Nicholas Murray, 50, 51


C

Camp Fire Girls, 4
Camp, Kimberly, 103, 107
Capital Research Center, 71
Carnegie Corporation, 22, 46, 49-56, 114, 158, 159
Carnegie Endowment for International Peace, 46, 50, 51
Carnegie Foundation for the Advancement of Teaching, 46, 49, 54, 61
Carnegie Institution of Washington, 46
Carnegie, Andrew, 1, 11, 14, 22, 27, 46, 52, 53, 159, 163, 213, 229
Carnegie-Mellon University, 46
Cassatt, Mary, 84
Center for Responsive Politics, 72
Center for the Study of Democratic Institutions, 40
Charities Act of 1601, 201
Charity Organization Society, 3
Charles, Marion Oates, 178, 181
Chenoweth, Helen, 77
Chernow, Ron, 10
Chicago Education Initiative, 63
Child Welfare League, 4
Children's Defense Fund, 54, 55, 61
Children's Television Workshop, 54

Christian Anti-Communist Crusade, 152, 153
Christian Freedom Foundation, 67, 69
Christopher, Warren, 55
*Chronicle of Philanthropy,* 46, 69, 71, 183, 199, 226, 227, 230
Chrysler Corporation, 43
Chrysler, Walter F., 83
Cialone, Frank, 137
Civil Rights Act of 1964, 222
Clark, Kenneth, 83
Cleveland Foundation, 6
Cliett, Eugene, 100
Coast Guard Academy, 228
*Coffee v. William Marsh Rice University,* 219
Colby College, 225
*Commonwealth of Pennsylvania v. Brown,* 218, 219, 223
Congress for Racial Equality, 43
*Connecticut College v. United States,* 221
Conservation Fund, 61
Cook, John E., 110
Coolidge, Calvin, 32
Corbally, John, 60
Cortright, David, 63
Council on Economic Priorities, 55
Council on Foundations, 4
Court of Chancery, 203-207
Cox Committee, 34
Cox, Mike, 45
Cromwell, James, 176
Crouch, Stanley, 62
Crowther, Samuel, 29, 30
Cutlip, Scott, 4
*cy pres,* 112, 117, 118, 203, 208, 209, 212-215, 219-221, 223-225, 229


D

Danforth Foundation, 140
Davidson College, 170, 184, 186, 187
Day, Alyesha, 138
De Mazia Trust, 90-92, 96, 98, 99
de Mazia, Violetta, 89, 91
De Rancé, 226, 227
deForest, Robert W., 3
Demopoulos, Harry, 181
Dewey, John, 80

## Index

Dewey, Thomas, 84
Diamond, Irene, 56
Dickerson, Janet, 136
Dobbs, Stephen, 120
Doris Duke Charitable Foundation, 175, 178, 180-183
Doris Duke Clinical Scientist Award Program, 183
Douglas, William O., 219
du Pont, Henry, 105
Duke
  Angier B., 187
  Anthony Drexel, 182
  Benjamin, 160-165, 168, 174, 187
  Doris, 164, 175-183, 185-187
  James Buchanan, 22, 159, 165, 182-184, 187- 189, 229
  Washington, 159, 163, 164, 174, 175
Duke Endowment, 22, 159, 161-163, 165, 167-169, 172-177, 184-189, 230
Duke Leadership Program, 187
Duke Power Company, 161, 184, 185
Duke University, 156, 166, 168-170, 172-174, 176, 178, 182, 184, 186, 187
Dulles, Allen, 124
Durden, Robert, 163, 165, 167, 184
Durkee, Robert, 141

### E

Eakeley, Douglas, 133, 134, 136, 140
Earth Island Institute, 120
Edelman, Marian Wright, 61
Edelman, Peter, 43
Eisenhower, Dwight, 35, 190
Eliot, Charles W., 1, 16
Ellison, Ralph, 61
Ellsberg, Daniel, 63
Equal Rights Amendment, 217
*Estate of Bernstrauch,* 223
*Estate of Buck,* 118, 214
Estate of Carlson, 216
Estate of Robbins, 218
*Estate of Scholler,* 215, 216
*Estate of Tomlinson,* 223
*Evans v. Abney,* 214, 219
*Evans v. Newton,* 219, 222

### F

Fanton, Jonathan, 63, 64
Fauci, Anthony, 181
Feigen, Richard, 104
Ferry, W. H. "Ping", 36, 37, 40
Few, William Preston, 163
First Amendment, 94, 221
Fisher, Mike, 99
Fitzgerald, Frances, 61
Flexner, Abraham, 16
Ford
  Benson, 42
  Cristina, 42
  Edsel, 26, 32-34, 44
  Henry, 26, 28, 33, 34, 38, 41, 68, 163, 189
  Henry II, 26, 34-36, 39-45, 230
Ford Foundation, 26, 27, 31, 33-45, 114, 158, 189, 230, 231
Ford Motor Company, 31-34, 37, 39-41
Ford, Gerald, 190
Fordham Foundation, Thomas B., 156
Foreign Missions Board, 11
Forer, Lois, 89
Forger, Alexander, 180
Fosdick, Harry Emerson, 20
Fosdick, Raymond, 18, 19
Fouhy, Ed, 73
Foundation for Economic Education, 67
Fourteenth Amendment, 218, 221, 222
Frank, Charles, 100
Franklin, John Hope, 61
Freeman, Gaylord, 60
Freeman, S. David, 43
Freer, Charles Lang, 78
*Freme v. Maher,* 224
Freudenheim, Thomas, 96, 108
Fund for the Republic, 36, 37, 38, 39, 40
Furman University, 170, 186, 187
Furman, James, 61

### G

Gabor, Zsa Zsa, 190, 193
Gaines, Ernest J., 62
Gaither, Rowan, 36, 41
Gallagher, Donald A., 226

# Index

Gardner, John, 54, 114
Garrett, Garet, 32
Gates Sr., William, 56
Gates, Frederick T., 1, 9-11, 13, 16, 21
Gell-Mann, Murray, 60
General Education Board, 14
Gibson, Eric, 96
Gill, James, 181
Gill, Steven, 140
Ginn, Edwin, 50
Girard College, 210-212, 218, 219
Girard, Stephen, 210, 218, 219
Girl Scouts, 4
Girls Clubs, 4
Gitlin, Todd, 63
Gladden, Rev. Washington, 10
Glanton, Richard, 89-96, 99
Glenmede Trust, 75
Goheen, Robert, 123, 126, 136, 137
Golden Nugget Corporation, 194
Golden, Daniel, 139
Goldwater, Barry, 152
Goodpaster, Andrew, 124, 126, 128
Goodwillie, Eugene, 125
Gospel of Wealth, The, 47, 48, 49, 51, 229
Gother, Ronald, 194, 195
Grace, J. Peter, 226
Grebe, Michael, 159
Greene, Jerome W., 16
Greenfeld, Howard, 79, 84, 89
Greenlining Institute, 120
Gregorian, Vartan, 55, 56
Griswold, Erwin, 38
Grove City College, 69
*Guillory v. Administrators of Tulane University*, 219

## H

Hackney, Sheldon, 131
Hamburg, David, 55
*Hardage v. Hardage*, 215
Harmelin, Stephen, 104
Harper, William, 10
Harriman, Averell, 5
Harriman, Mary, 5, 18
Harrington, Sybil, 135
Harris, Robert, 112

*Hart's Executors case,* 209
Harvard University, 1, 5, 16, 18, 23, 38, 61, 156, 231
Harvey, Paul, 59, 64
Hayes, Walter, 43, 45
Heald, Henry, 41
Heartland Institute, 156
Hechinger, John, 139
Heffner, Chandi, 177, 178, 180
Hendrick, Burton, 51
Henry Ford Hospital, 28, 42-45
Henry Luce Foundation, 97
Heritage Foundation, 74, 149, 156
Herman, Walter, 104
Heyboer, Kelly, 137
Higginbotham, Jr, A. Leon, 95
Hilton
    Barron, 189, 193-197, 199
    Conrad "Nick" Jr., 190, 193
    Conrad N., 189, 193-195, 196, 198, 200
    Constance Francesca, 193
    Eric, 193, 195, 197
    Steven, 199, 200
Hilton Foundation, Conrad N., 189, 192-200
Hilton Fund for Sisters, 197, 198
Hilton Hotels, 189, 190, 193-197
Hilton Humanitarian Prize, 199
Historical Society of Southern California, 224
Hobhouse, Arthur, 207, 208
Hoffman, Paul, 35, 38
Hood. Sue, 102, 106
Hoover Institution on War, Revolution and Peace, 146
Hoover, Herbert, 146
Hope, Kenneth, 62
House Un-American Activities Committee, 37, 152
*Howard Savings Institution v. Peep,* 220, 221
*Hoyt v. Bliss,* 112
Hubbs, Donald, 194, 196, 197, 199
Hudson Institute, 72, 158
Hutchins, Robert Maynard, 26, 36, 40
Hutton, Lyn, 64

*Index*

## I

*In Re Certain Scholarship Funds,* 222
*In Re Estate of Crawshaw,* 225
*In Re Estate of Wilson,* 222
*In Re Los Angeles County Pioneer Society,* 223, 224
Industrial Workers of the World, 17, 18
Institute for Contemporary Studies, 157
Institute for Policy Studies, 63
International Center for the Disabled, 145, 148
International Committee for the Study of Infantile Paralysis, 145

## J

J. Paul Getty Trust, 97, 102
James, Arthur, 66
*Janey's Executors v. Latane,* 209
Jehl, Douglas, 76
Jewish Welfare Board, 4, 20
JM Foundation, 143, 145, 147-149, 157, 229
John Birch Society, 67
John, Erica, 226, 227
John, Harry, 226, 227
John, Paula, 227
Johnson C. Smith University, 170, 186, 187
Johnson, Alvin, 52
Johnson, Lyndon, 35
Joyce, Michael, 155, 156, 157, 158

## K

*Kamehameha Schools v. Equal Employment Opportunity Commission,* 221
Karl, Barry D., 1
Katz, Stanley N., 1, 62
Kazin, Alfred, 61
Kean, Thomas, 55, 56
Keller, Helen, 199
Kelly, John T.J., 93
Kennedy, Robert, 43
Keohane, Nan, 178, 181
Keppel, Frederick, 54
King. W.L. Mackenzie, 18, 19
Kirby, William, 59, 60, 226
Kissinger, Henry, 63

Knight, Christopher, 101, 107
Knights of Malta, 226
Koch Charitable Foundation, David H., 158
Kolakowski, Leszek, 61
Koret Foundation, 120
Kornblum, Carole, 116
Kreps, Juanita, 188
Lafferty, Bernard, 178, 179, 180, 182
LaFollette, Robert, 11
Lagemann, Ellen Condiffe, 54
Laghi, Pio, 226
Lake, Anthony, 132
Lamprey, Wayne, 112
Langfitt, Thomas, 69, 71
Lapidow, Seth, 136
Lawrence, Abbott, 4, 5
League of Women Voters, 72
Lee, Ivy, 17, 19, 21
Leeb, Brian, 125
Lenfest Foundation, 97
Lenfest, H.G. Gerry, 101
Lenkowsky, Leslie, 108
Leo, John, 62
Lerner, Robert, 71
Levi, Edward, 60
Lewis, John, 130
Lewis, Jr., Fulton, 38
Library of Congress, 205, 228
Light, Paul, 71
Limerick, Patricia Nelson, 62
Lincoln University, 84, 85, 89, 91, 95, 97, 98, 100, 101, 107
Lingle, Walter, 184
*Lockwood v. Killian,* 221
Long, Huey, 32
Loock, Fred, 150, 151, 157
Loock, Margaret, 151, 155
Los Angeles County Pioneer Society, 224
Lowry, William, 64
Ludlow Massacre, 17, 20
Lynch, Frederick, 49

## M

MacArthur
   J. Roderick "Rod", 57, 58, 59, 60
   John D., 57, 58, 60, 61, 226

*Index*

John R. "Rick", 58, 64
MacArthur Foundation, J. Roderick, 58
MacArthur Foundation, John D. and
  Catherine T., 57-61, 63, 226
Mack, John, 181
Mahoney, Roger, 195
Malato, Marie, 104
Malone, Ronald, 139
*Man v. Ballet,* 204
Manhattan Institute, 149
Manion Forum, 153
Mankiewicz, Frank, 43, 61
Manko, Joseph, 105
Marin Community Foundation, 109, 118-121
Marin Institute for the Prevention of
  Alcohol and Other Drug Abuse, 119
Marquis, Alice Goldfarb, 76
Martinez, Alejandro, 63
Martinez, Peter, 63
Marva Collins School, 156
Marymount College, 225
Massaro, Thomas, 100
*Matter of Wilson,* 223
Maurer, Jeffrey A., 180
Mayo Foundation, 192
McCardle, Carl, 83
McCarthy, Kathleen D., 2
McClary, Susan, 62
McDonough, Peter, 137
McGroarty, Daniel, 157
McGuire, Michael, 140
McNamara, Robert, 42
Michener, James, 82
Mikoyan, Anastas, 152
Milbank
  Elizabeth Milbank Anderson, 144
  Jeremiah, 143, 144, 148, 149, 157, 229
  Joseph, 144
Mill, John Stuart, 207
Miller, Arlen, 185
Miller, John J., 46
Mintz, Joshua, 64
Moordian, Patricia, 46
Moore, Bernard, 94
Moore, George, 205
Moore, Tex, 26
*Morice v. The Bishop of Durham,* 206
Morrison, Toni, 61

mortmain, 15, 201, 202
Mortmain Act of 1736, 204, 205, 207, 208
Mullanphy Trust, 214
Munitz, Barry, 102
Muravchik, Joshua, 57, 59, 63
Murphy, Starr, 14, 16, 20, 226
Murray, Charles, 156, 158
Musmanno, Michael, 88


N

Nagai, Althea, 71
National Alliance of Businessmen, 35
National Association for the Advancement of
  Colored People, 1, 4
National Audubon Society, 72, 120
National Cancer Foundation, 224
National Catholic War Council, 20
National Center for Neighborhood Enterprise,
  61, 149
National Commission on Civic Renewal, 73
National Conference of Christians and Jews,
  120, 191
National Council of Churches, 4, 67
National Council of La Raza, 55
National Parent-Teacher Association, 4
National Recovery Act, 32, 65
*National Review,* 39, 46, 134, 152, 153
National Urban League, 1, 55, 80
National Women's Party, 217
Natural Resources Defense Council, 72, 120
Nature Conservancy, 61
NBC News, 73
Nelson, Ivory, 101
New York Bureau of Municipal Research, 5
Nielsen, Waldemar, 26, 39, 43, 54, 227
Nixon, Richard, 147
Noonan, Patrick, 61
Norton, Eleanor Holmes, 61
Nunn, Sam, 74


O

Olasky, Marvin, 2, 158
Olin Foundation, John M., 23, 155, 230
Olin, John M., 23, 158, 230

## Index

Open Space Institute, 183
Ornstein, Norman, 72
Ott, Stanley, 92
Oursler, Fulton, 190

### P

Paley, Martin, 113, 115, 116, 118
Papp, Joseph, 61
Partners in Health, 199
Patino, Douglas, 120
Patterson, Gardner, 129
Paul E. Kelly Foundation, 105
Pei, I.M., 119
Perkins School for the Blind, 199
Perry, Glen, 104
Peters, Harvey, 150, 153, 155
Peters, Thomas, 121
Pew
  Ethel, 68
  Harriet, 70, 71
  J. Howard, 65-68, 70, 72, 75
  John G. "Jack", 70
  Joseph N. Sr., 65
  Joseph N., Jr., 64, 65, 68, 70
  Mabel Pew Myrin, 68, 70
  R. Anderson, 70
Pew Center for Civic Journalism, 73
Pew Charitable Trusts, 64, 65, 69-72, 74, 97, 103, 107
Pew Memorial Trust, 68
Philadelphia Museum of Art, 83, 90
Philanthropy Roundtable, 157
Phillips, William, 102, 106
Pierce, Lyman, 4
Pifer, Alan, 54
POINT Foundation, 120
Pope, Carl, 77
Pound, Roscoe, 213
Preminger, Eve, 179
PRINCO, 132, 134, 137, 139
Pritchett, Henry, 54
Public Advocates, 114-117

### R

Rader, I. Andrew "Tiny," 155
Reagan, Ronald, 147, 190
Reed, Cheryl L., 63
Reeves, Thomas C., 35, 39
*Register of Wills for Baltimore City v. Cook,* 217
Reichert, Joshua, 73
Rendell, Ed, 98, 101
Retirement Research Foundation, 59
Ricker College, 224, 225
Rimel, Rebecca, 69, 71, 73, 75-77, 100-103
Robert Wood Johnson Foundation, 74
Robertson
  Charles, 122, 124, 126-131, 141
  Marie, 122, 127, 128, 131, 141
  William, 126, 127, 132, 133, 135, 138, 142
Robertson Foundation, 122, 125, 128-142
*Robertson v. Princeton,* 122
Robinson, Russell, 189
Rock the Vote, 72, 75
Rockefeller
  Abby Aldrich, 15
  David, 22, 56
  John D., 1, 9, 13, 17, 19-21, 27, 159, 167, 226
  John D. Jr., 9-11, 13-15, 17-22, 27
Rockefeller Brothers Fund, 22
Rockefeller Foundation, 1, 12-22, 31, 159, 204, 226
Roosevelt, Franklin, 32, 176
Roosevelt, Theodore, 11, 51, 160
Root, Elihu, 51, 53
Rosenwald, Julius, 22, 23, 208, 214, 229, 230
Rossiter, Clinton, 38
Rothschild, Michael, 134
Rubin, Israel, 180
Rubin, Robert, 55
Rubirosa, Porfirio, 176
Rule Against Perpetuities, 201, 204, 215
Russell Sage Foundation, 3, 4, 14, 231
Russell, Bertrand, 80

### S

Sadler, Kenneth, 95
Sage, Margaret Olivia, 3
Sage, Russell, 3, 231

*Index*

Sager, Ryan, 77
Salk, Jonas, 60, 61, 145
Salvation Army, 20, 27, 225
Samuel I. Newhouse, Jr. Foundation, 91
San Francisco Foundation, 110-120
Sanford, Terry, 177
Saul Alinsky Institute, 63
Scaife Foundation, Sarah, 158
Scalia, Antonin, 80
Schneebell, Herman, 68
Scholler Foundation, 216
Scholler, Frederick, 216
School Choice Wisconsin, 156
Schwarz, Frederick, 152
Semans, Mary D.B.T., 182, 186, 187
Shalala, Donna, 55
Shapiro, Harold, 134
Shaw, George Bernard, 26, 27, 228
*Shelley v. Kraemer,* 222
*Shenandoah Valley National Bank v. Taylor,* 217
Shue, Andrew, 75
Shuster, Neil, 134
Siegel, Daniel, 63
Sierra Club, 72, 77
Simon, John, 114, 117, 119
Simon, William, 60
Sinclair, Upton, 17
Smith, Robert, 69
Smithsonian Institution, 15, 78, 96, 205, 228
Socolow, Daniel, 62
Sokolsky, George, 38
Solano, Carl, 98, 101
Soros, George, 56
Southcote, Joanna, 207
Southern Cross Foundation, 226, 227
Sozanski, Edward, 92, 96
Spectrum Center for Lesbian, Gay, and Bisexual Concerns, 120
Spencer, Herbert, 47
Spero, Joan Edelman, 182
Standard Oil Company, 13, 14, 161
Stassen, Harold, 84
*State v. Adams,* 201
Stefan, Louis, 92
Stidger, William, 31
Stimpson, Catherine, 62
Stine, Cynthia, 82, 83
Stokes, Carl, 43

Stokowski, Leopold, 84
Story, Joseph, 212
Sudarkasa, Niara, 94, 95, 97
Sumner, William Graham, 47
Sun Oil, 64, 65, 66, 68, 69, 72
Sussman, Arthur, 64
Swink, Jack D., 193

T

Taft, Robert, 35, 66, 152
Taft, William Howard, 14-16, 50-52
Tax Reform Act of 1969, 68, 185, 189, 193
Taylor, Allen M., 155
Taylor, Elizabeth, 178, 181, 190
Taylor, Paul, 74
*Thatcher v. Lewis,* 214
Thornburgh, Richard, 89
Thorndike, Josseph J., 3
*Thornton v. Howe,* 207
TIAA-CREF, 49
Tides Center, 72, 73
*Tilden v. Green,* 213
Tilden, Samuel, 213
Tilghman, Shirley, 133, 140
Tinari, Nick, 99
*Trammell v. Elliott,* 220
Treglia, Sean, 77
Trollope, Anthony, 201, 206
Trotsky, Leon, 80
Trudeau, Garry, 61
Truman, Harry S, 41
Trust for Public Land, 183
Tunnerman, Carlos, 63
Turner, Ted, 56

U

U.S. Commission on Industrial Relations, 18, 19
U.S. Olympic Committee, 60
United Mine Workers, 17, 185
University of Chicago, 10, 15, 36, 61
University of Maryland, 74
University of Pennsylvania, 61, 69, 74, 83, 84, 85

*Index*

## V

*Vadrnan v. American Cancer Society,* 223
Van de Kamp, John, 114, 115
Vandenberg, Arthur, 32
Vendler, Helen, 61
Venturi, Robert, 92
*Vidal v. Girard's Executors,* 212
Volcker, Paul, 140

## W

Walker, Robert D., 193
Wall, Joseph Frazier, 50, 51
Wallace, Henry, 72
Walsh, Frank, 18
Wanik, Harvey, 102, 106
Ward, Charles Sumner, 4
Waring, Thomas, 39
Warner, John, 73
Warner, Mark, 73
Washington, Jessie, 135, 139
Watson, Bernard, 98, 99, 101, 102
Weakland, Rembert, 227
Webster, Daniel, 210
Weil, Robert, 196
Wellington, Ralph, 104
Welliver, Judson C., 31
Weymouth, Lally, 43
Whelan, Francis, 196
White, Sherman, 95
Whitman, Christine Todd, 178, 181

Wickersham, George, 14
Wiegand, Harold, 88
Wiesner, Jerome, 60
Wildavsky, Aaron, 109
Wilder, Thornton, 37
Wilderness Society, 72
*Will of Neher,* 214
Williams, Roger M., 117
Willkie, Wendell, 66
Wilson, Woodrow, 5, 17, 49, 168
Wolinsky, Sid, 115, 117
Wood, William, 104
Woodrow Wilson School, 122, 124, 127-133, 137, 140-142
Woods, Arthur, 16
Woodson, Robert, 61
World Resources Institute, 63
World Vision, 199
World Wildlife Fund, 72
World Without War Council, 120

## Y

Yale Program on Non-Profit Organizations, 114
Yancey, Jenny, 63
YMCA, 4, 5, 20
YWCA, 20

## Z

Zaller, Robert, 108

**Capital Research Center** (CRC) was established in 1984 to study non-profit organizations, with a special focus on reviving the American traditions of charity, philanthropy, and voluntarism.

Since the 1960s, thousands of nonprofit advocacy groups have been set up to promote more government programs in areas once considered the domain of families, charities, neighborhood associations, and other voluntary organizations. The growth of government has increasingly supplanted the voluntary action and community-based problem-solving that the great observer of early American society, Alexis de Tocqueville, recognized as a defining feature of our society.

CRC specializes in analyzing organizations that promote the growth of the welfare state-now almost universally recognized as a failure-and in identifying viable private alternatives to government programs. Our research forms the basis for a variety of publications:

*Organization Trends,* a monthly newsletter that reports on and analyzes the activities of advocacy organizations.

*Compassion & Culture,* a monthly newsletter highlighting the work of small, locally based charities that help the needy.

*Foundation Watch,* a monthly newsletter that examines the grant-making of private foundations.

*Labor Watch,* a monthly newsletter on trends in labor union activism.

CRC serves public-spirited Americans who provide the backbone of American philanthropy. Our research on organizations that shape public policy provides insight into the world of nonprofit advocacy.

CRC is a nonprofit, tax-exempt, education and research organization operating under Section 501(c)(3) of the Internal Revenue Code. Our programs are financed through gifts from foundations, corporations, and individuals and through the sale of publications. We accept no government contracts or grants.

**Capital Research Center**
1513 Sixteenth Street NW
Washington, D.C. 20036
Telephone: (202) 483-6900
Fax: (202) 483-6902
www.capitalresearch.org.